Memory

Linda—with many thanks for an insightful yet provocative interview! With my best wishes!

10/03

Memory
Remembering and Forgetting in Everyday Life

Barry Gordon, M.D., Ph.D.

MASTERMEDIA LIMITED
NEW YORK

This book is meant for information and education. It is not a substitute for informed clinical judgment. If you have any significant concerns about your own memory, or if others do, you should see a physician or other appropriate health care provider.

Library of Congress Catalog Card Number: 95-078074

ISBN: 1-571-01031-9
ISBN: 1-571-01073-4 (Pbk.)

Designed by Michael Woyton
Manufactured in the United States of America
10 9 8 7 6 5 4 3 2 1

To my parents, Blanche and Bernard Gordon

ACKNOWLEDGMENTS

I have drawn from a number of sources, both implicit and explicit, for this work. My first debt is to my parents. Whatever combination of genes and environment they provided, it sparked a dual interest in both the mind and the physical world. Oscar S. M. Marin, M.D., came into my life in medical school, and the example of his omnivorous intelligence, boundless enthusiasm, and openness to debate have stayed with me long after our careers and lives separated. Ola A. Selnes, Ph.D., the Neuropsychological Director of the Cognitive Neurology Clinic at Johns Hopkins, has taught me a vast amount clinically and academically by his superb interview techniques, his scholarship, his synthesizing ability, his persistence, and his sincere concern for our patients. Alfonso Caramazza, Ph.D., my Ph.D. advisor, helped ensure by his own example the rigor of my own thinking and the need to consider all the options that were open to the human mind and brain. John Hart, Jr., M.D.'s explosions of associative energy have blazed some connections for me to follow. Guy M. McKhann, M.D., Director of Hopkins' Krieger Mind/Brain Institute, has encouraged my work and helped protect and foster my fledgling efforts for the past twenty years. Benjamin A. Miller and his family have been stalwart supporters of research on Alzheimer's disease at Johns Hopkins and elsewhere, and have helped fund some of my most important intellectual explorations. Renee Gordon, my wife, supported, encouraged, and edited me. Her own memory sets an enormously high standard (and luckily, I can tap into it when my own memory fails).

More immediately, the patients and others I have seen for memory problems—who necessarily must remain unnamed here—have been an endless source of inspiration and education. Thanks are due as well to their physicians, psychologists, social workers, teachers, and attorneys.

Special thanks go to David Mahoney, Stephen Foster, Barbara Gill, Barbara Best, and Jane Nevins of the Dana Foundation and the Dana Alliance for Brain Initiatives, for being so receptive to the idea of the book and for pushing its development. In Jane Nevins's case, much additional thanks are due for her editorship. I owe special thanks to the Dana Alliance for Brain Initiatives for having underwritten a large part of the financing of this book, and to Randy Talley of the Dana Alliance for his research. Susan Stautberg and her team at MasterMedia, Ltd., including my other editor there, Merry Clark, and Melinda A. Lombard, provided encouragement and experience in actually getting the book into print. Michael Woyton did enough layouts for *two* books.

Rachel Wilder, my co-author on several chapters, helped begin the initial outline and proposal of this book, and reviewed many other chapters as well. Susan Gorn reviewed the entire book; her editorial advice was always heeded. Edith Stern commented on the chapter on recovered "memories." Bobbi Katz had many useful suggestions on Chapter 18. Seema Kumar contributed research and some of the first-pass writing effort to several chapters. Sharon Powell, R.N., had helpful tips for memory improvement drawn from her experience in our Memory Disorders Clinic. Lisa Rossell and Melissa Allen, my research assistants at Johns Hopkins, were exemplary in finding articles and information for my professional needs, some of which also found their way into this book. Martha Trachtenberg's research was prompt and exhaustive, particularly for amnesia in the movies and amnesia in the newpapers. Barbara Jeffrey helped select the cartoons. Carol Johnson of Physician's Transcription Service transcribed my mutterings almost as rapidly as I said them. Brett Gordon helped select pictures for the memory test. Robert Glatzer created Figures 17 and 18.

My thinking has also benefited from my collaboration with my colleagues on the Charles A. Dana Foundation's Memory Intervention Subcommittee: Drs. Marilyn Albert, Jason Brandt, Murray Grossman, Kathleen Jantzen, Diane Jacobs, Richard Mohs, Yaakov Stern, and Katherine Bick. Jim O'Sullivan, in charge of the Memory and Aging project for the Foundation, has also had an indirect influence on this book as well.

Finally, it should be evident that this book rests, for the most part, on the scholarship, experimentation, and theorizing of other people. There are far too many to give credit here directly, although they can be found cited directly or indirectly at the end of the book, in the Appendices.

Any errors, omissions, or misstatements in this book are my responsibility alone. Of course, I'll blame my memory.

Contents

Foreword

WELCOME TO THE beginning of a fascinating adventure.

Memory seems as if it should be easy for us to understand. We think we know when to worry about it, and when not to. But around middle age—or watching those we love grow old—we are shocked to discover that memory seems to have acquired "a mind of its own." It deserts us when we need it or adds strange details that nobody else remembers. Then we become anxious about Alzheimer's disease, or perhaps a small stroke that went unnoticed, or maybe the wildness of youth came home to roost in our brain cells. And while we can count on our doctors to find disease or injury, they, too, have never been much better than we in telling why a healthy, uninjured brain would have trouble with memory or what we can do to help it.

But all that is changing. As Barry Gordon tells in down-to-earth, energetic, plain English, brain science is bringing memory out of the shadows for us and our doctors, too. Scientists are finding out how memory works and what contributes to, or interferes with, good memory function. Probably not even half of what is likely to be discovered about memory has been learned yet, but the news is exciting and astonishing. Best of all, it is encouraging: there are things we can do to improve a memory that is acting up, and things we can stop doing that make it shaky. And it matters tremendously, because memory is so close to the center of our existence as human beings.

The Dana Alliance for Brain Initiatives is very proud of sponsoring Dr. Gordon's work on this book. It is a great beginning for what we expect will be several books telling the non-scientific world about the new-found marvels of the brain. We have undertaken this mission because brain science has made astounding advances in recent years—progress not just in solving the riddles, but also in producing extraordinary strides toward treatments to relieve the suffering caused by neurological and psychiatric disorders.

Who are we to offer you this kind of information? The Dana Alliance as of now (late 1995) consists of 140 prominent neuroscientists, including five Nobel laureates. The organization was formed in November, 1992, in response to what seemed the surprising failure of the federally-declared Decade of the Brain to have any impact on the public.

Thirty-five concerned brain scientists gathered that late fall day on New York's Long Island, at the Cold Spring Harbor Laboratories of Dr. James D. Watson, world-renowned for his Nobel-winning work as co-discoverer of the structure of DNA. Dr. Watson and Dr. Max Cowan, chief scientific officer of the Howard Hughes Medical Institute, were the meeting organizers and the Charles A. Dana Foundation, of which I am the chairman, underwrote it.

The problem that led to the meeting was that the Decade of the Brain was supposed to develop public opinion about, and hopefully support for, brain research. For better or worse, policy makers in Washington were making increasingly difficult decisions about priorities for funding, and evidence was that brain research was already faring poorly in the competition for support. Yet, brain studies had reached the point in the previous 10 years where more had been learned than in all previous history. The discoveries would make a difference in the nation's health, happiness—and tax bill, because the cost of neurological and psychiatric disorders exceeds all other diseases combined. Why wasn't the public thinking about this?

Wrestling with the question, it became obvious that so much was being found, so quickly, that information to the public simply had not kept pace. No small factor was that the brain *seems* mysterious at best and just too scientifically technical for people to break down the laboratory doors for information. But science, as the saying goes, eventually moves from the bench to the bedside, and brain science was rushing toward that move.

Whether or not a public education effort brought better support or research, it also could be said that neuroscience now had to recognize a duty to share information with the public that would soon be making decisions about it in doctors' offices.

The educational effort we then began has turned out to be a wonderful experience for all the scientists in the Dana Alliance. We have been learning, even as we try to teach, not just how significant the frontier of brain research is in science, but its profound importance to every man, woman and child in our country.

We have worked with the news media to help reporters locate information and research; we have prepared radio programs, a series called

Gray Matters, that airs across the country; television programs are in the making. We present public forums on brain-related subjects such as successful aging and the brain and brain fitness. We provide materials to help people locate organizations with information and assistance for specific disorders from which they or their loved ones suffer.

And finally, *Memory* is dedicated to helping you benefit directly from the tremendous progress in brain research. We hope that you find Barry's book as exciting and gratifying as we do. We want you to know what we know, and to win when we win.

—BY DAVID MAHONEY
CHAIRMAN, THE DANA ALLIANCE
FOR BRAIN INITIATIVES

Introduction

EVERYBODY WONDERS ABOUT their memory; many are annoyed by it; some are worried. The fact that our memory does get worse as we get older (that is, after the age of 30), the fact that Alzheimer's disease is very frequent, now affecting Ronald Reagan in addition to four million other Americans, the fact that Alzheimer's will afflict up to 40 percent of people over the age of 80, and the fact that the youngest case of Alzheimer's was 35 years old, have all fueled people's concerns about their memory.

But real knowledge about memory and memory problems—as opposed to awareness of them—is rare. Few people understand how memory really works, and why it sometimes fails. It may seem odd, but people can have problems with their memory not only because they have too little, but because they have too much. Often, those who complain the most don't have a problem at all. Even stranger, those who *do* have the most problems often don't think anything is wrong!

This book will tell you what you can and can't expect from your memory, and why. It will tell you why many of the popular notions of memory are plain wrong, and in some cases are the complete opposite of the way memory actually works. I decided to write this book when, after several years dealing with students, patients, journalists, and other doctors, it became evident that even educated people are puzzled about memory. Most people are just not very well-informed about the mental mechanisms that science already understands quite well.

So I wrote this book to help show you how your memory works, and to suggest some ways you might improve it. Perhaps most important of all, I want to try to answer your questions about your memory, or that of someone you care about. I hope I can show you how to recognize a real memory problem, and offer some suggestions about how to deal with it.

The episodes I relate as my personal experiences actually occurred, and the people and patients I describe really existed. But to shield the true identity of my patients, while preserving the fundamental lessons of each case, I have deliberately modified aspects and details. Any resulting match to real persons, living or dead, is coincidental.

This book is not just about the problems that can occur with memory, but about its opportunities and virtues as well. The universe inside our heads is rightly even more important to us than the universe outside. Memory is a very large part of what creates our unique, personal universe, and what helps generate its infinite variety. So I hope that by showing you something about memory, I can show you something about yourself.

I have simplified in these pages. It's true that many scientists shun such simplification, feeling it cannot do justice to complex ideas. Sometimes, and in some circumstances, they are right. But some simplifications let us get our mental arms around the main trunk of an idea, which might not be possible if we tried to gather in all the branches and leaves at the same time. In such cases, simplification is the more accurate approach.

Finally, I followed a planned sequence in this book, but I also wanted to make it useful and enjoyable if your inclination is to read it in pieces, a paragraph, a chapter, or a section at a time. Front-to-back readers: Forgive me for the redundancy that was necessary to make this work both ways!

Part I

Myths and Worries

1

Common Memory Myths—Debunked!*

Which of the following statements about memory do you believe?

1. People can forget their identities—and get them back—from a blow on the head.
2. People tend to block out the memory of traumatic childhood events, such as sexual abuse.
3. Your memory gets worse as you get older, and you can't do anything about it.
4. Forgetfulness is a sign that something is wrong with your brain.
5. The more your memory problems bother you, the more serious they are.
6. A person can kill or hurt someone, and never remember it!
7. You lose 10,000 brain cells a day, and one day you just run out.
8. Those who think they have Alzheimer's probably do.
9. Comparing yourself to others is a good way to tell whether your memory is normal.
10. Everything you ever learned is locked inside your head. You just need to find the key to get it out.
11. Everyone is born with the same memory abilities, but some use it and others lose it.

NONE of these statements is completely true!

Human memory is a fickle thing, capable of performing astounding feats, and at the same time muddling the most mundane tasks. You cannot remember whether you turned off the burner before you left the house this morning, yet it is easy for almost anyone to learn and recognize more than 10,000 different faces. Ancient Greek orators routinely memorized seven-hour speeches. A man in India can recite 31,811 digits of the number Pi from memory. And a whole generation of

---

* This chapter by Rachel Wilder and Barry Gordon, MD., Ph.D.

Americans thinks they remember exactly what they were doing when they heard that John F. Kennedy was shot—some do, some do not.

Today, there is a great deal of hysteria over memory ability. One of the most frequently-heard complaints from older patients is failing memory. People worry that the first time they forget the name of an acquaintance, they may have Alzheimer's disease. A majority of Americans—67 percent— claim they experience memory loss, according to a 1993 study.

The truth is, however, that only a small proportion of people develop significant memory problems due to brain disease. Having some memory problems does not necessarily mean that something is wrong with your brain—it is often just the way memory works.

People seem to have unrealistically high expectations for their memories. It is important to realize that memory lapses can be *completely normal*, especially as one ages. We all occasionally misplace the car keys, forget a neighbor's name, or go to the store to buy milk and come back with everything but. It is hard to emphasize enough that even normal memory is far from perfect.

People forget, they confuse, they blur, they invent—and it may come as a surprise that this is part of the normal memory process. Contrary to popular belief, human memory is not exactly like a photographic record, or a file in a computer that can be "saved" and called up whole anytime, unchanged from the way it entered the data bank. Our biologic brains are not perfect memory machines, the way machines can be perfect.

But the fact that our memories are not perfect by machine standards does not mean that human memory should be belittled. Our memories represent a wondrous natural miracle worthy of appreciation—or even awe. And if it weren't for what seem to be some of the imperfections of our memory, we would not be human, nor as creative as we are. The apparent fuzziness of our memories, their meandering interconnections, are part of what helps us solve problems and make creative leaps.

Those who *do* have nearly perfect memories are not necessarily better off for it. As one such person (who worked as a store clerk) lamented, "Most people [find] that memory alone is rather useless." So perhaps we should not pray so hard for perfect memories—we might be unlucky enough to get them.

But we *can* improve our memories. There are simple, effective, time-proven techniques people can use to improve memory. We'll remind you of some of them.

Exactly *how* we remember—what physical changes takes place in the brain as we hear something, store it and later retrieve it—is still poorly understood. But the more scientists uncover about how the learning of nerve cells translates into the learning and memory we experience everyday, the more amazing these processes seem.

Perhaps because memory remains one of the greatest puzzles in neurology, myths about it abound. The eleven statements at the beginning of this chapter all represent common misunderstandings about memory. They are fantasy, not fact. Here are the short answers to these myths (answers that we will delve into in more detail in subsequent chapters):

1. People can forget their identities—and get them back—from a blow on the head.

This is the stuff of Hollywood movies, not reality. A whack on the head can disorient a person temporarily, so it is possible to forget your name for a brief moment, but rarely is the knowledge of who you are wiped out completely. (For more, see Chapter 31—"Girl Loses Identity and Saves the Plot")

2. People tend to block out the memory of traumatic childhood events, such as sexual abuse.

Publicly, controversy rages over whether emotional trauma makes you forget, or remember all too well. But scientifically, there is little disagreement. People, even children, are all too likely to remember a traumatic episode. These are *not* the kinds of memories you forget. A crisis or stressful situation triggers the "fight or flight response," and the release of hormones such as adrenaline. These hormones actually help *preserve* memories, not block them out.

And if you don't remember something the first time—can you be sure of the "memories" you do eventually "recall"? *No!* Study after study has shown that memories of past events are notoriously inaccurate and unreliable.

No issue has brought these known facts into sharper focus than the current argument over "repressed memories" of childhood sexual abuse. A divinity student sued a priest in 1994 for sexually abusing him as a boy. But then, after a great deal of publicity, the student reconsidered and withdrew the suit because, as he said in his retraction, he had learned that the memories he seemed to have recovered under hypnosis weren't reliable. Unfortunately, other people now remember these allegations all too well.

Many memory experts believe that, with encouragement, many people like the divinity student can easily conjure up *false* memories of early abuse, suddenly "remembering" incidents that never happened. These memories may even seem very real. But they're not. (See Chapter 35 — "I Raped My Children, But I Don't Remember It!")

3. Your memory gets worse as you get older, and you can't do anything about it.

Yes—and no. Yes, slight memory deficits are completely normal as you age. And no, you do not just have to live with them. A few simple strategies can help keep your thinking vibrant, improve the quality of your everyday life, and perhaps improve your memory ability. (See Part V—"Improving Your Memory")

4. Forgetfulness is a sign that something is wrong with your brain.

If we did not possess the capacity to forget, we would all go crazy. In a sense, being forgetful could be viewed as having too much of a *good* thing!

Take the case of a man who remembered too much and too intensely. "S" was a Russian man with near-total recall, whose amazing abilities were described in 1968 by the neuropsychologist A. R. Luria in a slim volume called *The Mind of a Mnemonist*. Though "S" forgot very little—sights, sounds, conversations, numbers—he had to work at remembering, and he could not rise above the particulars to sort out what was meaningful to the task at hand. Everyday life was very difficult for him as a result.

So the capacity to unconsciously filter our experiences, remember what is important, and discard the rest, is a skill to be treasured.

Although certain types of forgetting must be taken seriously, as they can signal the onset of a serious brain disease, most cases of absent-mindedness are normal—just the lapses to be expected in an imperfect system.

In many cases, forgetfulness can be helped, at least to some degree. It may just be a matter of simplifying your life so that you reduce "information overload." (See Chapter 21—"The Man with Too Many Mistresses" and Part V—"Improving Your Memory")

5. The more your memory problems bother you, the more serious they are.

Wrong again. In general, the more severe your worries about your memory, the less likely you actually have a memory problem! Memory *complaints*, particularly when they are extreme, usually do not reflect memory *ability* at all.

Aging or an emotional state such as depression or anxiety, for example, can cause your memory to worsen, it is true. But your *fears* about your memory can skyrocket in these conditions. And some people complain bitterly about their memory problems, even though their memory is normal and has never gotten worse! (See Chapter 15—"Spotting a Memory Problem.")

6. A person can kill or hurt someone, and never remember it!

Criminal law allows attorneys to present this defense. Lorena Bobbitt, the Virginia housewife who cut off her husband's penis, testified that she had no recollection of doing so. Research does suggest that it is possible that *a few* people may not remember *a few* acts of passion very well. But almost *everybody* can be expected to remember *something* of what happened. And *most* people can be expected to remember such passionate, violent acts all *too* well, reliving them over and over again in their minds. It is unlikely that such "amnesia" happens as often as it seems to be claimed. (See Chapter 31—"The Memory Loss That Usually Isn't" and Chapter 35—"I Raped My Children, But I Don't Remember It")

7. You lose 10,000 brain cells a day, and one day you just run out.

As an adult, almost all the regions of your brain *do not* lose brain cells as you get older. What you have heard to the contrary is wrong, contradicted by better research methods. You *may* lose some nerve connections. But it's possible that you can even grow new ones, or prevent the ones you have from withering, if you exercise your mind and brain. (See Chapter 9—"Making New Memories.")

8. Those who think they have Alzheimer's disease probably do.

The typical Alzheimer's patient generally does not worry about their memory—friends and family do. The person with Alzheimer's usually is not really aware of the severity of his problems.

Again, if you think you have a serious memory problem, you probably do not. If you do not think you have a memory problem, but others suggest you do, you may. (See Chapter 15—"Spotting a Memory Problem.")

9. Comparing yourself to others is a good way to tell whether your memory is normal.

There is a huge range of ability across the general population, and even a single individual experiences ups and downs in memory ability over the course of a lifetime. Between the extremes of super-memory and true memory loss lies a very broad range of what is normal. Just as some people have a talent for music or art, while others do not, some of us are naturally gifted at remembering some kinds of things and some are not. (See Part III—"Is Your Memory Normal?")

10. Everything you ever learned is locked inside your head. You just need to find the key to get it out.

Not true. Our memories are not so much locked away as they are rearranged and repainted. And we forget selectively, too. You may find the key, but expect that the room you step into has been remodeled. (See Chapter 18—"How Does Normal Memory Normally Behave.")

11. Everyone is born with the same memory abilities, but some use it and others lose it.

All memory abilities are not created equal, and they get even more unequal as we get older. This is true. But it is *not* clear why these differences occur at any age.

It is widely believed that keeping your mind sharp is the best way to improve memory. This is a reasonable belief. It is also true that there are some ancient, tried-and-true tricks that do work to improve memory. We'll talk about these in Part V. And there are some newer realizations about how memory works that can also show you how to improve your memory, perhaps in ways that will make more of a difference to you than the tricks. These will also be discussed in Part V. But whether such mental exercises are *why* some people seem to be better than others as they get older has never been proven. And it's likely that even if this is part of the reason—that is, if some people use these strategies naturally—there are still changes that happen with aging that are due to the brain itself, at least in some people. Perhaps even these can be affected by how you use your mind, but this isn't at all clear. (See Chapter 26, on aging and memory.)

Some people may not lose memory because they don't use it—they may lose it because they worry too much about it. (See Chapter 20, on the worried well.) Stop worrying, and your memory may improve. And if you take an even more positive attitude—just *believing* you are likely to remember something—you increase the chances that you will. So there are a number of things you can do to fight memory loss.

As you can see, there are a great many myths about memory. Let's try to get at some truths about memory, and especially about your own!

2

What Are You Worried About?

MOST OF US don't complain about our strength, our appetite, our breathing, or our heart rate. But we do complain about our memory! Karen Bolla and her colleagues did a survey of such complaints which illustrates how common they are. (See Figure 1).

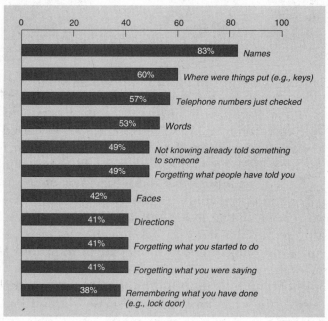

Figure 1

The general results of such studies have always been very much the same. As you can see from Figure 1, people complain most about memory for names, less often for the faces themselves. Forgetting where things have been put is almost as common a complaint as not remembering a name. A large number of people complain about forgetting phone numbers that they have just looked up or been told. Almost as many people find it hard to remember specific words. People forget that they have

Memory Concerns Increase with Age

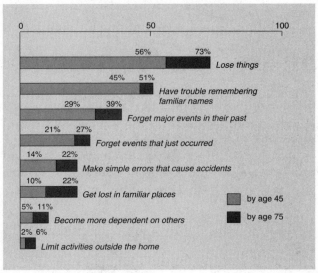

Figure 2

already told something to someone, and forget what people have told them with distressingly high frequency. Forgetting directions that you have been given is common, as is forgetting what you started to do or forgetting what you were saying. And, although less common, forgetting whether you have locked the door, put out food for the cat, turned off the stove, or really made sure that the refrigerator door was shut are extremely frequent complaints.

It is also very clear that the frequency of memory complaints increases with age, and that it doesn't take much of an increase in age to generate an appreciable increase in memory complaints. Moreover, while some of these kinds of memory problems can be trivial, at least some people feel they have had significant problems or potential problems because of their memory. A recent survey commissioned by the Charles A. Dana Foundation brought out this point. The results of this survey are illustrated in Figure 2.

Among people age 18-44, 14 percent felt they had made simple errors of memory that caused accidents. Of those 45 years of age and older, 22 percent felt they had made errors of memory that caused accidents. Perhaps one of the more surprising results of this telephone survey was that some people were even limiting their activities outside the home because of their perceived memory problems: 2 percent of the 18-44 year old group, and 6 percent of the older group.

Are these complaints and fears founded? What should you expect from your memory, or from anybody else's? What should you really be afraid of? What *shouldn't* you fear? And what can you do about your memory?

I could tell you the answers to these questions now—but you would not be convinced. To convince you, you have to know more about how memory actually works. To learn more about how memory actually works, you have to appreciate that memory means different things to different people. For some people, "memory" can mean learning something new; for others, "memory" means remembering something old. "Memory" is often used to mean mental abilities that are really not memory at all, such as attention and intelligence. People will blame their "memory" when what they really mean is that they weren't paying attention, or didn't understand what was being said even if they *were* paying attention. And, curiously, we use many memories that we usually do not *call* memory. Examples of these are the memories—which we call skills—that allow us to throw a ball accurately, and to ride a bicycle without falling. (And some of these skills may be in our spinal cords, not in our heads! But they are memories just the same.)

To get to know how "memory" really works, and to get to know your own memory, I would like you to try the following exercises. These exercises are meant to get you to appreciate the differences between some of these different types of memories. Call them tests if you want, but they have no right or wrong answers. Their main purpose is to have you *feel* for yourself how you work different mental muscles with different types of "memory."

At the end of each exercise, I'll briefly describe what was probably happening in your mind and brain with each type of memory.

Part II

Coming to Know
Your Own Memory

3

Remembering Old Memories

© The Walt Disney Company

Exercise #1

Is this character familiar? Almost everyone who is old enough to be reading this book has been exposed to Mickey Mouse —as a child, as a parent, as a grandparent, or perhaps as all three.

If you *know* Mickey Mouse, then, is that a surprise? No, but it does show some important things about you and your memory. It shows that you *did* have exposure to the popular culture including Mickey Mouse, and that you *did* learn his likeness and his name. So it shows that your mental mechanisms for at least these very strong memories and strong words are intact. And it also shows that you are not lying—not about this, at least.

Perhaps you can recognize Mickey Mouse as familiar, but not recall the name. This is not impossible, and may actually happen more than we care to admit. The familiarity of Mickey Mouse's picture is determined in the visual areas of your brain. If these get activated with the recognition, then your brain, by looking for that activation, can determine that you have just seen something familiar—but may not be able to express what it is that you have seen. You may not be able to express what it is you have seen because your language abilities, which are in a different area of your brain than vision, are somehow damaged. But if this were the case—that is, if you have this language damage, which is called aphasia—then it would probably already have been evident in almost everything else that you tried to say or understand.

But suppose your language system is otherwise completely intact, and you somehow can still not find the name "Mickey Mouse"? That might be because, familiar as the visual image is, the connection between the visual image and its name may be weak or rusty in you. Or the name itself ("Mickey Mouse") may be weak. Either way, you will not be able to activate the name "Mickey Mouse" with enough force to get you to say it outloud. You will have the tantalizing experience of having it "on the tip of your tongue," and perhaps may even be able to say that it is two words, and three syllables, and recognize it instantly if you hear it—but not be quite able to say it out loud.

And there's another possibility. The image of the stalwart mouse may trigger not only the connections to the name "Mickey Mouse," but also to the name "Mighty Mouse," or "Jerry" (the mouse of the "Tom and Jerry" combination), and so forth. These different names may fight each other inside your mind and prevent the right name from getting strong enough. Walk away from the picture, let these other influences die down for a little bit, and suddenly the name "Mickey Mouse" may pop into your head: not because it has gotten stronger, but because its competitors have gotten weaker. This is another possible mechanism of the "tip of the tongue" phenomena. It is very likely that these same kinds of competition also play a very big part in the ordinary problems we have in finding the names of people we know.

YOU SAY YOU DON'T KNOW MICKEY MOUSE?

Suppose you say you don't recognize Mickey Mouse. What does this show us about you and your memory?

You may have had an incredibly impoverished cultural background by American standards. But that should have already been evident, from knowing something about your background and by talking to you.

Suppose you had a background that almost certainly included exposure to Walt Disney characters. But you still say you don't recognize Mickey Mouse. What could this mean?

It could mean that the actual memories of Mickey Mouse *could* have melted in your brain. The memories that were lost could have been the visual memories of what Mickey Mouse *looked like*. Or the ones that disappeared could have been the memories of the *name* "Mickey Mouse." Or the memories that were the *connection* between the image of Mickey Mouse in your head and his name could have been destroyed. (To show that there is a connection between pictures and names, and this has to be learned, consider the fact that virtually nothing we see has the name stamped on it. You have to learn what the names of things are. Usually this learning takes place long before the time when you would now consciously remember doing so, but it was learning nonetheless. And even as an adult, you can appreciate that not everything you could picture has a name that you know (for example, what is the perforated material that you tear off of computer printed checks and sheets?) And not everything you can name has a picture (try visualizing The Truth).

However, the memories of things such as Mickey Mouse's image, name and the connection between them are things you were probably exposed to relatively early in life. They are almost certainly something you have been exposed to over and over again. So they are almost certainly memories that have been deeply embedded in your brain, and spread across multiple connections. To eradicate such memories would require major brain damage, perhaps even damage spread across many regions of the brain. A stroke can do such damage. So can a severe head injury or Alzheimer's disease, in the late stages. But the effects of such massive damage would hardly be confined to just memories of Mickey Mouse. So if such damage were the cause of your not remembering Mickey Mouse, it should be evident to almost everybody.

Assume you had a standard American cultural background, and you do not have massive brain damage. Yet you still say you cannot recognize the picture, nor can you give it a name. What does this imply?

There are two major possibilities, in theory. One is that your lack of memory is only at the conscious level. Unconsciously, you know Mickey Mouse's picture and you know his name, but you are not saying it because somehow your mind is suppressing this knowledge and keeping it out of your consciousness. But can this happen? Almost never, if it ever happens at all. If people suppress such memories, it is usually only for their own autobiographical memories, the memories that affect them. It is almost never for such a benign and omnipresent picture as that of Mickey Mouse. But some cases of this type of odd suppression have occurred. They represent bizarre puzzles on the borderline between Neurology and Psychiatry (see Chapter 33, "Forever Fourteen")

But what is more likely is the other theoretical possibility: you really do *know* Mickey Mouse, but you just don't want to say that you do. It is a conscious decision.

I occasionally see people who claim such losses. One was a journalist in his fifties. He claimed to have written extensively about popular events for the prior thirty years. He had gotten an electrical shock while holding a public telephone on a work assignment. Afterwards, he didn't make exorbitant claims about his problems; he only claimed that he could not work again. One of his apparent problems came out only on our testing: he could not remember the names or faces of almost any public figure within the past three decades—John F. Kennedy, Lyndon Johnson, Jimmy Carter. For an otherwise intact functioning individual, this would have been suspicious enough. But he also showed curious islands of preserved memories. He recognized Lynda Carter, who played Wonder Woman on the TV show, but not Jacqueline Kennedy Onassis. He recognized Buddy Rich, the jazz drummer, but not Frank Sinatra. He would have had to have had a very unusual cultural background, and a very curious adult life, to have had such memories together with such gaps!

Exercise #2. Recognizing old memories

Recognizing Mickey Mouse was, well, "Mickey Mouse" (easy). Recognizing the following pictures is likely to be much harder, but try them anyway (answers next to each set):

Picture 1

Picture 2

Picture 4: Bobby Jones
Picture 3: Fredric March
Picture 2: Jack Dempsy
Picture 1: Edward G. Robinson

Picture 3

Picture 4

Picture 8: Walt Disney
Picture 7: Gene Autry
Picture 6: Amelia Earhart
Picture 5: Lillian Gish

Picture 5

Picture 6

Picture 7

Picture 8

Picture 9 Picture 10

Picture 11 Picture 12

Picture 9: Eleanor Roosevelt
Picture 10: Bing Crosby
Picture 11: Veronica Lake
Picture 12: Groucho Marx

Picture 13 Picture 14

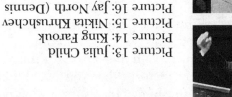

Picture 15 Picture 16

Picture 13: Julia Child
Picture 14: King Farouk
Picture 15: Nikita Khrushchev
Picture 16: Jay North (Dennis the Menace)

Picture 17 Picture 18

Picture 19 Picture 20

Picture 17: Marlo Thomas
Picture 18: Malcolm X
Picture 19: Telly Savalas
Picture 20: Burt Reynolds

Picture 21   Picture 22

Picture 21: Patty Hearst
Picture 22: Dinah Shore
Picture 23: Billy Graham

Picture 23

Don't panic; this exercise is hard for everyone! For most people, these faces are not as famous as Mickey Mouse's, and as you undoubtedly noticed, many of them date from a long time ago. The pictures are of people who first became famous in the 1920s through the 1970s. There was a deliberate effort to find some people who dropped out of the public eye after their period of fame, so you would not have been reminded of them constantly. I will explain the reason for that shortly.

The main reason for giving you pictures that you may know, but probably not very well, is so that you can feel for yourself what parts of your mind are straining. Normally, your mind delivers answers to you quickly and smoothly, so fast that you cannot be aware of the mental machinery that produces them. But when the machinery slows, or stutters, or jams, as may have happened with these pictures, then you can appreciate the mechanisms at work. Let's look at the pictures again, and I'll explain what probably went on as you tried to identify them.

First, look back at the pictures you could not recognize *at all*, the ones that caused you to doubt ever having seen such a face before. But even though you didn't know who the person was, I am sure the pictures gave you clues that your memory of the world could interpret. The style of the photograph, and the set of photos it appeared with, probably suggested to you the decade in which the person lived. The people themselves gave further clues. Frederic March (Picture 3) is movie-star handsome and poised, precisely the character type he played in the movies. Jack Dempsey (Picture 2) is obviously athletic, obviously defiant. In how many other sports do men wear no other uniform but trunks and tank top? You could go through a similar process with every other picture that you failed to recognize at all. I am sure you will find that, with many of them, you actually *know* a great deal about them, even if you don't remember them at all!

What you exercised on the pictures you did not remember was the *thinking* part of memory. Memory is partly collections—of pictures, of names, of facts—but if that were all your memory is, then it would be no more than a file cabinet or a photo album. What makes human memory vastly different from a cabinet or album is that it is *active.* Your mind is constantly finding connections between the pieces in your memory, constantly acting like a detective trying to find out what these pieces mean and how they interrelate.

You have two different kinds of engines in your mind, powering this active memory. The most fundamental engine is an **unconscious** one. Your mind automatically uses connections between different pieces of information. Most of these connections, you already have in your mind. But some connections have to be created, and these connections then become forms of memory in their own right.

The connections are made for many reasons. *Time* is one; memories you learn around the same time are connected because of it. *Space* is another connector; things that went together in space—for example, items on your kitchen counter, or furniture in a room—became linked by the space they occupied.

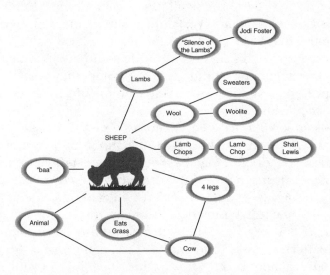

Figure 3: The memory network: Individual memory items and their connections. Some of the connections are known to you consciously, but some are not.

Meaning and *purpose* are among the biggest connectors. Things similar in meaning or purpose get connected very easily, and usually with multiple connections. Figure 3 on page 21 illustrates the connections that might flow from a single word in your mind, the word "sheep."

The connections between pieces of memory create a network of pathways that can be activated at any point. Information coming into your mind activates memories. These, in turn, activate other memories through existing links. The process seems to be very much like what happens when water pours into a dry riverbed. It races along existing channels, activating whatever it touches. And what is activated can, in turn, activate other memories. If there is more than one connection between memories—if connections exist that loop back—then the different activations may reinforce each other. The reinforced set of activations may then excite others, and eventually a complete memory (or memories) may pop into consciousness. So the combination of recognizing an athlete, a defiant posture, and a boxer's attire, may come together to activate names you remember of people who fit that combination: Rocky Marciano perhaps, or perhaps the right answer, Jack Dempsey. And these activations may, in turn, trigger others: Joe Louis, Muhammad Ali.

The activations we have been discussing occur unconsciously and automatically. You cannot be aware of the connections themselves, only of the points that they activate. Nor can you stop the spread of activation. You may not *want* to think of Muhammad Ali whenever you think of another boxer. But almost certainly, a faint memory of Ali is evoked in your mind. Because of individual differences, psychologists do not usually demonstrate this effect by showing pictures of people. Instead, they show that automatic activations exist for other things, such as words. For instance, showing the word "doctor" automatically activates meanings associated with "nurse."

Some of these links between memories obviously exist in the world we all share. Referring back to Figure 3, almost all people have had enough experiences with *sheep* and *cows* to connect them to "four legs" and "animals." Most people will also connect from *sheep* to "lamb chops" and "wool." But a few people may have links to other items that are idiosyncratic, or at least far-fetched. From *sheep* to "Woolite" or to "Jodie Foster" are examples of such idiosyncratic, unusual associations.

(Your pattern of links in memory—your pattern of associations—says a great deal about you. You can find such links in your mind by starting almost anywhere and jumping to wherever the next activated link takes you. Psychologists use techniques such as *free association*—the classic psychoanalytic technique in which you say whatever's on your mind, and go wherever your thoughts lead you—or the *Rorschach test*—in which you voice whatever thought an otherwise-meaningless figure activates—to get at the unconscious network of your memories and the unconscious influences on your personality.)

(Another point: the links are memories themselves. They may fade, but they may not be completely erased. So a bad or inappropriate link may continue to haunt you. Perhaps for you, the sight of a rose activates the memory of thorns, from having stumbled into a rose bush in childhood. You may eventually learn more pleasant associations to a rose, but time and experience may not be able to eradicate all vestiges of that original connection, whether good or bad.)

The links between memories, and the spread of activation through them, are part of your mind's automatic mechanism for making memory an active tool of thought and feeling. But you are much more aware of the other mechanism your mind has for memory—the *conscious* probing of these networks of associations. This conscious probing probably occurred when you studied the pictures of people famous long ago, particularly the ones you didn't recognize at first. "It looks like an actress", you'd say. "What actresses from the 1930s do I know of?" The list of actresses that come to your mind is then plugged into your automatic network. They may spark a response, or nothing. You examine the responses again; you open up levels of your memory that you wouldn't ordinarily use. "It couldn't be somebody really famous, or I'd have recognized her by now. Who are some not-so-famous actresses of the 1930s?" Conscious probing, examining, and re-probing lets you extract maximum value from your automatic network of associations and allows you to "remember" things that were really not accessible to you at first.

4

The "Memory" That Isn't
Memory—Remembering What
You Couldn't Know

BECAUSE OF THE combination of conscious and unconscious processes, you can "know" the answer to something that you really never learned. To see what I mean, try this exercise:

Exercise #3. What is the length of the ship, the *Queen Elizabeth II*?
  (Select the answer you think comes closest.)

  a) 100 feet
  b) 300 feet
  c) 1,000 feet
  d) 5,000 feet
  e) 10,000 feet

Many people will correctly answer (c) 1,000 feet. (The actual exact length is 963 feet.) But even if you answered correctly, you almost certainly did not really know how long the Queen Elizabeth II actually is. Where then, does your answer come from? It comes from pulling together different facts in your mind, using your reasoning ability, double-checking your answer, pulling in more facts that you might need, and checking these against the answers I have given you. In short, it is a highly interactive process that draws on a large number of sources of information. The sources can be different for different people. Most of us will probably know that the Queen Elizabeth II is a large ship. An engineer might know what approximate size a large ship should be. If you own a pleasure boat, you may have an idea that a large ship would be ten to twenty times as long as yours. If you had seen pictures, you could imagine how big people are in relation to the size of the ship and extrapolate from there. But notice, also, that the other choices also contain an enormous amount of information. Some are clearly impossible (100 feet, or 10,000 feet—almost two miles long!). This eliminates two out of the five choices, and raises your chances of getting the answer correct, even if you know next to nothing about ships in general, and the Queen Elizabeth II in particular.

In short, it is not just your memory itself—not just your basic ability to remember faces and facts, nor how many faces and facts you have remembered—but also your unconscious links between memories, and your thinking ability, that determines how good your *real-world memory* is going to be. Of course, you probably already noticed another difference between the exercise with faces that you took, and the exercise about the Queen Elizabeth II. The exercise with faces required you to *recall* the names. Let's now exercise your memory for people and events of earlier eras by having you *recognize* the answer.

5

Recognizing Old Memories

Exercise #4. Check your memory of earlier eras with this exercise. Pick the best answer (answers are given at the end of the set of questions).

1. Amelia Earhart's companion on her ill-fated journey around the world was:
   (a) Tom Johnson
   (b) Charles Noonan
   (c) Dan Munroe

2. Mickey Mouse originally debuted as:
   (a) Steamboat Willie
   (b) Mr. Mouse
   (c) Mouseketeer

3. In 1930, a new planet was discovered. That planet was:
   (a) Uranus
   (b) Jupiter
   (c) Pluto

4. The Hindenburg exploded while trying to land in:
   (a) New Jersey
   (b) New York
   (c) Germany

5. The first American to travel in space was:
   (a) Alan Shepard
   (b) John Glenn
   (c) Yuri Gagarin

6. The first human heart transplant was performed by:
   (a) Dr. Michael DeBakey
   (b) Dr. Denton Cooley
   (c) Dr. Christiaan Barnard

7. Muhammad Ali was originally known as:
    (a) Cassius Clay
    (b) Jack Morgan
    (c) Wilt Chamberlain

8. The role of Annie Sullivan was played by which actress
    in the 1959 movie *The Miracle Worker*:
    (a) Patty Duke
    (b) Anne Bancroft
    (c) Lauren Bacall

9. "7AA" became famous as:
    (a) An advertising slogan
    (b) A War Bond rating
    (c) Greta Garbo's shoe size

10. The Dionne Quintuplets were born in 1934 in
    which country:
    (a) United States
    (b) Canada
    (c) France

11. Ho Chi Minh City was originally named:
    (a) Saigon
    (b) Hanoi
    (c) Peking

12. The acronym WIN stands for:
    (a) Whip Inflation Now
    (b) Microsoft Windows®
    (c) Winning in Numbers

13. When George McGovern ran for president in 1972,
    his first named running mate was:
    (a) John Dean
    (b) Thomas Eagleton
    (c) J. Carter Libby

14. Woodstock was:
    (a) a film festival
    (b) a ski resort in Colorado
    (c) an outdoor musical festival

15. In 1945, an airplane crashed into
    (a) Wrigley Field

(b) The Empire State Building

(c) The Verazanno Narrows bridge

16. The Symbionese Liberation Army was headquartered in
    (a) Guyana
    (b) Sri Lanka
    (c) California

17. Martin and Osa Johnson were
    (a) An ice skating team of the 1920s and 1930s
    (b) A wildlife photography team of the 1920s and 1930s
    (c) A vaudeville team of the 1920s

18. Amie Semple MacPherson was
    (a) An evangelist
    (b) A suffragette
    (c) A health fad leader

19. Which U.S. president was responsible for reopening diplomatic relations with China?
    (a) Gerald Ford
    (b) Richard Nixon
    (c) Jimmy Carter

20. In the popular *Thin Man* series of movies, William Powell starred with which of the following leading ladies:
    (a) Katharine Hepburn
    (b) Myrna Loy
    (c) Carole Lombard

21. Thor Heyerdahl sailed the Pacific on an raft and later wrote a book about his experience. That book was entitled
    (a) *Aloha Hoi!*
    (b) *Wind, Sun, and Waves*
    (c) *Kon Tiki*

22. Jackie Kennedy popularized the
    (a) Pillbox hat
    (b) Double breasted jacket
    (c) Knee-length skirt

Answers to the questions of Exercise #4:

1. Amelia Earhart's companion on her ill-fated journey around the world was (b) Charles Noonan.

2. Mickey Mouse originally debuted as (a) Steamboat Willie.

3. In 1930, the planet (c) Pluto was discovered.

4. The Hindenburg exploded while trying to land in (a) New Jersey.

5. The first American to travel in space was (a) Alan Shepard.

6. The first human heart transplant was performed by (c) Dr. Christiaan Barnard.

7. Muhammad Ali was originally known as (a) Cassius Clay.

8. In the 1959 movie *The Miracle Worker*, the role of Annie Sullivan was played by (b) Anne Bancroft.

9. "7AA" became famous as (c) Greta Garbo's shoe size. MGM released her shoe size to fight a widespread rumor that she had big feet.

10. The Dionne Quintuplets were born in 1934 in (b) Canada.

11. Ho Chi Minh City was originally named (a) Saigon.

12. The acronym WIN stands for (a) Whip Inflation Now.

13. When George McGovern ran for president in 1972, his first named running mate was (b) Thomas Eagleton.

14. Woodstock was (c) an outdoor musical festival.

15. In 1945, an airplane crashed into (b) the Empire State Building.

16. The Symbionese Liberation Army was stationed in (c) California.

17. Martin and Osa Johnson were a husband-and-wife team of wildlife photographers in the 1930s.

18. Amie Semple MacPherson was (a) an evangelist of the 1930s.

19. (b) Richard Nixon was responsible for reopening diplomatic relations with China.

20. In the popular *Thin Man* series of movies, William Powell starred with (b) Myrna Loy.

21. Thor Heyerdahl sailed the Pacific on a raft and wrote (c) *Kon Tiki.*

22. Jackie Kennedy popularized the (a) pillbox hat.

These questions probed your memory for things you once knew in a different manner than did the faces and people you were asked to identify earlier.

One important difference was that they were in **words** rather than pictures. And many of the questions asked for information you would have known only through words. (You probably would not have known Greta Garbo's shoe size by just seeing pictures of her shoes.) Word memory is a different kind of memory than memory for pictures or scenes; it resides in a different part of the brain. People can normally differ from one another, in having one type of memory that works better than the other.

Another way the memory probed by these questions differed from that tested by the pictures was that the questions also asked about **events**, not just people. Memory for events may be different than memory for people. And some people may be more attuned to people than events or vice versa.

But most important, these questions gave you a chance to *recognize* the answer, rather than *recall* it. The pictures earlier did have some component of recognition, too—you had to recognize the face to answer the question correctly—but *recalling* the name was the crux of the answer. Because recall questions are much more open-ended, you really had to *know* the specific piece of information in order to say it. In the multiple-choice recognition test, you have two pieces of information (the question, and a set of possible answers). You "answer" the question by searching your mind for a connection that makes the most sense between one possible answer and the question. So a multiple-choice recognition memory test does not test one type of raw memory power as strongly as a recall test does.

To recall something, you must call together the to-be-remembered information in your mind and say it in some form. How well you can call together that information depends on both the adequacy of the clue that you were given (or figured out) and the way you reconstruct information in your mind. It also depends upon how easy it is to express that to-be remembered information in the first place. An example: name a popular English singer of the 1960s with an unusual name.

There were many popular English singers in the 1960s, so this clue doesn't help an enormous amount. What do I mean by unusual name? To think of this one, you have to go through the list in your head. To bring that list to mind, you have to call up the names themselves. The fact that they are unusual makes it more difficult to call them up. What about Engelbert Humperdinck?

"Engelbert Humperdinck" was the one I had in mind. Anyone who lived through the '60s and early '70s could hardly escape hearing his songs. But his name may not have been anywhere close to the tip of your tongue. The sounds of the name itself are not the usual sounds of modern day English, and their combination is certainly unfamiliar. It is simply hard to remember such a name, and hard to get such a name out of your mouth.

But when you saw it, didn't you easily *recognize* that "Engelbert Humperdinck" was the right answer? This difference between recalling and recognizing is very important in memory. In general, you more easily recognize something than recall it. You are asking less when you ask for recognition memory than when you ask for recall. With recognition, you ask for a feeling of familiarity, or the triggering of an association; your actual memory does not have to be completely accurate. But with recall, you actually have to dredge up all the information, and get it out *exactly*. This is, in general, why you almost certainly find it much easier to *recognize* a person's face, voice or name than to *say* the person's name, what they looked like, or what they sounded like.

Here is another important difference between recognizing and recalling something: All other things being equal, the *easier* it is to **recognize** something you have learned, the *harder* it is to **recall** it. Probably, the reason has to do with how we use *familiarity* to recall and recognize. Less-familiar items stand out more when we try to recognize them. But the less familiar something is, the harder it is to bring it into mind for recall.

In everyday life, recall and recognition are often talked about interchangeably, but they are not the same type of memory. They actually probe different kinds of memories and do it in somewhat different ways. And to do best in either one, you actually have to study differently for one than the other. For a recall test, you must make yourself fluent in the answers you need to come up with. For a recognition test, you have to create (and find) as many links as you can in your mind; you need not go through the trouble of actually *learning* the items themselves as thoroughly. If you are one who "doesn't take tests well," the differences between recall and recognition may explain it: how you are tested is mismatched with how you remember.

INFANTILE AMNESIA

What about your oldest memories of all—your memories of your childhood?

Most adults find it impossible to recall events that occurred before the age of three. This has been termed "infantile amnesia." (As with most things involving memory—and human beings in general—variation among individuals is vast.) Why this barrier to recall? Several reasons. When we are that young, we do not learn very well. We may not be paying attention; what is important to us later as adults is meaningless to us as children. We may not even learn very well the things we try to learn. The systems to lock in information may not be as efficient. But perhaps even more important, the web of interconnections that an adult has, that serve to lash down memories and tie them into a larger system of remembered experiences, is lacking. In addition, many memories that could occur before age three, occur before the child has language, or appreciable language. Therefore, they may be locked into a nonverbal store, but not be accessible to the language system that later develops. And finally, later memories overlay prior memories, in much the same way that memory for the first person you meet in a receiving line may be partly wiped out by the flood of faces and names that follow.

6

Learning, Repetition, Time, and Memory

CONSIDER AGAIN THE pictures you tried to identify, and the people and events you were asked about. What made even the ones you *knew* you knew (or knew once!) hard to remember, and certainly harder to remember than Mickey Mouse?

You may not have learned these people or events as well in the first place. They may not have been as exciting, as memorable, as Mickey Mouse (Those ears! That face! That squeaky voice!).

And pictures of Mickey Mouse have been repeated over and over again for you. Each repetition would strengthen your memory. But many of the pictures and events I tested you on, you would have learned only once. You would not have had the benefit of repetition to make them stronger. (Of course, I cannot be completely sure of this. You might like to leaf through old *Life* magazines or history books. But if this were a *real* test, I would have asked you about this. And you might have told me so yourself.)

Also, most of the pictures and questions in the tests were from quite some time ago. Memories may fade a bit with time itself. Old memories are usually harder to reach than newer memories. But, by itself, the time that has passed since you learned something may not be the major culprit; it may be the mileage you have put on—all the other memories and experiences that came between when you learned something and when you're asked to remember it. Your memories may not get erased, but they may get overwritten and interfered with. Either way, older memories will be harder to remember.

Pictures of Mickey Mouse therefore have a double advantage. Not only have they been repeated, but they've been repeated endlessly (or so it seems). So it is likely that you last saw Mickey Mouse much more recently than you saw or heard about any of the other people or events. This is another reason why these were harder to remember than Mickey Mouse.

But the faces I presented to you and the events I asked about, were purer tests of some aspects of your memory than was Mickey Mouse. Too much is involved with memory for Mickey; it is impossible to disentangle why any one person remembers Mickey at all. But the faces and the events have fewer of the memory complexities that Mickey carries. With these, you should be able to feel aspects of memory that the strength of Mickey's memories floods and obscures. One aspect is the sense of familiarity, which we will discuss next.

7

Familiarity, *Déjà Vu,* and the Other *Déjàs*

TURN BACK TO the old photos of famous people and examine again one that you thought you knew, but did not have the slightest idea of the name. You were experiencing an example of how your memory for the picture actually has two different parts: the sense of *familiarity* that you appreciated, and the *specific* knowledge of who it was, which was lacking in this case. A large part of the sense of familiarity—particularly the very first sense of familiarity that you feel—originates from calculations your brain performs before you become conscious of *who* you are looking at. The sense of familiarity itself does not even have to become conscious. In some peculiar kinds of memory loss, even the conscious knowledge of familiarity is inaccessible. Such people cannot tell you whether they are looking at somebody who is familiar or not. But deeper in their brain, the sense of familiarity may still be there. Their pupils will dilate with interest and recognition, their heart rate will increase, and they will sweat just a bit more than otherwise.

DÉJÀ VU ALL OVER AGAIN

Sometimes, this unconscious, primitive feeling of familiarity that our brain automatically estimates gives us some surprises. You look down a street, and *know* that it is familiar. The shops, the buildings, the trees, even the trash cans—you *know* you have seen them before. You have *been there* before.

The *déjà vu* experience—literally, in French, "already seen"—which is the feeling that something is familiar even though you have never seen it before—is a common one, as are other *déjà* experiences: *Déjà entendu* is the feeling that, at some prior time, you heard what you are hearing now, even though that is not true; *déjà eprouvé* is the feeling that you have already done an act or had an experience which you have actually never done before; in *déjà fait,* you have the feeling that

35

what is happening to you now has happened to you exactly the same way before. *Déjà pensé* is the feeling that you have already had the same thought before; *déjà raconté* is the feeling that the story you are hearing, you have already heard before.

Many people think *déjà vu* and related *déjà* experiences are abnormal, perhaps because these experiences probably occur more dramatically in people with diseases such as epilepsy affecting the temporal lobe, or schizophrenia and other psychiatric conditions. Some people even interpret the *déjà vu* experience as evidence for past lives: You thought the scene was familiar because you experienced a similar scene in a previous life.

But *déjà vu* is *not* abnormal; between 30 and 70 percent of otherwise normal people have experienced it at some time. And for some people, it can be quite common.

You do not need to invoke the possibility of past lives to explain the *déjà vu* experience; mind and brain actually explain it quite well. To understand *déjà vu* and related experiences of familiarity, you need to understand only two things about the way our memories and our minds work.

First, our minds are always trying to find *approximate* matches for things we see, hear or experience; it is the nature of our memories to try to generalize, to extract the universal. A street scene *does* look like another street scene, certainly more than it looks like a cow or the face on a dollar bill. Your mind readily extracts the gist of what you perceive, and readily activates the memories that have similar gists. It is far from clear how it does so. It may be that the mind extracts general features from the street scene: the straightness of lines that represent the street; blobs that represent trees or people; larger blobs that represent cars; a blur that represents motion. Or it may use more esoteric methods. *Holograms, Fourier transforms*, and *distributed coding* are all mechanisms that have been invoked to explain how the brain processes information in a way that identifies the essence of the information, as well as its specifics. But however it is done, it is clear that our minds can do it.

Familiarity is the second mechanism needed to understand *déjà vu*. The brain seems to try to determine whether something is familiar using many different methods. It uses many different bits of information and uses many different levels of information to do so. For example, if you look at your toaster, your brain determines that it is familiar from the specifics of that particular toaster, but also from the general sense you have of "toasterness." So even a toaster you have never seen before will still be familiar to you in some way, because it *is* similar to other toasters you have seen or know about. Taken together then, little fragments of familiarity can add up to create a sense that something is familiar, when it actually is not.

To get a feel for how this might operate, examine these "objects" created by my colleague, Dr. John Hart, Jr.:

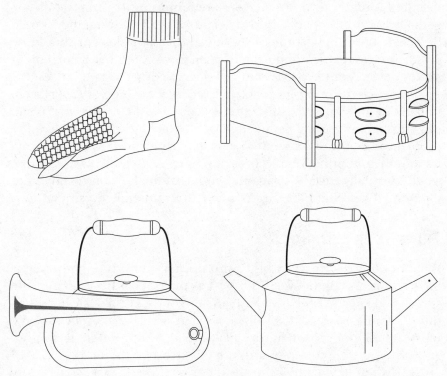

These may seem somewhat familiar. But at the same time, you know that they are not right. That is because they are made out of pieces of real objects, but put together in unfamiliar ways. The pieces trigger your sense of familiarity even though the object as a whole makes your mind shout "impossible!"

The fact that the feeling of *déjà vu* and related experiences are so common in one particular form of epilepsy—epilepsy originating in the temporal lobes—is one important clue that the brain mechanisms involved in calculating and evaluating familiarity are in the temporal lobe. (The temporal lobe, amygdala, and hippocampus are pictured in Figure 7, Chapter 14, page 71). It is very likely that these senses of familiarity are somehow associated with a structure in the tip of the temporal lobe, called the amygdala, a mass of neurons involved in regulating emotions such as fear and laughter, among others. The amygdala sits just in front of, and next to, the hippocampus, a structure that you will see me refer to again and again. The hippocampus is critically involved in signaling the brain that it must lock in memories. It seems reasonable that the brain would put the system involved in deciding whether or not memories are important (the amygdala) together with the system involved in deciding whether or not they should be saved (the hippocampus)—because what is important should be saved, and what is not important should not be. So this arrangement makes perfect sense, as does our proclivity to d*éjà vu* experiences.

Jamais vu is the opposite problem from *déjà vu*. Familiar things seem unfamiliar and strange. Although less common than *déjà vu*, it is still not unusual for normal people to have this feeling at times. When the problem is due to disease, the major culprit again is epilepsy beginning in the temporal lobes. This again suggests that the pathways that would normally carry information about familiarity run through the temporal lobe. When they are blocked, everything seems strange.

TRUST YOUR FEELINGS?

What often goes wrong in otherwise normal individuals, however, is incorrect cross-talk between the system that says "who it is" and the system that judges familiarity. You can talk yourself into believing something is familiar, and, if you repeat it often enough, it *will* become familiar. This is one reason for the advice to go "with your gut feeling" in answering test questions. Your gut feeling can be the more unbiased sense of whether you know the answer or not, whereas you could probably talk yourself into believing almost anything if you give yourself enough chance. On the other hand, your conscious probing of your own memory might uncover information your initial gut reaction never appreciated. So whether you should go with your feelings, or ponder your answers, is still an individual decision. It depends upon how much you know, and how skilled you are in making your conscious probing work for you.

KNOWING THAT YOU ARE LIKELY TO KNOW

Examine the pictures of famous (and not so famous) people again. If you find yourself telling yourself, "If I had seen this person before, I would have surely remembered him!", then you are experiencing another aspect of memory: your ability to tell how memorable something is going to be, even before you try to learn it. While this is the basis for a coy introductory line—"If we had met before, *surely* I would have remembered *you!*"—it nonetheless is true. We can estimate how memorable a face, a phrase or an event is likely to be for us, and then further use this as a guide to whether we remember it or not. If the face *is* memorable, but you have little or no real recollection of having seen the person before, then you probably did not. You would have remembered better if you had. But if the face is *not* memorable, then even if you had seen it before, you might still have no memory. So you have to be more careful about saying "no."

ARE YOU CAUTIOUS OR RECKLESS WITH YOUR MEMORY?

Making a memory decision is one thing. Deciding what to do about the memory is another. If you see someone you think you recognize, should you say hello? If you really do know the person, and you say hello, everything is fine. But if you really do *not* know him, and you say hello, you risk embarrassment—perhaps even accusations of harassment! But if you really do know the person, and *don't* say hello, then it looks as if you snubbed them. Of course, if you really don't know them, and don't say hello, you are fine.

Notice that you have exactly the same *knowledge* of whether or not you know the person in each case. It is what you *do* with that knowledge that differs.

Sometimes the factors that sway your thinking are conscious. Sometimes, they are unconscious. Either way, the existence of such biases and influences on decisions made about memory are very well known.

Biases are part of the reason for differences in memory performance between different people. Two people can know the same amount, or have the same amount of memory. But one may be reckless to respond. He'll have many answers—many will be right, but many will be wrong. The other person may be very reluctant to respond. She'll have few answers—but all her answers will be right. (Which is the right strategy depends upon the situation.) But even though their memory abilities may *seem* to differ, and their test scores certainly will, their **actual** memory abilities are not different at all.

SLIPS OF THE MIND

Automatic activation does not last very long by itself—perhaps one half-second or so. But it can be constantly refreshed. So if you are discussing money, whether you realize it or not, thoughts of "bank", "wealth" and perhaps even the shimmer of "gold" are almost literally dancing in your head. These activations subtly guide the paths of your thinking.

Activations and their connections can extend far beyond our original ideas and thoughts. "Bank" can trigger "Thank" (a sound association), or activate "river bank" as well as the right meaning. These associations are actually not incorrect. After all, they really *are* connected. But they have no sustaining connections—no other links that lead from the original stream of thought—and they get no additional activation along the way. So their activations quickly die out, or are snuffed out by the activations of other, competing thoughts in the same set of nerve cells. As a result, they usually cause no trouble.

But if you are not careful, or if you really *are* thinking of going fishing when you should be thinking of your bank job, then these activations might get strong enough to produce a conscious result, a slip of the tongue (or of the mind). If you observe yourself, you can even tell what types of activations caused these slips. Slips of the tongue that involve meaning arise from activation in the network of meaning. Slips of the tongue that involve sound arise from activation in the network of sounds that you speak.

"I JUST CAN'T PLACE IT!"

You see a face. She looks familiar. But where did you see her before?

You look at a book. It looks familiar. But where did you see it before?

If you *had* seen these before and you can't remember where, when or any of the circumstances, you are not alone. This *amnesia for the source (source amnesia)* is very common. It does not mean that something is wrong with your memory; it is just the way that memory works.

We *should* have source amnesia for some things, because where or how we learned them is not important. At some time in your life, you probably learned that the capital of France is Paris, that four quarts make a gallon, and the Pythagorean theorem. But if you can recall in detail the *circumstances* of your learning these facts—the face of your history teacher as she pointed out the capitol of France, the place on the blackboard where your teacher wrote out the Pythagorean theorem, or the back of the milk carton where you first came to realize that four quarts made up a gallon—then either you have an extraordinary memory, or you were paying attention to the wrong things. The important point of the history lesson was not everything that was happening in the class at that time, but the basic fact that Paris is the capital of France. You *should* have forgotten the rest, because you should not have spent much mental energy learning it in the first place. It was unimportant.

That is why a certain amount of source amnesia is to be expected. And a certain amount of what feels like source amnesia is also to be expected, because you will always be better able to recognize that something is familiar than place *exactly* why it is familiar. To place where, when or how you learned something requires a more detailed memory than just knowing that it is familiar. The memories you have of where, when and how you saw something may be in your mind, but they are probably weak. Individually, these memories are certainly weaker than the sum of all of them put together. But it is the sum of all of them put together that may make something seem familiar. So, you can have a substantial sense of familiarity—the sum of your individual memories— even though each individual memory may be too weak to register, just as a pile of sand can be heavy even though each individual grain of sand is too light for you to appreciate.

8

Your Own Old Memories

WHAT ABOUT YOUR own memories? Obviously, these are vastly more important to you than pictures of almost any public figure. Because they are so important, and so central to who you are, researchers believe that such memories are either stored with special strength, or treated in some special way by the brain. However, it is precisely the uniqueness your own memories that makes them extremely difficult to test in any scientific way. How does somebody, who is not you, know what you have experienced?

It *is* possible to make a good approximation of the truth, but it takes intense work. Later in this book, in "Forever Fourteen" (Chapter 33), I describe the results of memory testing of a fifty-four-year-old man we called "J." "J" seemed to have lost his memories—*all* of his memories—back to age fourteen and before. To test "J's" memories from his entire life, my colleague Dr. Michael McCloskey and his associates had to do an enormous amount of background work; to find what "J" *should* have remembered from his past, they had to find out what his past had been! So Dr. McCloskey and his team went to "J's" original home town, and checked in the archives there. They found pictures showing how streets had looked and the buildings and businesses that had been present in different decades. This way, they could show him pictures of scenes from the town he may have experienced, as well as ones from before and after the time he spent there. They collected his school records to get a complete index of his teachers. They interviewed his family and friends to find out who he knew or should have known. From all this material, they were able to create a set of comprehensive tests of "J's" past life. They complemented this testing of his own memories with tests for public figures and public events like the ones I have shown you here. Months of effort, and many people, were involved. Obviously, this degree of investigation is not something that can be done with everybody.

When such autobiographical memories can be checked, it is common to find out that any one person's memory is likely to be very different from what really occurred at the time. One important reason is *selectivity*. You don't pay attention to everything, and different people pay attention to different things. Therefore, participants in the same event are likely to have different recollections of it because of selectivity alone. When I was six, my parents took me and my young brothers on a three-day drive to Florida. It was to be an adventure for us all. My parents have very strong memories of the drive down, and of the weary attempts to keep three small children under control. But I have a strong memory of the trip, too: I remember a manta ray being hauled up onto the dock. I remember the scene vividly, and my father has confirmed all the details. But that is *all* I can consciously remember of the entire trip.

In addition to simple selectivity, there are many other reasons why our autobiographical memories are likely to differ from what really occurred. Such memories are subject to twin phenomena—distortion and self-perpetuation of distortions. All memories can be tainted by these influences, as we will discuss (Chapters 18 and 35). But these are perhaps particularly likely to occur with our own personal memories. Memories are modified when we recall them, modified again when we save them in our minds. With important personal memories, this cycle may be repeated many times. This reinforces and solidifies the memories, but it may also alter them beyond recognition by anyone else there at the time. So our own memory, of our own life, has many reasons to be considerably different from the real experiences we had—not just distorted, but at times totally incorrect. If you want to test this yourself, just bring up questions at any family reunion!

9

Making New Memories

THE EXERCISES SO far have stretched your ability to get at memories you once had. How do you create new ones? You exercise that ability in the next several sections.

Before we begin, there is an important point to make. You almost never create totally new memories. You are never told a story, for instance, in a totally alien language, about a totally alien culture, and asked to remember it. Instead, you hear the story in sounds that are already familiar to you, in words and sentence patterns that are already familiar to you, and in connection with events and people that are probably at least somewhat familiar to you. What you try to remember is the particular arrangement that is new, the association—with time or place or other people—is what makes that a "new" memory.

The difference is important, because much of what we call "learning something new" actually involves taking something we already know and giving it a tag of some kind. The tag may be a sense of time ("I saw Uncle Albert just yesterday"). Or it may be a tag for place ("I saw Uncle Albert at the train station"). Or it could be a sense of familiarity ("I know that person from somewhere"). Or the tag that we create may actually be a link between two known items ("Mark met Shelley at the party, and now they're always together").

It is possible to learn completely novel information—sounds, images, object, or actions. But it is much harder to learn something really new than it is to learn *about* something you already know. To see this, which of the patterns of dots in Figure 4 will you remember better?

Both are made out of the same parts (dots), and both have the same number of parts. But one is in a totally unfamiliar arrangement, and is very difficult to learn. The other, in a familiar arrangement, is easy.

This exercise is not entirely academic. The dot pattern you just saw is something like Braille, or any other pattern that is unfamiliar at first. It takes a lot of effort to learn such patterns from scratch. But, once you've learned them, they become units in your head; you can use them to build other, bigger, memories. We go through exactly the same

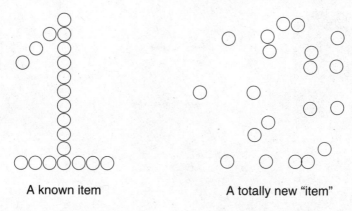

A known item   A totally new "item"

Figure 4: An item you already know, and a totally new "item." Which is easier to remember?

process when, as children, we learn the parts of letters, then the letters themselves, then the words that letters can make. (Of course, in this natural form of learning, we often try to learn several things at once—the parts of letters and the letters themselves, the letters and the words they make up.)

Unless we are learning a new language, a new form of art, or new music, most of the learning we are interested in as adults is a more prosaic type of new learning. This is what we shall exercise next. Again, try to feel what mental muscles these examples make you use.

Exercise #5. Learning new faces

Study the faces on the next two pages. Allow yourself five or ten seconds for each. Then take the test of your memory for these pictures that follows the two pages.

Picture 24

Picture 25

Picture 26

Picture 27

Picture 28

Picture 29

Picture 30

Picture 31

Which of these faces were you *just* given in the test? (Answers are at the bottom of the page.)

Face A

Face B

Face C

Face D

This was an exercise of your **long-term** or **permanent** memory for pictures. Don't be worried about how you did (or didn't do!). This was not a real test—the book would have had to been too long to make it a *real* test. Because if we have anything to be proud of as human beings, we can be proud of our picture memory. People can be shown a series of *ten thousand* pictures like the ones you just had, and get 99 percent of them correct. Human beings are very visual animals. So our ability to process and remember visual things that are very important to us—and pictures of people's faces fall into this category—is truly extraordinary.

I called this **long-term** or **permanent** memory, even though you were tested only a few seconds after studying the last picture. That is because I am trying to avoid a confusion in the way popular terms like "immediate memory," "short-term memory," and "long-term memory" are used. For the types of memories we are testing here, and the next ones we will test, there are really only **two** *kinds* of memory storage systems inside your head (as we will discuss in Chapter 14, "How Your Brain Remembers," there are probably a large number of memory storage systems inside your head—these are the two *kinds* that are present).

The first is an **immediate memory**. This acts like an immediate echo box (for sound) or a quick glimpse (for vision). For sounds, this echo box memory can last seven to ten seconds, but not much longer. For vision, this image memory probably lasts no more than half a second under most circumstances. These types of immediate memory very likely represent the actual firing of nerve cells inside the brain, the immediate record of what you heard or saw. These immediate memories correspond to what your tape recorder can pick up as you are recording, or what your video camera sees at the moment it is aimed at a scene. Memories that are taken out of permanent storage are also placed into this activated form.

The **long-term** or **permanent memory**, in this analogy, is what is *on* the tape. It has been recorded, but it is not active. It probably lies latent in the connections between nerve cells, or deeper within individual nerve cells themselves. To get at permanent memory, it has to be reactivated. It has to be played through the speaker or be painted on the video screen.

These are the two main systems that people have for learning. And it is very likely that the two systems are active simultaneously. The patterns that you hear or see dance along the neurons, while at the same time the connections between the neurons are learning those patterns to be able to re-create them again, later. So unlike the tape recorder or the video camera, where the immediate activation is kept separate from the long-term storage on tape, our brains probably combine the two. At the very least, very much the same areas of the brain are used for the immediate registration as well as the permanent storage.

During the test for memory for faces that you just took, you would not necessarily have been aware of the immediate visual memory that you had. It does not last very long under normal circumstances, and the moment you moved your eyes to the next picture, the pattern of activity that represented the last picture would have changed to reflect the new one, the one you were looking at at the moment. But the nerve cells would remember that pattern of activity. Although dormant, the potential for re-establishing that pattern will remain within the connections between them. It can be activated again, and brought into active memory and consciousness, in a number of ways: by seeing the same image again, or by seeing or recalling something connected with that original image.

10

Immediate Memory

IF YOU WANT to get a better feel for what one of the immediate memory systems is like, you need to test your *digit span*. To do this test properly, you really need somebody reading these digits to you and then asking you to recall them. The tester should read one number at a time to you, at about one per second. They should read the whole line of numbers and then pause. The pause is your signal to repeat back the numbers to them. The examiner can keep track of the ones you get right by checking them in the book. Ready?

Exercise #6. Digit Span Test

> 3 7 4—test
> 8 1 6 5 7—test
> 3 1 6 8 9 2 4 7—test
> 5 9 6 3 2 1 7 4 8 6 2 9 3 4—test

What did you notice? The short list was very easy. You probably were not even conscious of having the numbers in your head, but when your tester paused, they tumbled out.

But then, when the list of numbers lengthened to five, six, or seven items, you probably discovered you were having troubles. The numbers would seem to vanish from your head as new numbers came in. So you would discover that you really were not able to remember much beyond seven numbers or so.

When you tried even longer lists, your examiner may have noticed something peculiar. You tended to give out first the numbers from the very end of the list, then a few from the beginning, and then perhaps a few from the middle.

What you were doing with these lists was testing the capacity of your **immediate memory**, the one that deals with sounds and words. Normally, it seems to hold about seven items, plus or minus two. (Its *real* capacity is three to four items, but we won't get into that here.) This immediate memory for digits and words works something like an echo box. But unlike an echo box, this one cannot hold more than about seven items. Any new item coming in randomly displaces one that is already there. This is why you suddenly had problems when you exceeded the capacity of this immediate memory store.

With the longer list, **long-term** memory was coming into play. The items circulating inside your echo box, the immediate memory, had a chance to be learned, to become part of a more permanent memory. The ones that particularly had a chance to be learned were the ones that came in first, at the beginning of the list. When you are asked to recall a list that exceeds the capacity of your echo box, the typical strategy people use is to first dump everything that they have in their immediate memory (the items at the end of the list), and then recall the strongest items in their permanent memory. The strongest items in permanent memory are the ones that came in at the beginning of the list. The numbers in the middle of the list are not in immediate memory, and had the least chance to be put into permanent memory, so recall for these is weakest, and most erratic.

What do we use our immediate memory for? The almost trivial use of this immediate memory is when you try to remember a phone number. Most people will notice that they have trouble repeating more than seven digits of a phone number they have just heard. This is the limitation of your immediate memory.

The major purpose of immediate memory seems to be that it is part of a scratch pad system that we use in our minds to keep track of what we are hearing and to try to understand it. This can be shown in several ways. In the extreme, there are people who have very poor immediate memories for words because of damage to the brain, where the damage is so limited that it only seems to affect this type of immediate memory. (Such cases are uncommon. Usually, damage in this region of the brain is associated with damage affecting other speech functions.) People with this problem typically cannot repeat back more than one or two digits at a time. And they have problems with accurate comprehension of what they hear, because they cannot keep track of all the clauses and redirections we normally juggle in our minds.

This use for immediate memory can also be shown in normal people. Two researchers at Carnegie-Mellon University in Pittsburgh, Drs. Patricia Carpenter and Marcel Just, have shown that people's comprehension of sentences and stories, and of text in general, is related to their immediate memory: The bigger the immediate memory, the better people seem to be able to understand.

Some people *seem* to have poor comprehension, and *seem* to have an immediate memory problem. But in my experience, usually they are just not paying attention. If you are really not *trying* to remember a set of digits, or something else is distracting you, then your digit span will not be very good.

One way we have of checking this clinically is to read the digit list to people forward, but ask them to give them back in reverse order. Normally, recalling a set of digits backward is a much harder job than just letting them rush out of your immediate memory store. However, some people, who are not paying attention or not finding it very interesting to do the digits forward, become much more interested and challenged with the digits backward. They do better with them backward than they do forward. This is one of the pieces of evidence I might use to show a patient that his immediate memory is actually intact, but what is wrong is that he is not paying attention well enough.

11

Long-term Memory for Pictures, Lists, and Stories

Exercise #7. List learning.

Once we move beyond immediate memory, we enter the realm of more permanent memories. The long list of digits you tried out above gave you some indication of how permanent memory could sneak into a situation. If you tried to learn a longer list of words, and repeated it over and over, you will see an even better example of permanent memory. Try reading through this list of words just once, then look up from the page and try to recall it:

> plate
> wheel
> glass
> tire
> hood
> window
> gas
> light
> trunk
> keys
> spare

When you read through this list of words, you began filling up your immediate memory. But the items you read were also getting tagged as new, long-term memories. You probably did not remember many of the words the first time you read the list through. (In fact, you may not have been able to repeat more than about six or seven words, the capacity of your immediate memory.) If you kept repeating the list, though, gradually the connections would become stronger, and eventually you would remember the entire list perfectly well. (These connections are, in fact, fairly permanent. They may fade with time, so much so that you would not even remember after awhile having learned the list. But I could probably demonstrate that some connections were still there by showing that, if I gave you this list again, you would do better than you would have if you had never seen it before.)

You may have noticed something about the list that gave you a shortcut. Learning new connections is difficult, but if you can resurrect connections you already have, then your job of remembering will become much easier. Did you notice that these items were all the components of a car? (Your mind probably did so subconsciously, even if you did not appreciate the fact.) Realizing that connection makes your whole task of learning the list a great deal easier.

The process of finding connections can be, as we have seen before, both automatic and conscious. Either way, it provides a very powerful glue for our memory. It also provides a very convenient way for us to tag whole groups of items together within our mind. Instead of remembering a list of ten or fifteen disconnected items, you remember just one—*car*.

The categorization you just experienced is what was called *semantic categorization*. It is based on *meaning*. Other types of categorization or clustering are possible. For example, you could group items together by where they are located. Or you can make associations between items that you have to learn and items that you already know by rhyme, for example. You can try to make acronyms for things you have to learn, in the same way that you can make USA stand for United States of America. In the extreme, if you can find in what you have to learn a pattern that is the same as what you already know, you have a powerful hook for remembering that information. For example, try to remember the following series of digits:

$$3\ 1\ 4\ 1\ 5\ 9\ 2\ 6\ 5\ 4$$

If you recognized this as the mathematical number *Pi*, then you have replaced what you were trying to learn with what you already knew, and your job of remembering it becomes much, much easier.

It took us a little while to get here, but now we are actually at the point of better understanding the kind of memory that is one of the most important for people: memory for meaningful connected events, actions or stories. We rarely have to remember lists of unconnected words, but we often have to remember lists of things to get at the supermarket. In real life, very few people ask us to remember random digits.

But we all have to remember stories of who said what to whom, where, when and why. Our memory for such stories or connected events is not something separate from the memories we have just examined. It is actually built out of these more basic memory processes. As a result, it shares their virtues, their limitations, and their faults.

Exercise #8. Your memory for stories.

Read this story and try to remember it verbatim. Write it down while you are recalling it, if you like. You'll have a chance to compare how well you do to how well a "natural" mnemonist, "V.P.," did with the same story, in Chapter 19. I should warn you now, though, that while I am asking you to remember the story immediately, V.P.'s memory was so good that he had to be given more of a handicap: his memory for the story was tested *six weeks* after he first read it! But don't get discouraged, and don't peek!

> One night two young men from Egulac went down to the river to hunt seals, and while they were there it became foggy and calm. Then they heard war-cries, and they thought: "Maybe this is a war-party." They escaped to the shore, and hid behind a log. Now canoes came up, and they heard the noise of paddles, and saw one canoe coming up to them. There were five men in the canoe, and they said:
> "What do you think? We wish to take you along. We are going up the river to make war on the people."
> One of the young men said: "I have no arrows."
> "Arrows are in the canoe," they said.
> "I will not go along. I might be killed. My relatives do not know where I have gone. But you," he said, turning to the other, "may go with them."
> So one of the young men went, but the other returned home.
> And the warriors went on up the river to a town on the other side of Kalama. The people came down to the water, and they began to fight, and many were killed. But presently the young man heard one of the warriors say: "Quick, let us go home: that Indian has been hit." Now he thought: "Oh, they are ghosts." He did not feel sick, but they said he had been shot.
> So the canoes went back to Egulac, and the young man went ashore to his house, and made a fire. And he told

everybody and said: "Behold I accompanied the ghosts, and we went to fight. Many of our fellows were killed, and many of those who attacked us were killed. They said I was hit, and I did not feel sick."

He told it all, and then became quiet. When the sun rose he fell down. Something black came out of his mouth. His face became contorted. The people jumped up and cried.

He was dead.

— Story from F.C. Bartlett, *Remembering: A study in experimental and social psychology.* London: Cambridge University Press, 1932, as reprinted in Hunt & Love, 1972.

Notice that in "learning" this story, you did not recall it verbatim. It is hard to recall each individual word, and in some ways it is good that you do not, because the real importance of the story is in its meaning, its gist. But notice also how there are different levels of meaning and gist in this story. If you thought it was only referring to the travails of some young men in a canoe, you would remember some information about the story. But if you understood this was a story about American Indians, and ghost warriors, you would understand a great deal more. You would not only understand the story itself better, but you would also discover that the story would become another piece in your mental picture of American Indians. The memory of Indians in canoes fighting with arrows would become not just a part of this story, but also part of your images and memories of American Indian tribal culture and warfare.

This may seem like a great deal to expect of one story. But it is, in fact, how memory—the memories that we really want—really work. Memories build upon other memories. They are interlocked with each other, and reinforce each other. So what we really mean when we speak of our memory is not a collection of isolated bits of information, but actually a fairly strong structure made out of these smaller, weaker elements.

Sometimes this structure of memory causes problems. New information that tries to get into our memory, if it is truly new, gets twisted and trimmed and stretched to fit the spot available. It can be pushed in, and make something of a new spot—that is, alter memory—but not without itself being somewhat altered. This is why what people remember tends to fit their expectations, and may actually even be completely shaped by their expectations and prior experiences.

The good side of this constructive interactive process is that it builds a very much stronger memory system out of building blocks that are individually much weaker. The web of connections we build up in our memory—that we *call* our memory—is what we use to capture knowledge. Each individual strand of memory may be too poorly positioned to catch anything, or too weak to hold whatever it does touch. But collectively, the elements of our memory, and the connections between them, can catch information coming at us on the fly, make sense of it almost immediately, and lock some of that passing information in permanently.

This is one of the major virtues of human memory, and one of the major ways human memory differs from computer memory. The memory of a computer is much more accurate. It is much faster. It can be much vaster than human memory. But memories inside of a computer all exist in isolation from each other. They do not have this wondrous web of latent connections that make our memories real tools for our thinking.

THE TYRANNY OF THE OLD

The difficulty that our brains have in forming completely new memories, combined with the flexibility they have in trying to fit incoming information, creates situations in memory with far-reaching consequences.

Our brains try to force incoming information into the forms that already exist in memory. So if an incoming perception doesn't quite fit what is in memory, our memories are likely to trim it or stretch it to fit the already existing patterns. On one hand, this is a useful adjustment. It allows us to recognize faces, even though the perspective in which we see them may be different than the original; it also allows us to make creative jumps across similar types of incoming information. But the other side of this transformation is inimical: it means that what we "perceive" and what we "remember" may not be a completely true copy of what came in. This is especially true as the incoming information is more and more deviant from what is already in our minds. Probably the extreme example of this is hallucinations, in which the incoming information is minimal, even nonexistent, and the information actually is stretched out from pre-existing slots inside our minds. We hallucinate based on our experience, and our cultural experience. We will see an unfamiliar shape as a familiar one and try to force it into the mold we already have for it.

12

Our *Truly* Unconscious Memories

THE MEMORIES YOU DIDN'T KNOW YOU HAD

Our minds and brains make use of enormous numbers of memories that we may not always appreciate as being memories at all. To get a feel for some of these memories, examine the following picture:

Exercise #9. What do you see?

Michael E. Leonard, based on a photo by Ronald G. James

Figure 5. What do you see?

Did you spot the dog in Figure 5? (Now that you know there's a dog there, look again. It may take a few seconds to pop out.) Your "memory" of dogs and street corners connected the dots and blobs in this picture for you, and let you recognize the meaningful pattern they made.

If you want other examples of this other type of memory, try the following mental exercises:

Exercise #10.

1. Describe how you make a cup of coffee. Now, do it—or imagine doing it.
2. Describe how you drive a car. Now, imagine doing it.
3. Describe how you get dressed in the morning. Now, do it or imagine doing it.

The difference between doing something and talking about it, and what you experienced perceiving the dog in Figure 5, above reveals a very important type of memory: memory that is **implicit**. (Among the other terms applied are **unconscious** and **procedural** memory.) This is the type of learning or knowledge involved in doing something such as riding a bicycle, driving a car, making coffee or dressing yourself. It is also the kind of memory involved in reading and speaking. It is called implicit memory because you don't have to speak out loud about it or be able to describe it to do it. In fact, often you can't describe what you do easily in words; you can only do it.

It seems likely that this kind of memory is the memory that occurs because of changes in the connections between nerve cells that are *directly* involved in doing the activity. The connections between the parts of these circuits can become strengthened (or weakened). We probably have a great many types of implicit memories and memory systems, but this is still hotly debated by researchers.

Implicit memory is clearly a very fundamental form of memory. It is undoubtedly the basis, in some way, for the other types of memory we have discussed. However, implicit memory is not the kind of memory that most people imagine when they discuss memory. Nor is it the kind of memory that most people worry about losing.

Part of the reason that implicit memory has not been a focus of attention is that very little seems to affect it. It is not easily "forgotten" —do you ever "forget" how to ride a bicycle? Drive a car? Forget how to see the dog in Figure 5? In general, implicit memory can only be damaged when many of the connections in the brain are severely damaged, as occurs in the later stages of Alzheimer's disease or in severe brain damage.

Therefore, realize that I am deliberately neglecting an enormous area of memory when I neglect implicit memory—but that we all do.

Our memory exercises are finished. Now to reconsider where all these different kinds of memory and memory processes are located in the brain.

13

How Your Memory Works—
Everyday Examples

THE PRECEDING EXERCISES have focused on parts of memory. Here, we will
discuss how everything works together. To do so, let's trace what happens when you do remember someone or something that you want to
remember.

LEARNING A PERSON'S NAME—LEARNING SOMETHING NEW.

You are introduced to "Rachel" at a party. Your ears registered a sound,
and in the cerebral cortex of the left temporal lobe the sound is con-
verted into an internal code that stands for the word "Rachel." This is
an important step. What your brain has done is taken the raw sound
and broken it down into the sounds and syllables of English that you
know. So rather than having to deal with all possible sounds in all possible combinations, your brain only has to deal with a few: the syllables
"ray" and "chel." In this auditory sound system, you have not yet learned
something new. You have relied on *old* knowledge of the sounds of
English, knowledge that you acquired when you were growing up and
first learning to speak the language. If you had not known English,
then the sounds in "Rachel" might have been very strange and new to
you. They would not have fit into any of the categories you already had,
and it would have been very difficult for you to even begin to *hear* the
name, let alone remember it. But you do know English. And you have
also heard the name before, so you can treat it as a familiar chunk, not
as a completely new combination of sounds.

What happens next is that the internal code for "Rachel" (the sound
chunk) will persist for a few seconds in a kind of echo chamber within
your head. You will probably not be conscious that it is echoing there.
You don't even have to be paying much attention; what you hear automatically goes into this echo box. (This echo box is why you can repeat
the last part of what you've just heard, even if you haven't been listening.)

But items in the echo box can get erased, as you would very quickly discover if you tried to learn a string of names in succession. After about the seventh name you heard, you would begin forgetting the first ones. You would feel as they had completely disappeared from your head—and you would be almost completely right. The echo box has a capacity of about seven words. New words coming in tend to crowd out some of the words that are already there. The ones that get pushed out are lost forever. This is an **immediate memory** system. It holds some information—in this case, the sound of words—for a short period of time. If you try to add too many, as you did, you erase some of the ones already there—those names are lost. Even if you keep below the limit of seven items, and did nothing else, the information in this immediate memory would gradually fade. As you've probably discovered for yourself, though, you can maintain the contents of the echo box by rehearsing things to yourself, repeating them in your mind.

But *you* don't have a chance to repeat Rachel's name to yourself because someone else has just walked over to you at the party, just after you were introduced to Rachel. Nonetheless, the information associated with the name "Rachel" has not been lost. Automatically, the activation in your head produced by the sound "Rachel" was associated with activations in other regions of the brain, those produced by all that was happening when you heard the sound of her name. This includes such things as your mental image of what she looks like, the sound of her voice, what the conversation was about, perhaps even what you are eating. For Rachel herself, this activation may well have included what you were wearing. At the same time, the mental activation produced by the word "Rachel" and the image of what she looked like are also making contact with all your other memories of other Rachels, other images of people who might have something in common, and perhaps even other associations. For example, someone well versed in the Bible may automatically make an association with Rachel as a Biblical character. Somebody else with a different background might associate the "Rachel" with Rachel Ward, the actress. Yet another background would lead to an association with Rachel McLish, the bodybuilder, Rachel, the sister or cousin, and on and on.

The echo box for the sound of the word "Rachel" is quite temporary, and quickly erased. Its permanent learning took place when you were a child, and the sounds of your native language were engraved into this box. Now, it can no longer learn anything new, permanently. But, other processing and memory systems, such as the ones that associate meaning to a word, and the ones involved in vision, still have a great capacity for learning in you as an adult—they probably have an even greater capacity than they did when you were a child. (These other types of memory systems also have immediate memories, their own temporary activations. However, we are usually not so aware of them, because they are so far along the chain of processing. But general anesthesia or electroshock can show that these memory systems also have a temporary component, when they erase the temporary activations in these regions of the brain.)

In these other processing systems, the temporary activity in the brain caused by meeting Rachel can become locked in more permanently. Although the temporary activity disappears, different aspects of it can be evoked by the proper stimulus (for example, seeing Rachel again, or hearing her voice, or hearing about the party at which you first met). With this appropriate stimulus, the activity that once represented Rachel can be rekindled, and give you again some aspects of the experience that came with the original memory.

Although we call this process "learning something new", you can see that actually this aspect of learning involves something old as well as something new. You already knew the sounds of the English language. You already had connections with other people and other images and perhaps associations to other Rachels and other parties. Because of this, there was already fertile ground for the "new" activity coming in, to allow it to link with what you already knew. So not everything associated with learning about Rachel had to be learned from scratch. In fact, from this account, you could see how "learning" about Rachel would be easier in some ways the more you already knew about things that might be related in some ways to her, and to the experience of meeting her. You would then have more spots already partially prepared in your memory to put information about Rachel, and more links between those spots that you could use to find information about Rachel again when you had to search for it.

What if you truly had to learn something totally new? What if you were the first person to leave Earth and go to an alien's party? You meet an alien named "ZUBZP", who not only sounds nothing like Rachel, but who looks nothing like anyone you've ever met before. Your memory for Zubzp's name is likely to be fairly poor, because you would lack the pre-existing slot you had for Rachel's name, and all the possible connections between Zubzp's name and other material in your head. This lack of prior knowledge is one reason why your memory for new situations and new materials can be quite poor.

Apart from this, it is also true that not everything you see or that goes by you in the world gets locked into your permanent memory. What helps information get locked in? Paying attention is important. Being interested is also important. These seem to be the signals the brain uses to tell the processes that solidify or harden memories to start to work. These processes take the temporary nerve cell activity and lock it in as changes in connections between the nerve cells. In this way, selected aspects of the world that are rushing by you can be locked into your memory and the rest safely allowed to fade away. This process of locking into memory is called **consolidation**. But these changes do not have to take place, and for most of what rushes by you, they do not. You let it go by, and it gets lost forever.

Consolidation can begin with even a single experience. You can aid it by repeating the experience to yourself. By going over the events you experienced, you will lock them more and more firmly in your memory, and build more and more connections between what you experienced and what you already know. You may also discover new connections between them all, that will further strengthen the web you hold these memories in.

This rekindling and chewing on your memory is a common process. We all think back to periods in our childhood and call them up again in our minds. The process of calling these memories up helps refresh them and restore them in our memories.

But there is a danger to this recall and restorage. We don't perceive the world exactly as a video camera or an audio tape recorder would. In part, this is because our mental processing capacity can't be as great as these machines. Therefore, rather than hearing or seeing exactly what happened, what we hear or see is what our brains can handle. And we remember in part by relying on what we have already experienced. Therefore, our mind is always trying to force our perceptions into the molds created by our existing memories. As a result of this molding process, even our first memory of an event may be different than the truth. And these alterations are particularly likely to happen as a result of the process of reawakening memories and chewing on them and reprocessing them. The "memories" that result may well be torn, shredded, stretched, pounded, modified, mixed with other memories, and often changed beyond recognition.

This misregistration, and subsequent process of alteration, are entirely normal. They are exactly the same as the standard telephone conversation effect. Often, when people repeat one conversation to another, they add, subtract and modify, and mix different conversations together, so that the final "conversation" reported often bears little resemblance to the actual conversation. Well, in some ways you have multiple telephone conversations with yourself, through your memory. You call up a memory in your mind, examine it, modify it without realizing, and then put the changed memory back into storage again. As a result, some memories of things that you are absolutely certain about may not really be what you once saw. Your parents and grandparents and cousins and brothers and sisters can probably tell you many episodes where your memory of events is entirely different than theirs.

My sister-in-law had a tonsillectomy at age nine. A few years after the tonsillectomy, she had absolutely firm memories of being driven by her mother from the hospital to Foster's, a small coffee shop in San Francisco, and being given milk. She can describe the sequence perfectly, remembers the soothing coldness of the milk, and can describe the location of the Foster's. Now, as an adult, twenty years later, she swears this all happened. Only—her mother says it *didn't*. Her mother *did* pick her up from the hospital. And there *is* a Foster's where the woman remembers it to be. But they drove straight home from the hospital. And the woman's story is implausible to the mother anyway. "Why would I have given you milk?" her mother exclaims. "I was told not to give you anything to drink for a while!" But my sister-in-law sticks to her story.

You *can* still trust your memory—but the known unreliability of memory, and such examples, should teach you the limits of this trust.

Most of the time, of course, such modifications of memory, and whatever trust we put in our memories, even if it is misguided, are fairly harmless. However, if one comes to rely upon such memories when a significant event is the issue, such as childhood sexual abuse, then the situation can be vastly different. People can be utterly convinced that their memory is accurate. But what is recalled may have very little, if no, relationship to any actual event at all, because of the normal inaccuracies of memory and this automatic reworking process.

WHERE IS IT STORED?

The process we have discussed, of learning something "new," takes place in many different regions of the brain. The initial processing of what you see or hear takes place in the specific region of the cortex of the brain. There are specific areas of the cortex devoted to different functions. For sound, the region is in the left temporal lobe (the part of the brain on the left just above and behind the ear). For vision, it is in the occipital lobes (the part of the brain in the very back of the head). For touch, the connection is in the parietal lobes (the part of the brain extending up from the ear to the top of the head). And for smell, there is a system at the very top of the nose, inside the head, where smells are registered.

These are the places where temporary processing occurs. After the initial registration of the sensation, at steps further along from these areas, there is further processing and extraction of information from the signal coming in. The sounds of a word are interpreted as a meaning, the lines of an image are interpreted as a face. Where the processing takes place is also where more permanent memories for that type of material will be stored.

But the most critical parts of the brain of all, for this particular scene of new learning that we have discussed, are two areas on both sides of the brain (see page 71). One is on the inner part of the temporal lobes, and it is called the hippocampus. The other is the thalamus, deep inside the center of the brain. The hippocampus and the thalamus seem to be the central station for deciding when something is truly important and for sending out the signal to other regions of the brain to lock the memory in (to consolidate it). When the hippocampus is damaged, your immediate memory will still work properly, and information coming in will still be able to make contact with the information that is already inside your head. But you will not lay down any new information and therefore learn really nothing new. This is true amnesia. Case histories of true amnesia are given in Chapter 28 ("The Unfinished Baseball Season").

REMEMBERING A NAME—RETRIEVING OLD INFORMATION

Another common situation is when we have to remember something we once learned. You remember a party you were at and you remember meeting a woman there. What was her name?

You may not remember because you may not have learned her name in the first place. You may have had a little too much to drink. So although you were awake, and seemed to be functioning reasonably well, you were not locking in memories as strongly as you could have without the alcohol. As a result, you may have experienced what heavier drinkers call an "alcoholic blackout." This is not a true blacking out. They do not lose consciousness. Instead, their memories are blacked out because they never had them in the first place. This can also happen to people without alcohol. If someone is not paying attention to something (for example, in driving), then the locking-in mechanisms of memory don't work because there is no need. As a result, when you think back to where you have driven, you can't remember where you had been or what you had been doing. This is normal. But it is definitely exaggerated by things such as alcohol, sleep loss, and by drugs which directly or indirectly interfere with the normal memory consolidation process. For example, Halcion and other sedative drugs may cause apparent blocks in memory consolidation, and resulting gaps in memory.

But assume you *were* paying attention, and you did learn the name the first time, so it is now somewhere inside your head. The problem of retrieving what's-her-name is now very much like finding a paper that you know is somewhere in your files. What the brain uses to index its location are clues that have been associated with that name or information. For example, you remember being at the party. Therefore, you call up the information about the party in your mind (what you can remember of it!) and hope that the links from that information will lead you to the name or to some other aspect of Rachel that you then use to get to her name. You may call up the image of the party as you walked in the door, as you were standing around and picture to yourself the people standing around there. Why can you do this? Because for most people, visual memory is very, very good. Your visual memory may also be good enough to do this. But there are differences among people in memory. Someone else might have a different pattern of memory abilities, with more verbal memory skills and less visual memory abilities. They may remember Rachel's name more directly and not even remember exactly the face that was connected with it. The method you use depends upon *you*; no one method is more "correct" than another.

The information about Rachel is stored exactly where it was when you first learned it, that is, in the cortex and related areas involved in processing different aspects of "Rachel" (her voice, her face, the conversation, the food). The search process can be automatic or it can be deliberate. The automatic search process seems to rely upon the automatic connections you have already established between aspects of Rachel and her name. These automatic connections happen very quickly and you may not even be aware of them occurring. Her name may simply pop into your mind or you might suddenly flash the scene and remember her name instantly.

However, you may also rely upon a more deliberate search strategy. You may force those connections or you may force different clues to bring up other clues, probe them consciously and gradually find in that mix or mess the information you need. Most of us have used this method, and are very conscious of our search. You may have the same ultimate result, but it's a much slower process than the automatic search mechanism. This slower, conscious process is probably very strongly dependent upon the frontal lobes, whereas the automatic links seem to be established within the cortical regions where memories are stored.

Whether unconscious or conscious, there are many possible routes your mind can use to try to find the information about Rachel. Having different routes to "Rachel" has pluses and minuses. In some ways you will be better off if you have many more connections to her name, or to information about her, because you will then have a better chance of finding a route that leads to her name, the correct one.

But—if you have many different routes to follow, you might also be led down the wrong one. Your mental wanderings may be waylaid by similar information, by misremembered circumstances, by miscues. You may even find the right name, but about the wrong person (very embarrassing should you actually meet, and tell her what you think you know!).

The system involved in retrieving memories varies somewhat depending upon the age of the memories. The consolidation process we discussed above, orchestrated by the hippocampus and thalamus, seems to take days or weeks, or perhaps sometimes months, for memories to get completely hardened. The hippocampus is required during this hardening period. Therefore, if the hippocampus is damaged, pre-existing memories (that is, information you learned before the damage occurred) will have a tendency to gradually fade away. This is one explanation of why in some diseases people will seem to forget information. This is a true forgetting, a true loss of the memory, never to return.

Another form of true forgetting is when the memories are truly lost, because you've lost the nerve cells and connections in which they are stored. But normally, this does not happen. It only occurs in some brain diseases such as Alzheimer's disease, or in severe head injury, or in stroke, where the nerve cells are actually damaged or destroyed.

Forgetting in normal people is not due to loss of nerve cells, and probably not even to evaporation of existing connections. What is probably more often the case in normal people is a combination of problems: one is that the memory is still in existence, but that it has been misplaced. The cues and connections to it have been lost or weakened, so it can't be found. Another, more serious problem, would be that the brain cells carrying the information have been reused, to carry newer, different memories. So, in this case, while the memories the nerve cells carried have not "evaporated," nor are they "lost," they nonetheless have been scribbled over and will be difficult to identify.

In essence, our memories grow as a kind of tapestry sewn over patterns already there. You start out life with your memory as something of a clean slate. But as you acquire more and more patterns, it becomes harder and harder not only to see the original patterns that were there, but for each new pattern to be distinctive from the other ones that were already laid down. This is probably a very major part of the reason why we find it hard to remember old memories. The fragments of them that were strung together have been reassembled and used again and are hard to find in their original configuration or original connections. As an example, imagine that when your slate was relatively clean, you learned the name "Barry" and any associations connected to Barry. But then you met another Barry or heard of Barry Goldwater and Barry Manilow and Berry Gordy. All of these Barrys and related sounds and words are not stored completely separate from the original. Instead, they are tagged on or attached to the original name (at least in part). Therefore, when you try to retrieve your memory for the original Barry, you may well have a confusion because of all the additional information attached to it. As a result, even though your "memory" of the word Barry has gotten stronger and stronger, your ability to actually get information from that word or know what it exactly refers to may have somewhat weakened.

Because this is the way our memories work, a large part of remembering something better is not necessarily learning it, but organizing it so you can *find* it, and keep it distinct from other, somewhat similar memories. That is, you have to be clear that one Barry writes the songs, whereas another Barry writes these words. You have to sharpen the division between them to be sure which is which. This sharpening process is one that clearly must be there, but one about which relatively little is known. It seems to be a large part of the reason why experts, who know so many facts (which would normally confuse a memory), can get at them better than a non-expert who may seem to know as many details (because the expert has his or her facts organized, the non-expert does not).

WHOLE BRAIN

It is often assumed that words and language are on the left side of the brain, and faces and images on the right. This is a convenient approximation, but it is too inaccurate for us to understand our *memory* for words and pictures.

That is because what we call memory for words and pictures in everyday life is usually highly constructive; it uses your whole brain. The fragment of a memory of a word activates a part of an image; the part of an image triggers another burst of words; these words ignite a series of images; and so it goes. The actual memories we produce come from many sources. It is possible to establish memories in the mind that are pure, and to test them in ways that eliminate much of this bouncing around inside the brain. Such memories can be tied to more specific brain locations, and to more specific sides of the brain. But most memories are only weakly dependent upon a particular site or side. They use your whole brain as you normally use it—completely—as in everything else that you do with your mind.

14

How Your Brain Remembers

THE PRECEDING EXERCISES and examples have given you a feel for *how* your memory works, and touched on some of the brain machinery that is involved. Here, I will tell you in more detail about *where* these mechanisms are located in the brain, and how they are thought to operate.

The basic map of where your memory occurs is easy to understand:

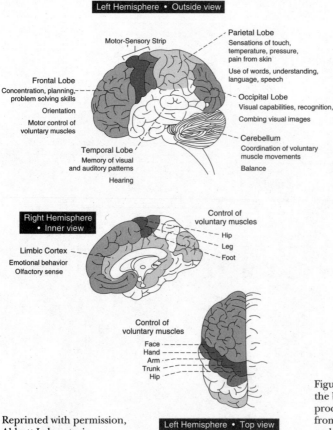

Reprinted with permission, Abbott Laboratories

Figure 6: The regions of the brain involved in processing information from sound, sight, touch, and other functions.

Registration. The type of information you're receiving determines which region of your brain is active (for a schematic, see Figure 6). For example, words are initially processed in the language regions of the brain, pictures initially in the visual regions.

Immediate memory. When information comes into a region, it comes in as a pattern of nerve cell activity. This nerve cell activity normally persists for just a short period of time—seconds or less.

Permanent (long-term) memory. If the information in this temporary pattern of activity is to be permanently stored—and most is not!—it will be saved within the same regions of the brain. Saving the patterns of activity consists of changing nerve cell connections so that the pattern of activity can be called forth again, at some later time. To do this, some nerve cell connections are *strengthened*, while others may be *weakened*. These changes are relatively permanent, although the changes may take weeks or months to completely solidify.

Even though the solidification occurs in the regions of the brain that contained the original activity, the *signal* to make the solidification occur came from other regions. The best known of these regions with such signaling functions are the **hippocampus** and the **thalamus** (see Figure 7). The hippocampus is on the inner side of the temporal lobe; the thalamus is located deep within the center of the brain (see Figure 7).

Memory access. Remembering what you've learned may be a simple matter of just reactivating a latent memory—for example, by seeing a picture again and recognizing it as familiar. In this case, the memories get reactivated in the region of the brain where they were first stored. The measurement of *familiarity*—the sense of how familiar something is, or how recently

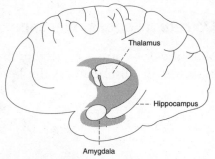

Figure 7: A transparent representation of the left side of the brain, showing the thalamus, hippocampus, and amygdala

you learned it—seems to be done in parts of the temporal lobe, particularly in or near a structure called the **amygdala**, which sits just in front of the hippocampus.

This simple memory retrieval operates very quickly. You can decide that a picture is familiar to you or not in less than one-half a second, measuring from the very start of the time you see the picture to the start of when you say "yes" or "no." Once the picture has been registered in your brain (which takes about two-tenths of a second), it takes you about two-tenths of a second to actually make the decision, and about another two-tenths of a second to say your answer. (The total time it actually takes you is a little less than the time you spend on each stage, because some of these stages can overlap. You start deciding a picture is familiar or not while the image of the picture is still developing within your mind.)

More often, though, as we have seen, remembering what you have learned is much more complicated, because the information you need is not directly available. So your brain's job is to try to find the best answer to what you've been asked to remember. To do this, you use the initial information you were given to activate information in as many different parts of your brain as possible. If this is not successful, you then broadcast these activations to other regions, to try to elicit other memories that may be of help. Because finding each piece of information can take two-tenths of a second or less, and because many searches can occur simultaneously, even in the same region of the brain, you can retrieve and test an enormous amount of information in just a second or two.

This, in outline, is how explicit memories are formed and found in your brain. Let us now consider some parts of this anatomy in more detail, and then go through some examples of remembering and learning, to see how the pieces all fit together.

DIFFERENT CODES, DIFFERENT REGIONS

Memories for words are different than memories for pictures. The brain basis for this distinction is the best understood—or at least, the best

Figure 8: Some of the many mental codes produced by hearing the word "red."

mapped out—of all the brain differences for different types of memories. In most right-handed people and about 60 percent of left-handed people, the left side of the brain is the one that is responsible for language. In these individuals, it also seems as though it is the left side of the brain that is responsible for verbal memories, while the right side of the brain is the one mostly responsible for visual memories. In about 40 percent of left-handers and in very, very few right-handers, both sides of the brain are more equal in how they perform verbal and visual functions. For these individuals, this specialization for memory functions is less marked.

Memory in the brain is not based on what you got from the world *outside* your head, but instead is based on what you created from what you got *inside your head.* That is, if you are asked to remember the word "red", it is not remembered as a single item, as the spoken word, although that is perhaps the way it feels to you. Instead, the information in the word is unpacked and distributed over multiple memory systems in multiple brain regions, as shown in Figure 8, opposite.

Refer to Figure 8. First the *sounds in the word* ("re" "eh" "deh") are deciphered, using memory of the English language as a guide. Then the word as a whole sound ("red") is recognized, again using your memory for language. Next, the meaning of the word is found. Notice that a spoken word such as "red" is ambiguous. It can mean the color, or it can mean the process of reading. Both senses of the word are probably activated, depending upon the context. And finally, associations to the meaning of the word and to the concepts it evokes can be triggered. The word "red" may bring up an image of the color, particularly in the visual system of the brain. It can bring up a feeling of heat, a sense of danger, a glimpse of the devil and the fires of hell, or of communism, even Warren Beatty (the movie *Reds*). Most of these associations appear to be unconscious, and not under conscious control. But no matter what particular chain of associations you have, the word "red" is different *inside* your mind than it is *outside* of it. It has been translated into different parts, and the parts are saved in a number of places.

As a result of this translation process inside your head, some of the things you think are single memories are really not—they are many different memories, drawing on many different regions of the brain. Musical lyrics are perhaps a good example: memory for the words is probably kept in a somewhat different place than memory for the melody. So people can lose one, and not the other. But also, because there is this double storage, if there is some damage to one or the other type of memory, you may be able to compensate through your remaining memory. This may be one reason why people who have had strokes that prevent them from speaking may nonetheless still be able to sing a song!

Besides separate memory regions for words and for vision, separate memory regions have also been identified for such functions as touch or feel, for sounds apart from the sounds of language (sounds such as the noise of a lawnmower or the bark of a dog), and for aspects of movement. As you can see, these large subdivisions seem to be based on the nature of the input to the brain, or the nature of the action the brain takes. Within these large divisions, it is known that there are still finer subdivisions of processing and of memory. In the brain system we use for spoken language, for example, there are separate subsystems, and separate memories, concerned with the sounds of speech itself (such as those in the languages we know), with the sounds of words as a whole, and with word meanings. There are certainly even finer subdivisions than these. Chapter 34 ("A Shark Has Four Legs, Doesn't It?") gives some inkling of how bizarre these subdivisions may be.

A dramatic illustration of where different codes in the brain are located, and how quickly the brain can shuttle information from one code to another, comes from studies performed by my colleague Dr. Nathan Crone, in conjunction with Drs. John Hart, Jr., Dana Boatman, Ronald P. Lesser, and myself. Dr. Crone recorded the electrical activity directly from the surface of a person's brain, while he was naming a series of pictures out loud. The recording was done through a large number of small electrodes, which had been placed over the surface of the brain in order to map this individual's seizures, and to help determine what parts of the brain should be removed to help his seizure disorder. These electrodes were embedded in a sheet of plastic, which had been left in over the brain while the skull and scalp had been closed over on top of it. In this way, the electrical recording could be done while the patient was completely awake and alert, and completely able to cooperate with the testing.

Memory for the names of pictures is generally an implicit type of memory, as was discussed in the last chapter. Nonetheless, the brain regions involved, and their sequence of activation, is probably similar in many respects to those which would be used for remembering the name of someone whose face or picture you've just seen.

This sequence is shown below, in Figures 9 through 13. The image of the brain shown is that of this patient's very own brain, reconstructed in three dimensions from a special MRI scan.

You See An Apple

What is Happening in Your brain

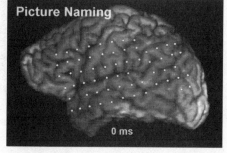

Time

0—The start

Figure 9: The left side of one person's brain. White dots represent electrodes placed on the surface of the brain, as part of planned surgical treatment for epilepsy. The patient has been told to name the picture out loud. At the very beginning, when the picture has just appeared on the screen, there is no change in the brain's electrical activity, indicated here by the smallness of the dots.

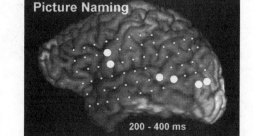

2/10-4/10 seconds

Figure 10: Even by 2/10 to 4/10ths of a second after the picture has come up on the screen, there is activation of areas involved in the visual processing of the picture, and the processing of the sound of its name (shown by the large white dots, which represent changes in the electrical activity of the brain underneath those particular electrode positions). The motor areas responsible for controlling the face and tongue are also activated. This activation is either for the specific sounds themselves (that is, the movements required to produce them) or just in preparation for producing the movements. When this person was told to look at the picture without saying the name out loud, these motor areas did not get activated as much).

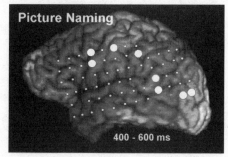

4/10-6/10ths of a second

Figure 11: By 4/10 to 6/10ths of a second after the picture has come up on the screen, the visual and sound regions remain activated, as are the motor regions, but now activation is also seen in the sensory regions of the face.

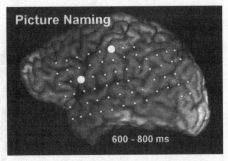

6/10-8/10ths of a second

Figure 12: By 6/10-8/10ths of a second, activation from the picture has died away in the visual and sound regions, even though the picture is still on the screen. The motor activation is also dying down. The patient is just about to *begin* to say the name of the picture.

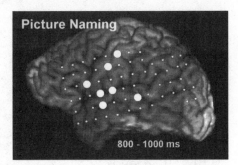

8/10-10/10ths second

(1 second)

YOU

START

TO SAY

"APPLE"

Figure 13: On the average, the patient has *just* started to say the name of the picture by 8/10ths of a second after the picture has come on the screen. In this time period, just after the name has begun to be said, there is activation of the top part of the left temporal lobe, which was not seen before. This is from the name being spoken out loud, which is activating the part of the brain that normally hears and interprets the sounds of words. Notice that this region was *not* activated even by the "name" when it was internal [see Figure 10, above]; the codes for the internal sound and the external sound are different, and are in different areas of the brain.

IMMEDIATE AND PERMANENT

The dynamic activation of regions of the brain with naming also illustrates another important feature of how memories exist in the brain. The *same* memory can be in two different forms in the brain. One is the **activated** form. This is when the nerve cells are actually firing, and the connections between them (the wiring) are actually humming with activity. This activation can come about because we are perceiving something directly. Or it may occur because something in your mind triggered the memory. Either way, this is the **active** state for memory. In this form, your memory is part of the ongoing activity of the brain. And just as part of that ongoing activity of the brain is your *consciousness*, your activated mental window, memories in active form can be part of your consciousness.

The inactive form of memory is actually the **permanent** or **long-term** one. It is the pattern of connections between nerve cells that can *recreate* the original pattern of nerve cell activity, the active form. In Dr. Crone's experiment, the permanent memory was what allowed the patient to remember that "apple" was the name for the picture that he was shown. Being shown the picture awakened a burst of electrical activity which was the neural code for the word "apple." This electrical activity was not present before the patient was shown the picture of an *apple.* In fact, I suspect it was the furthest thing from his mind at that point, while he was waiting for surgery with a set of electrodes inside his head. But it could be triggered, and that triggering showed both his long-term memory for the word (which we could not otherwise see), and his immediate brain activation (which we could).

FLEXIBILITY AND CAPACITY OF LONG-TERM MEMORIES

There are different long-term storage sites for memory, in different regions of the brain. As we have seen, they differ in the *code* or the type of information that they store. But they also differ somewhat in how much they can hold, how easy it is to store information in them, and how long they hold that information.

The brain region that stores the *sounds of our language* seems to have a malleable period in early childhood coincident with exposure to the sounds of one's own language. We have to *learn* what the particular sounds of our native language are, and what aspects of sound are important to our language and which are not. In English, "L's" and "R's" are very distinct. In Japanese, they are not. Conversely, some other languages (such as Thai) recognize differences that English does not, such as that between the "p" sound in *pill* and the "p" sound in *spill.* You can *feel* this difference if you hold your hand up in front of your mouth while you pronounce them—the "p" in "pill" has a puff of air with it, while the "p" in "spill" has none. But if you speak only English, you cannot *hear* this difference—because English does not treat them separately. For a language that does, the two "p's" are as different as an "L" and an "R" are to us.

We normally automatically learn about the differences that matter in our language, and those that do not, in early childhood, when we learn to understand speech and to speak. This is also when this region of our brain seems to be able to adapt. Any child can learn to listen and speak in any language, if they start early enough. But once past childhood, for most people this brain region seems to become frozen, at least as far as new learning is concerned. It will readily process the sounds of our language, but not pass any others. And it cannot *learn* any new sounds, at least not easily or well. This is one reason why people who learn a language after about the age of 6 almost always have an accent, and why the Japanese find it very difficult to learn the "L" and "R" difference that seems so easy to us: For most people, that region of the brain has ceased to learn, ceased to change.

In contrast, further on upstream from hearing words, the memory store responsible for learning new **word meanings** remains flexible, and it expands thoughout life. This store takes up information more slowly than the one that processes the sounds of the language, but it has a vastly greater capacity and an enormous persistence. Perhaps because word meanings are widely distributed over the brain, or perhaps because they are so deeply embedded in several spots, knowledge of word meanings tends to be one of the most resistant to most types of brain injury, particularly the kinds of brain injury seen with otherwise severe diseases such as Alzheimer's disease.

Long-term **visual memory** is even more impressive. We can remember pictures or scenes for years. Normal people can see 10,000 pictures in rapid succession and reliably recognize a large proportion of them on testing immediately after.

MAKING THE TEMPORARY PERMANENT—CONSOLIDATION

The temporary activation of a single memory store can sustain the information for seconds, and perhaps even somewhat longer. However, these patterns will eventually die away. Or they will be replaced by others. Or they may even be abolished by anesthesia. To get them back, the dancing patterns of electrical and chemical activity have to be put into a different code, one based on the strengths of connections between nerve cells. This is what we have meant by solidifying memories; its more formal name is **consolidation**. This consolidation process is almost certainly the fundamental process involved in learning something new. What it results in is the capacity of the brain region to somehow recreate the active pattern that was once there.

Temporary activation and long-term learning for each information code takes place within each region of the brain that was responsible for the initial processing. But the trigger for the consolidation process probably comes from elsewhere. Not all information passing through and transiently activating is saved. Only information that is most relevant, most congruent with information already present, or most important, gets stored. The neuroanatomic structures responsible for this triggering are thought to be the hippocampus, thalamus, and probably some other connected regions as well. Without them, the transfer to long-term storage does not take place.

It is very likely that this process of consolidation is not one process, but many, with many different time scales. Psychologically, whether information has been saved in this permanent memory store for several seconds or several years seems to make no difference. However, for at least the first several weeks or months, a "hardening" of the neural connections seems to occur. In the absence of the hippocampus and associated structures, this hardening does not take place, and so these memories remain excessively fragile and prone to dissolve.

These critical roles are known partly from the experiences of human beings who have had damage to these regions. It does not matter much what causes the damage. It could be a stroke, viral inflammation of the brain, or even surgical removal. But regardless of the cause of the damage, the result is the same if it is severe enough. The affected person is wide-awake and alert, and can carry on a conversation—up to a point. They can remember what they once learned. Their temporary activations of memory work normally. But they cannot learn anything of explicit memory that is new. So they forget where they are, who you are, and what they have been doing almost immediately, and can never get this information back. And, because of the fragility of memories that they learned just before they lost their hippocampus or other brain region responsible for their condition, they may also lose some memories from the days, weeks, or months just prior to the onset of their illness. This condition is called the **amnestic syndrome**. A case is described in Chapter 28, "The Unfinished Baseball Season."

IMPLICIT AND EXPLICIT MEMORY

The memories affected by the amnestic syndrome are the memories we can explain, recognize, and recall. They are the memories we can take out of the recesses of our mind, consciously examine and talk about. These kinds of memories include memories for facts ("Where were you last April?") and memory for familiarity and identity ("That picture looks like someone I know—yes, it's Larry!").

But the devastation caused by the amnestic syndrome leaves one other large class of learning and memory intact. These are the memories involved in reading words, driving a car, and playing an instrument. These memories are unconscious and direct. You show you know how to play tennis, not by telling someone how to do it, but by going out there and hitting the ball over the net (and hopefully, hitting it back again if you have any skill!). These types of memories have been termed *implicit* or *procedural* memories. They do not seem to require conscious awareness, control or access. They, instead, seem to be directly burned into the circuitry of the brain. This type of learning and memory resists most kinds of brain damage, unless the damage also directly affects the circuits involved.

And such learning is totally unaffected by damage to the hippocampus or thalamus, even though such damage devastates a person's ability to learn new information explicitly. Patients with the amnestic syndrome are still able to learn how to throw a ball, ride a bicycle, play tennis, and drive a car. But they will not consciously learn about the experiences they have had. They will not be able to tell you what game they played in, what bike they bought, who they played in tennis, or where they drove. Taken to a tennis court, they will deny ever having seen the court before, and deny knowing how to play. But put on the court, they will hit the ball with all the skill they have learned.

Although all this seems fairly compelling evidence for two different types of memory systems, there are still many questions about this distinction. It is possible that declarative memories arise in some fashion out of procedural ones. It may even be the case that declarative memory is necessary for some aspects of procedural memory, for example, in learning vocabulary.

One reason for the interest in these two types of memories is that implicit memories seem to be unaffected by aging, or by conditions such as Alzheimer's disease (until the disease is advanced). If we could understand why damage to the brain does not affect one type of memory, we may understand better how to attack the problem of memory loss.

NERVE CELLS AND MEMORY

The memories that concern us in everyday life—whether they are explicit memories or implicit memories—are far removed from nerve cells, just as our everyday world of food, cars, and people is far removed from the atoms that make them up. One example of a nerve cell is shown in Figure 14. Figure 15 shows how nerve cells can be interconnected, in schematic form.

Even a relatively small region of the brain, such as the one activated by the picture of an "apple" in the brain images shown above (Figures

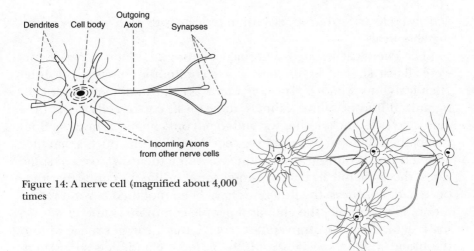

Figure 14: A nerve cell (magnified about 4,000 times

Figure 15: Nerve cells and a schematic of their connections. Nerve cells can have thousands or even tens of thousands of connections.

9 to 13), contains an enormous number of nerve cells, perhaps 10 to 100 million. These neurons can have an vast number of connections—ten to a thousand or more times as many. The brain as a whole has been estimated to have 10 billion neurons or more.

A magnified view of a connection between nerve cells is shown in Figure 16. An important fact to understand is that, while nerve cell

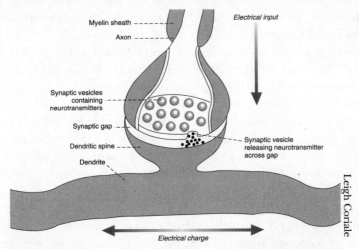

Figure 16: Internal operation of a synapse (one of the dots in Figures 14 and 15) shown in more detail. Incoming electrical activity leads to the release of neurotransmitters across the gap between nerve cells, which causes a change in the electrical activity on the other side (the other neuron). (Illustration adapted with permission from P. Russell, *The Brain Book*. New York: Penguin, 1979, page 39.)

activity is electrical, nerve cells communicate with each other by releasing chemicals.

(This chemical release is a heritage of our past. When our ancestors were all just single cells, the only way to communicate was by releasing chemicals into primordial oceans. Later, as collections of multiple cells organized into primitive animals, the easiest way for cells to get messages across to one another was still to put out chemicals into the fluid that bathed them all. When nerve cells developed, it appears that they adopted this existing transmission system for their own use. In some cases, these chemicals have retained some of the functions that they once had. In others, the functions have been modified beyond recognition. For example, the chemical people commonly know as *adrenaline* is actually a neurotransmitter as well. But it can get released into the blood when a special gland, the adrenal gland, gets stimulated. Adrenaline signals *all* the cells of the body to get ready for an emergency. It forces sugar into muscle cells, and slows down the digestive system. But adrenaline also operates deep within the brain, in the connections between some sets of nerve cells.)

Memory at the nerve cell level is thought to involve changes in the strengths of connections between nerve cells. These changes can be both increases and decreases in the strength of connections. Since neurotransmitters are the major way nerve cells communicate from one to another, changes in the way neurotransmitters are released, and changes in the way neurotransmitters are received or interpreted by the nerve cell at the other end, must clearly be important in the formation of memory.

However, because we are concerned with the memories that come into our conscious experience, it is important to place our current knowledge of "memory" at the nerve cell level in the proper context. The memories that we are conscious of are not discrete files or pages inside our heads. Instead, they are a product of the electrical activity of an enormous number of nerve cells and nerve cell endings. Some of these nerve cells and nerve cell endings are probably clustered together, and we identify them as specific regions of the brain. Other nerve cells involved in what we feel is a single memory probably are scattered widely all over the brain. The firing of the nerve cells is also probably spread out over time, as well. A single nerve cell takes about one-thousandth of a second to fire. However, the memories we see with techniques such as direct electrical recording seem to occupy a period of time at least two hundred times longer than this.

One way to picture this relationship between nerve cell firing and

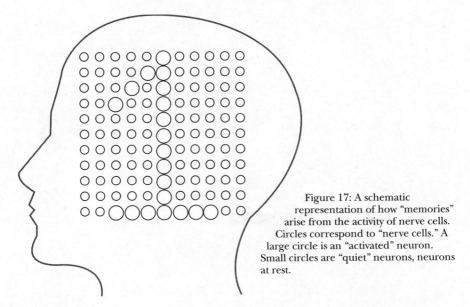

Figure 17: A schematic representation of how "memories" arise from the activity of nerve cells. Circles correspond to "nerve cells." A large circle is an "activated" neuron. Small circles are "quiet" neurons, neurons at rest.

our conscious memories is shown in Figure 17. In the picture, our conscious memory or knowledge of the number "1" can be seen to result from the coordinated firing (and lack of firing) of a large number of individual nerve cells, shown here as the circles in the figure. In the illustration, each pattern is represented in about 120 "neurons." So there is a ratio of one conscious "memory" to 120 "neurons." The ratio in the real brain is not known, but is clearly one to many millions.

One other point to make about Figure 17 is that memory depends as much upon which nerve cells are turned OFF as it does upon which nerve cells are turned ON. The "1" in the illustration is defined not only by the nerve cells which are *active*, but also by those which are *inactive*. We often imagine that memory is a matter of *strengthening* connections in our mind, but actually memory may be as much a matter of *weakening* connections.

This schematic for memory can also illustrate what it might mean at the nerve cell level to have memories "weaken." We do not know why memories seem to fade. One possibility is that the actual connections *do* weaken eventually over time.

However, another possibility is that the connections remain strong. In this case, how is it possible that the memories that they contribute to still fade?

One way this is possible is illustrated in Figure 18. Figure 18 is meant to show the same set of nerve cells, learning different items. "1" has a

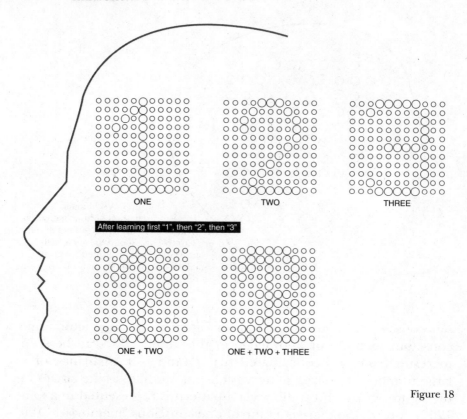

ONE   TWO   THREE

After learning first "1", then "2", then "3"

ONE + TWO   ONE + TWO + THREE

Figure 18

distinct pattern of nerve cell activations; "2" has a distinct pattern; "3" has a distinct pattern. But after learning "1" and "2" together, the patterns begin to overlap, and are less separable. They become even more indistinct when "3" is added into the mix. This is one possible reason why memories can be both permanent at the nerve cell level, but still lost to us: even if they are not erased, they can get overwritten.

MEMORY IN THE CONNECTIONS

Refer again to the magnified—and simplified—view of a connection between nerve cells shown in Figure 16. Neurotransmitters moving from one side to the other convey the signal that the first nerve cell has fired. How much neurotransmitter is released, and how receptive the second nerve cell is to it, help determine whether the second cell will fire also, or not.

The basic mechanisms for memory at the nerve cell level must be within the cells themselves, but *where* within the cell is still unclear. Memory may be the result of changes in the nerve cell membrane, in chemical pathways within the nerve cell, or even within the DNA of the cell itself. Current research suggests that *all* of these can get modified when a nerve cell "learns."

The mechanisms that have been uncovered for these changes are *extremely* complex. Fortunately, these mechanisms seem to be working properly in almost every human being. In fact, the only examples of problems with these basic learning systems are ones that have been *created* in the laboratory: fruit flies, snails, and mice bred to have missing genes, and missing memories as a result. If a human had such a problem, it should be obvious. But no human cases have ever been reported.

Part III

Is Your Memory Normal?

15

Spotting a Memory Problem— Checklists and Explanations

THESE CHECKLISTS ARE meant to highlight and help explain some of the warning signs for memory problems.

One checklist is for you to complete. The other checklist is to be completed by someone who knows you (your spouse or a good friend). To be more accurate, you *must* have someone else rate your memory. And if your spouse's or friend's evaluation suggests you should go see a doctor, DO SO—even if you do not think you have to go.

These checklists are not a substitute for your own judgment, your spouse's or a friend's, or a doctor's opinion. So, regardless of anything in this book, **if you are worried about your memory, or if other people are worried about your memory (*especially* if other people are worried about your memory), go see a medical professional.** At the end of this section, I describe how to prepare for a doctor's visit about your memory.

FOR YOU TO FILL OUT
(Please circle the answer that you feel best describes you)
1. **How old are you?**
   (a) Less than 45
   (b) 46-65
   (c) 65-75
   (d) 76 or older

(a) *If you are less than 45*, you probably do not have to worry about having a serious memory problem. While mild memory loss associated with aging may begin even by the thirties, most people will hardly have felt its real effects. While diseases affecting memory—such as multiple sclerosis or tumors—can occur in this age group, it is rare for the first and only sign of the disease to be memory loss. Alzheimer's disease, and conditions related to Alzheimer's disease, are extremely rare under age 45. Most memory complaints from people in this age group are from overwork and overstress. In addition, serious depression, which certainly affects people in this age range, can also affect memory.

(b) *Between ages 46 and 65,* especially at the later end of this range, people are more likely to notice problems with memory, such as remembering names. Serious brain diseases that might affect memory—such as Alzheimer's disease—are extremely rare before age 60, and remain uncommon even through age 65 (probably less than one-tenth of one percent risk per year). Depression, anxiety and overwork, however, are still common threats to memory in this age group.

(c) *Ages 65 to 75.* In this age group, the risk of Alzheimer's disease increases, but the risk of actually developing Alzheimer's is still less than one percent per year. Depression remains a possible cause of memory problems. For people in this age range, there is a higher risk of stroke and of heart or blood vessel disease, which can affect the brain and memory. And people in this age group are more likely to be on medications, some of which can adversely affect thinking and memory (See Chapters 23 and 24, on drugs and alcohol).

(d) *Ages 76 or older.* Above age 75 or so, aging itself is more likely to have a more noticeable effect on people's memories. Numerous studies have shown that, by age 75, many people become more forgetful. For most people, forgetfulness is still part of aging. However, above age 75, and particularly above age 80, the risk of developing Alzheimer's disease is much higher. The risk increases considerably with age, so much so that about 30 to 40 percent of people in their eighties will develop Alzheimer's disease.

Often, the Alzheimer's disease that affects older people seems to be a slower disease than the one that affects younger people. It begins more gradually, and may take longer to produce noticeable effects. Because of the high risk of Alzheimer's, and because it may be harder to identify if you are in this age category, it is even more important that you have a competent health care professional evaluate your memory problems.

   2. How would you rate your memory?
     (a) Really bad—I forget everything!
     (b) Not too bad—but I forget more often than other people.
     (c) Normal. Like everyone, mostly I remember, but sometimes I forget.
     (d) It's perfect. I never forget anything.

(a) *Really bad*—you can relax a bit. Keep in mind the old saying that "the more you complain, the longer you live." In general, the worse you think your memory is, the less likely it is that you have a serious brain problem. There are at least two reasons for this. First, if you *really* had a serious memory problem, then you would not remember what you forget; you would not even be aware that you had a memory problem. If you can remember everything that you have forgotten and the details of how you forgot it, then you are showing that at least part of your memory is working quite well.

Second, if you really did have a brain disease such as Alzheimer's, you would be much less likely to think your memory is terrible—even though it may be! That is because the damage to the brain caused by Alzheimer's frequently affects areas of the brain that impair your knowledge of your own abilities. So people with Alzheimer's tend to minimize or ignore the memory problems that they have.

(b) *Not too bad, but more often than other people.* You may have a realistic appraisal of your own memory. If you are concerned that it is worse than other peoples' or worse than it should be for you, or if you think it has gotten worse in the last year, then getting it checked is reasonable.

(c) *Normal with occasional forgetting.* You may *be* normal. However, if you had Alzheimer's disease, you might think the same thing. If your spouse or friends do not notice anything wrong with your memory, then you can relax. But if they have been rumbling about your forgetfulness, then it would probably be best if you got it checked.

(d) *I never forget anything.* If we can believe you, this is wonderful! You should make a living showing off your memory skills! You should volunteer for memory experiments!

But, without knowing more about you, it is more likely that your memory is not so extraordinary. It may be good, but not perfect. No one has a perfect memory for everything. In one study of ten people who thought they had extraordinary memories (volunteers who presented themselves after hearing a radio program), only one probably had a memory that was better than average. Even people with amazing memories in some areas, such as the mnemonists described in Chapter 19, do not remember everything. V.P., a man who never forgot any story he ever read, could not remember people's faces.

3. **What kinds of things do you forget? Important things? Things that really inconvenience you, interfere with your work, or perhaps even endanger you or other people? Or do you forget minor things, so it's just an annoyance, but not a real problem in your life?**

Forgetting important things—work that you *had* to do for your job, turning off the range—is a sign of a more severe memory problem than is forgetting things of little or no consequence. However, even if your memory is bad, this doesn't necessarily mean that you have a serious medical problem such as Alzheimer's disease. Depression, for example, can sometimes cause marked forgetting.

    4.   Do you feel your memory problem began suddenly, or gradually?

      (a) Suddenly, within hours or a day or two.

      (b) Gradually, so slowly I'm not actually sure when they began.

    (a) *Suddenly, within a few hours or a day.* Sometimes, people suddenly notice problems that have been there for quite a long time. It may be because they are forced to do something that requires memory, or they may experience a particular episode of forgetting that may really highlight the forgetfulness. But, if memory problems seem to begin suddenly, in hours or a day or so, then that may be an important clue to what caused the memory problem. A head injury (that the person may have forgotten!), a stroke in an area of the brain that affects memory only—these are all the sort of possibilities that a medical professional can sort out.

    (b) *Gradually, so gradually I'm not certain when it began.* Many times a person with a memory problem may not remember when it began, because of the problem itself. However, people also will not be able to remember when a memory problem began if it starts very slowly and imperceptibly. To try to pinpoint the time, we ask people to think back to a time when their memory was normal. Was it a year ago? Five years ago? Twenty years ago? In memory loss due to aging, people are often fairly certain that their memory five or ten years ago was better than it is today. But they often think that it hasn't changed that much over the past few years. In the memory loss due to Alzheimer's, memory worsens much more quickly. The Alzheimer's sufferer, unfortunately, may not be aware of this, although family members will notice a definite decline over a year or two. And because the condition begins so slowly, it's natural that different people may have different impressions as to when they first noticed a problem.

    5. Do you feel that your memory has worsened in the last year, in general?

      (a) Yes

      (b) No

    If you *think* your memory has worsened, it *actually* may have worsened or your *perception* of it may have worsened. Either way, you should consider a medical evaluation. If you feel that your memory has not worsened during the last year, you may be normal. Or, if you think you do have something of a memory problem that just hasn't changed lately, you may simply be experiencing a memory problem related to aging, stress or depression. Remember, if you have a real memory problem, you may not necessarily be fully aware of the extent of your memory problem or whether your memory has truly gotten worse.

6. **Have you had periods of time in the last year when your memory has improved** *a great deal?* **Periods such as over the weekend or while you've been away on vacation?**
   (a) Yes
   (b) No

Everybody's memory ability shows some fluctuations. We all have good days and bad days, good hours and bad hours. But if you think you have a memory problem, and your memory has gotten appreciably better at times, then this usually indicates that the cause of your memory problem is not in your brain itself. With very few exceptions, brain diseases don't fluctuate *that* much. Most likely, something is interfering with the way your brain is working. But be encouraged: the fact that it can get better, even if only briefly, is a sign that the interference has not had any permanent ill effects.

While memory problems that improve periodically usually do not mean significant brain disease, they may well mean that you are depressed, anxious, or otherwise disturbed about something. The fact that your problem can get better is good evidence that it can be helped. Seek attention for it.

7. **How do you think your spouse or close friends or relatives would rate your memory?**
   (a) Really bad—I forget everything!
   (b) Not too bad—but I forget more often than other people.
   (c) They think it's normal. Like everyone, mostly I remember, but sometimes I forget.
   (d) It's perfect. I never forget anything.

(a) Really *bad.* If you feel that those who know you well may think your memory is bad, then you should consider seeking a medical opinion. Of course, you may not have anything wrong with you. But the earlier you find out, the better off you will probably be.

(b) *Not too bad, but I forget more often than other people.* If your spouse or close friends think you are more forgetful than other people, then they are probably right. Your forgetfulness may be nothing more than normal aging (distressing as that may be), depression, drug side effects, or an uneventful lifestyle. In any case, a check-up by a medical professional may be advisable.

(c) *They think it's normal. Good remembering, occasional forgetting.* That's good. But if their evaluation of your memory is significantly different from your own (from Question #2 above), then you should ask yourself, why are our impressions different? Are you hiding things from your spouse or friends, so that they can't really tell how bad your memory is? Or are they aware of the same episodes of forgetting that you are, but don't treat them as harshly as you do? Or do you think they are simply trying to minimize your problem? Again, a medical evaluation may help ferret out the problem.

(d) *Other people think your memory is perfect.* If other people think this about you, then either your memory truly is perfect, or your friends are being overly kind. Almost everybody has memory lapses, sometimes.

8. Do you find that you remember something that you forgot after you are reminded of it?
   (a) Yes, all the time, or almost all the time
   (b) Yes, sometimes
   (c) No, never.

If you can remember what it is you forgot after being reminded, this is certainly a clue that whatever your memory problem, it is relatively mild. Some memory of what you forgot remains, and can be tickled by the reminder. If only sometimes you remember what you forgot after reminded, this may suggest that your memory problem may be more troublesome. Of course, even in this case, the problem could be due to something as simple as distraction, absentmindedness, or depression. If you never remember what you forget, this may mean that your memory loss is more severe. The solution may be simple, but a real problem seems to be present. You should be checked by a medical professional.

9. If you are having memory problems, did you also have any major medical problems around the time they began?

Major medical problems you have, that began around the time your memory problems began, may be a clue to your memory problems. By themselves, medical problems may not necessarily mean that your memory is at risk. But sometimes, people fail to connect the onset of their memory problems to a stroke (which can show itself as temporary weakness of one part of their body, or temporary blindness), major operations (of the heart or blood vessels, for example), or new medical problems that have led to changes in medications. If any of these have happened to you, you should consider a visit to a medical professional who can use these clues to begin to uncover the cause of your memory loss.

10. **Were there any changes in any medications that you take, or in how you took them, around the time your memory problems began?**

This can often be an important clue that, instead of something being wrong with your brain itself, medications may be at fault. Although medication problems are unusual as a cause of memory loss, they can cause them, or make them worse. Your medications and the dosages should be checked. Also, sometimes, people get confused and take the wrong dosages, at the wrong times, or on the wrong schedule. So how you are actually taking your medicines should be checked.

11. **Do you drink substantial quantities of alcohol regularly? Are you frequently tipsy or drunk?**

Drinking to excess frequently can be a danger flag. An occasional glass of wine or a beer with dinner is probably not going to cause memory problems. But some studies have suggested that heavier social drinking can worsen a person's mental ability and memory. In one study by Dr. Elizabeth Parker and her associates at the National Institute on Alcohol Abuse and Alcoholism, the amount of social drinking in men was correlated with mental problems resembling those of premature aging. An extra drink of alcohol was associated with the equivalent of aging an additional 2.4 to 3.7 years on a mental test.

Heavier drinking, to the point of frequent tipsiness or drunkenness, is known to cause memory problems. Some people seem to be more sensitive to the effects of alcohol, but there is no way of predicting whether you will be in this category. The brains of heavy drinkers can be damaged by a Vitamin B_1 (thiamine) deficiency, by toxic effects of alcohol, and often by the effects of the drinkers' frequent falls. The lack of Vitamin B_1 seems to be due to the poor diet of many drinkers, and the fact that metabolism of alcohol seems to use up B_1. Interestingly, taking B1 on a regular basis while continuing to drink heavily will not necessarily prevent this problem.

12. **How are your spirits? Do you feel really depressed, anxious, unhappy?**
    (a) I feel really depressed, anxious, or unhappy.
    (b) I feel fine; my spirits are good.

Depression and anxiety, more often than any other problem, go hand in hand with memory complaints. Depression or anxiety can impair your memory somewhat, but more important, these conditions can make you *feel* that your memory is terrible. They can also make you easily distractible, apathetic, and unable to perform well. Luckily, these conditions are usually treatable.

Some diseases that affect memory do not alter a person's spirits at all, although the disease can alter the way you view your memory. For instance, patients with Alzheimer's disease often feel just fine, and do not appreciate how serious their condition is. So, even if you feel fine, if someone close to you is concerned about your memory, you should consider seeking a medical opinion.

FOR YOUR SPOUSE OR CLOSE FRIEND TO FILL OUT
(Skip this yourself)
INSTRUCTIONS FOR THE SPOUSE OR CLOSE FRIEND: Please circle the answer that you feel best describes the person you are rating. Although I have used a "he" for the questions and answers, they apply to a woman as well.

1. **How old is he (or she)?**
    (a) Less than 45
    (b) 46-65
    (c) 65-75
    (d) 76 or older

(a) *If he is less than 45*, you probably do not have to worry about his having a serious memory problem. While mild memory loss associated with aging may begin even by the thirties, it will have hardly made its real effects felt in most people. While diseases affecting memory can occur in this age group—such as multiple sclerosis or tumors—it is rare for the first and only sign to be memory loss. Alzheimer's disease, and conditions related to Alzheimer's disease, are extremely rare under age 45. Most memory complaints from people in this age group are from overwork and overstress. In addition, serious depression, which certainly affects people in this age range, can also affect memory.

(b) *Between ages 46 and 65*, especially at the later end of this range, people are more likely to notice problems with memory, such as remembering names. Serious brain diseases that might affect memory—such as Alzheimer's disease—are extremely rare before age 60, and remain uncommon even through age 65 (probably less than one-tenth of one percent risk per year). Depression, anxiety and overwork, however, are still common threats to memory in this age group.

(c) *Ages 65 to 75*. In this age group, the risk of Alzheimer's disease increases, but the risk of actually developing Alzheimer's is still less than one percent per year. Depression remains a possible cause of memory problems. For people in this age range, there is a higher risk of stroke and of heart or blood vessel disease, which can affect the brain and memory. And people in this age group are more likely to be on medications, some of which can adversely affect thinking and memory (See Chapter 23 and 24, on drugs and alcohol).

(d) *Ages 76 or older.* Above age 75 or so, aging itself is more likely to have a more noticeable effect on a person's memories. Numerous studies have shown that, by age 75, many people become more forgetful. For most people, this forgetfulness is still part of aging. However, above age 75, and particularly above age 80, the risk of developing Alzheimer's disease is much higher. The risk increases considerably with age, so much so that about 30 to 40 percent of people in their eighties will develop Alzheimer's disease.

Often, the Alzheimer's disease that affects older people seems to be a slower disease than the one that affects younger people. It begins more gradually, and may take longer to produce noticeable effects. Because of the high risk of Alzheimer's, and because it may be harder to identify if he is in this age category, it is even more important that he have a competent health care professional evaluate his memory problems.

2. **How would you rate his memory?**
    (a) Really bad—he forgets everything!
    (b) Not too bad—but he forgets more often than other people.
    (c) Normal. Like everyone, mostly he remembers, but sometimes he forgets.
    (d) It's perfect. He never forgets anything.

A word in advance of the explanations: Provided that you know him reasonably well, and have a chance to see him in everyday life, what *you* think of his memory is a fairly reliable guide to how good—or bad—it actually is. Therefore, in general, I give far more weight to the impressions of a spouse or close friend than to his own.

Of course, there are exceptions to this. Sometimes a spouse sets extremely high standards. Usually, in this case, the spouse will admit that the other has had memory "problems" as long as they have known each other. Sometimes spouses or friends haven't known each other very long, so there is really no way to compare.

We have to be particularly concerned in May-December unions where the spouse who is complaining (typically the younger mate) may simply not be used to the forgetfulness that can occur with aging. Or complaining spouses may even have ulterior motives, such as getting themselves declared their spouse's guardian.

(a) *Extremely bad, they forget everything.* If this is a change for your spouse or friend (see Question 3 below), then this is a major danger sign about his memory. I would urge you to convince him to have it checked by a professional.

(b) *Not too bad, but more forgetfulness than other people.* If you think his memory is worse than that of other people in general, and you have known him long enough and well enough to be able to say that, then again, I would urge you to have him see a medical professional. His memory problem may be nothing more than an annoyance, the memory loss due to aging, or it could be due to something else that might be simple, and simple to correct—depression, excessive medication, poor diet or inactivity. But it should be checked, so that whatever can be done is done.

(c) *Normal. He has a memory just as good as everyone else's.* You almost certainly do not need to be concerned about his memory—and neither does he. The only exception: when some very intelligent people begin to develop memory loss, they may be so adept at covering up the problem that even their spouses or friends do not notice, at least at first.

(d) *It's perfect—he never forgets.* Since *you* say so, I have to believe you. Can you persuade him to volunteer for medical research, so we can find out more about how his memory can be so perfect?

3. **What kinds of things does he forget? Important things? Things that really inconvenience him, interfere with his work, or perhaps even endanger him or other people? Or are the things he forgets only minor ones, so it's just an annoyance, but not a real problem in his life?**

Forgetting important things—work that he *had* to do for his job, turning off the range—is a sign of a more severe memory problem than is forgetting things of little or no consequence. However, even if his memory is bad, this doesn't necessarily mean that he has serious medical problem such as Alzheimer's disease. Depression, for example, can sometimes cause marked forgetting. And depression can often be helped.

4. **Did his memory problem begin suddenly, or very gradually?**
   (a) Suddenly, within hours or a day or two.
   (b) Gradually, so slowly I'm not actually sure when it began

(a) *Suddenly, within hours or a day or two.* Sometimes people *notice* memory problems suddenly, even though the problems have been there for quite some time. This seems to happen most frequently after an illness, often a hospitalization, when the person's problems with memory become much more evident in the new circumstances. You may find that, after he was admitted to the hospital for a routine procedure, he seems to be confused. He doesn't remember why he is there, doesn't remember the day of the week. He may get agitated and more confused, particularly at night. (This is called "sundowning.") Once outside the hospital, back in his own home, he will usually improve considerably. However, it may take several weeks for the confusion and nighttime agitation to clear.

This inability to adapt to new situations often signals that he has problems with memory and other functions. He has been able to get along well in familiar surroundings, but mentally just cannot keep up when circumstances change or become unfamiliar.

Sometimes, even when we know the person has a condition such as Alzheimer's disease that does *not* begin suddenly, nonetheless it seems to. Family members tell us about a sudden episode of memory loss, with everything being downhill from there. These usually remain puzzles to us.

But if the memory loss really does begin suddenly, then that is an important clue that it may be due to a medical condition such as a stroke in the areas of the brain that control memory—the thalamus or hippocampus. A stroke in those regions may cause little or no paralysis or weakness anywhere else in the body, and may not affect the person in any other way. So it might be very hard to detect. Or, sometimes, a memory loss may begin suddenly because a person has injured his head, and not remembered it.

Or something else may have happened to him—very, very rarely, a condition such as seizures could trigger memory problems. Whether the problem begins suddenly or slowly, it should be evaluated by a medical professional. But if it begins suddenly, this may be a clue that the cause is not a degenerative brain disease like Alzheimer's, but instead something from which he may recover.

(b) *Gradually, so slowly that we're not really sure when it began.* If you cannot be sure when the memory problem began, or if you, your family and friends argue as to just when you each noticed it, then this is a sign that it began very gradually. Frequently, such memory loss becomes apparent to other family members at family gatherings such as Thanksgiving, Christmas or birthdays. People who have not seen him in a year notice that he doesn't remember the names of the grandchildren quite so well, or that he just seems forgetful.

Some may think it went back two or three years, some may only notice it at this last event. Memory loss due to aging creeps up on a person very slowly. Usually, it is hard for anybody to see a change, even over a five- or ten-year period.

The memory loss due to Alzheimer's disease also creeps up, but it progresses more quickly. On the average, it takes family members about three years to become convinced that something is going wrong, and bring the affected person in to see the physician. So if you are still arguing among yourselves as to when the problem really began, or if not everybody is still completely convinced that there *is* a problem, this is not unexpected. Situations like this—where there may be some doubt in some people's minds—are precisely the situations in which you need the objective evaluation of a medical professional.

5. Do you feel that his memory has worsened in the last year, in general?
   (a) Yes
   (b) No

(a) *Yes, it has gotten worse in the last year.* This is a sign that not only is there a memory problem, but also that something is making it worse fast enough for you to notice. Conditions such as Alzheimer's disease can do this. So can some unusual conditions such as blood clots on the brain, conditions which build up a pressure inside the brain, or certain kinds of brain tumors. The list of diseases that can make memory worse this way is quite long. *You* should not be making the diagnosis, a medical professional should be.

(b) *No, no worsening over the past year.* Memory loss that doesn't change appreciably over a year means whatever is causing it is either very slow, or is itself not changing. Memory loss due to aging is like this. Memory loss due to stroke can be like this. In fact, memory problems caused by a stroke may actually seem to improve over a period of time. Memory loss due to anxiety or depression may fluctuate, but may wind up at the end of the year much like it was at the beginning. And if the memory loss is truly about the same after one year, it makes a condition such as Alzheimer's disease much less likely. Alzheimer's disease can have periods of relative quiescence, lasting from one to three years, but these are relatively uncommon. So if the memory loss is not changing, it does raise the chances that the cause is much less serious than would be the case with Alzheimer's disease or some other brain conditions such as tumors, blood clots, or increased pressure.

6. **Has he had periods of time in the last year when his memory has improved** *a great deal?* **Periods such as over the weekend or while he's been away on vacation?**
    (a) Yes
    (b) No

(a) *Yes, there have been periods of time when his memory has improved a great deal.* This is a good sign. It means that whatever is going wrong with his memory has not permanently damaged it. Often, this means that the memory problem is due to a condition such as anxiety, depression, or even just simple lack of effort. Serious brain diseases, such as Alzheimer's or brain tumors, would rarely allow a person to improve dramatically. So, if his memory has already shown it can get better by itself, it is more reason to expect that it will get better with treatment.

(b) *No. There have been no periods when his memory has improved a great deal.* Lack of improvement does not prove that he has a serious memory problem or a serious disease affecting memory. Even mild memory problems can persist unchanged.

7. **How do** *you* **think** *he* **thinks you are rating his memory?**
    (a) Very much different—I think his memory is much *worse* than he does.
    (b) Very much different—I think his memory is much *better* than he does.
    (c) The same—I think his memory is the same as what he thinks it is.

(a) *Very much different—I think his memory is much worse than he does.* This is a cause for concern. Not only do you think his memory is bad, but it also implies that he is not a very good judge of his own memory abilities. Diseases that affect memory only—which are relatively rare—often leave a person still able to give some sense of whether his own memory is good or bad. But diseases such as Alzheimer's destroy not only memory, but also judgment and self-awareness. Such people often think that their memory is quite good, or only a little bit of a problem. So this difference between your opinion and his is even more reason to seek medical attention.

(b) *Very much different, I think his memory is much better than he does.* This tends to be a good sign. How you rate his memory is probably more accurate than his own rating. And the fact that a person is a much harsher judge of himself often implies that his memory problem is due to depression, anxiety or self-monitoring. (Self-monitoring people are overly critical of everything they do and watch themselves constantly. If you watch yourself constantly, you are going to interfere with the way your mind works, and make your memory problems much worse.)

Rarely, people can have memory problems, realize that they do, and hide these problems from others. But such cover-ups are rarely perfect, even though the person may offer a good "explanation" on one or two occasions why his memory "slipped up just then." If you have seen him in situations where he has had to use his memory, then you have a fairly good idea of how well his memory works.

(c) *The same.* What this means depends in part on how good or bad you think his memory is. If you both think it is bad, then it deserves an evaluation. If you both think it is good, then you can both relax.

   8. **How often does he remember something that he forgot after you remind him of it?**
       (a) All the time, or almost all the time
       (b) Sometimes
       (c) Never.

(a) *All the time, or almost all the time.* This ability to be reminded of things he has forgotten is a good sign. While he is forgetful, he has enough memory remaining to remember what he did forget.

(b) *Sometimes.* This is cause for some concern. If he can only sometimes remember what he forgot, it implies that his memory problem is more severe than if he could always remember with reminding.

(c) *Never.* This is cause for definite concern. It implies that his memory problem is more severe. Such a severe memory problem should be checked.

   9. **If he is having memory problems, did he also have any major medical problems around the time these memory problems began?**
       (a) Yes
       (b) No

(a) *Yes, he had major medical problems around the time his memory problem began.* The clues to the cause of this memory problem might be in the medical condition he suffered. Was it a stroke? An operation? Cancer? A reaction to drugs? Pneumonia? Only a trained medical professional can confirm the connection, but it would be important to let a professional know about what had happened.

(b) *No, I know of no problems around the time his memory problem began.* This lessens the chances that a sudden medical problem was the cause of the memory problems. But, sometimes people can have strokes causing memory problems that do not show up any other way. A medical professional will have to look for causes that are not necessarily obvious.

10. **If he is having memory problems, have there been any changes in his medications?**
     (a) Yes
     (b) No

(a) *Yes, he did have a change in his medications.* As with medical problems, this could be a clue that the medication change is causing the memory problems, or at least making them worse. It is not common for drugs to cause memory problems. But because the memory problems they do cause can often be so easily treated, a physician should consider this possibility in every case of memory loss.

(b) *No.* Drugs are less likely to be a cause of his memory problems, but the drugs he is taking should still be reviewed to make sure they are not causing or exacerbating his memory problem.

11. **Does he drink appreciable amounts of alcohol regularly? Does he get tipsy or drunk regularly?**

Drinking to excess can be a danger flag. An occasional glass of wine or a beer with dinner is probably not going to cause memory problems. But some studies have suggested that heavier social drinking can worsen people's mental ability and memory. In one study by Dr. Elizabeth Parker and her associates at the National Institute of Alcohol Abuse and Alcoholism, the amount of social drinking in men was correlated with mental problems resembling those of premature aging. An extra drink of alcohol was associated with the equivalent of aging an additional 2.4 to 3.7 years on a test of mental ability.

Heavier drinking, to the point of frequent tipsiness or drunkenness, is known to cause memory problems. Some people seem to be more sensitive to the effects of alcohol, but there is no way of predicting whether he will be in this category or not. The brains of heavy drinkers can be damaged by a Vitamin B$_1$ (thiamine) deficiency, by toxic effects of alcohol, and often by the effects of the drinkers' frequent falls. The lack of Vitamin B$_1$ seems to be due to the poor diet of many drinkers, and the fact that metabolism of alcohol seems to use up B$_1$. Interestingly, taking B1 on a regular basis while continuing to drink heavily will not necessarily prevent this problem.

Heavy drinking is not unusual, even among the elderly. And, sometimes, people drink in secret. So alcohol is always a factor to consider in memory loss. How reversible the effects of drinking are, is not yet known.

12. How are his spirits? Do you think he is depressed, anxious, or unhappy?

(a) Yes, depressed or anxious.

(b) No, it seems like his spirits are good.

(a) *Yes, he seems to be depressed or anxious.* Depression or anxiety by themselves can impair memory ability. They certainly do not help make it better. He should seek the help of a trained professional.

(b) *No, his spirits seem to be good.* His spirits, therefore, can not *explain* his memory problem. But good spirits are, unfortunately, also no indication that he does not have a real memory problem, even from a serious disease. Sometimes, people with Alzheimer's disease are inordinately cheery. Cheery or sad, if you think he has a memory problem, you should urge him to get an evaluation.

WHAT TO DO IF YOU THINK YOU HAVE A MEMORY PROBLEM . . .

IF YOU THINK YOU HAVE A SERIOUS MEMORY PROBLEM, THEN YOU SHOULD SEE YOUR DOCTOR FIRST. DO NOT TRY TO DIAGNOSE YOURSELF!

EVEN IF YOU DO NOT THINK YOU HAVE A MEMORY PROBLEM, BUT OTHER PEOPLE WHO ARE CLOSE TO YOU OR KNOW YOU REASONABLY WELL THINK THAT YOU DO, THEN YOU SHOULD DEFINITELY SEE A DOCTOR OR ALLOW OTHER PEOPLE TO TAKE YOU TO A PHYSICIAN. Most people who have memory complaints are really not able to judge their own memory very well. Do not try to do so yourself!

A family doctor, general practitioner, or internist should be the first medical professional to hear about your problems. They can evaluate your general health, determine if there are any illnesses, drugs, or drug interactions that might cause difficulties, and refer you as necessary to individuals who may be more expert at diagnosing and managing the particular problem that you may seem to have. Such experts might include neurologists, neuropsychologists, psychologists, and psychiatrists. Again, this first step should be to your family practitioner, general practitioner, or internist. They can then determine if a referral to a specialist is necessary.

There is, of course, a reluctance to find out the answer, because of dread about what the answer might be: Alzheimer's disease. A brain tumor. Alcoholism. AIDS. Multiple sclerosis. Encephalitis. It is not unusual that *fear* prevents people from coming to see a doctor.

For example, I once had a patient for whom I had excellent news. She was an older woman, who had several years of memory problems. I assumed that she was worried about Alzheimer's disease, as most people her age are. I was able to reassure her that her memory problem was not due to Alzheimer's disease. But she was clearly not reassured by what I had said. She continued to look distressed and distracted. As I got happier, and her family got happier, she looked more and more anguished. Finally she blurted out, "It's a brain tumor then, isn't it?"

I was astonished. Nothing that she had told me was bothering her was even remotely similar to the effects of a brain tumor. But that was what she was *really* worried about! She was afraid of brain tumors, but not of Alzheimer's disease! I never would have guessed that. I have since tried to make it a practice in appropriate cases to ask people what it is that really *worries* them. Do they have any questions or concerns that I have not been able to get to? If *you* have such concerns, bring them up.

Most complaints of memory loss are NOT due to Alzheimer's disease.

Many people with memory complaints will be suffering from depression or anxiety; there is nothing fundamentally wrong with their brains. Their memory abilities will return when their depression or anxiety clears.

Many people with memory complaints will simply be experiencing normal memory loss due to aging. This is annoying, it is true. But it does not necessarily mean that you have Alzheimer's disease, or that you will develop Alzheimer's disease.

In some people, memory loss might be due to such things as drug side effects, hypothyroidism (low thyroid), or a wide variety of conditions which can be detected and solved. A number of studies of patients with dementia—a more severe condition than just memory loss—have shown that even in this group, about 11 percent had problems that could be totally (8 percent) or partially (3 percent) reversible. These estimates are probably higher than the true frequency of reversible problems in dementia. But they do show that there is often some reason to hope for a reversible problem, even when the condition is more severe than memory loss alone.

Whatever the cause of your memory problems, *you will be better off if it is detected early, rather than too late.* If the problem is treatable, you will have a better chance of recovery of your memory if the problem is caught early. And if is not, you will have more of an opportunity to plan.

So don't delay. If other people really think you have a memory problem, or if you are really concerned about your memory, go see a doctor.

Again, a warning: if you think you have a significant memory problem, or if other people think you have a significant memory problem, DO NOT USE THIS BOOK TO TRY TO DIAGNOSE YOURSELF! People are complicated, and memory is complicated. There is really no substitute for actual clinical knowledge and actual clinical experience.

TO WHOM SHOULD YOU GO?

Sometimes people want to go directly to a memory specialist. But, generally, you should go to your primary care doctor first. Although your family practitioner or internist may not be an expert in memory itself, you will still need a basic medical check up, and assurances that there are no problems with the rest of your body that could cause memory loss, before you see a memory specialist.

HOW TO PREPARE FOR THE DOCTOR'S VISIT

Diagnosing a memory problem is often a detective problem. You can help yourself and help your physician help you, if you give him more of the clues. So I suggest that you, and if possible someone who is close to you and who knows you reasonably well (a spouse, good friend, or grown child) help provide the necessary information to your doctor.

HOW WILL MY MEMORY BE CHECKED?

How your memory is checked will depend upon what you complain about, and what problems your physician perceives.

Memory checking should at least include an interview about what the problem is (if possible, from both your point of view and that of others close to you).

Testing of memory and related functions can take from five minutes to two hours or more. Not only should memory be checked, but also other mental functions as well. These may include vocabulary, arithmetic ability, your ability to draw a set of figures, and the like. These tests will give your doctor a sense of your skills, and can help determine if you have problems in areas other than memory. This is important for diagnosing conditions such as Alzheimer's, since Alzheimer's disease usually affects more than just memory.

Generally speaking, the longer the testing, the more reliable and accurate it is likely to be. In my clinic, we find that a single visit that includes two to three hours of testing is usually both necessary and sufficient for giving an accurate clinical diagnosis, to the extent that is possible from a single visit.

Memory testing might be done through the offices of a neurologist, psychiatrist, or clinical psychologist with special expertise in neuropsychology. *Medical interpretation* of the results of memory testing, however, requires a physician. This could be your own primary care provider, specialist in geriatric medicine, a neurologist or psychiatrist. What matters most is whether the physician has experience with memory disorders in general and with the particular kinds of memory disorders that you *might* have. This may well be the physician who specializes in Alzheimer's (since serious memory loss *can be* Alzheimer's disease). Sometimes, it takes the concerted efforts of several physicians and other medical care providers, working together, to adequately understand an individual's case and give him or her the best possible advice.

No matter who you see, be prepared for the fact that it may not be possible to have a definitive answer on your first visit. Although the visit will undoubtedly give you more information about your condition, it may be necessary to wait a year or more to see if anything objectively changes with your memory (either up or down). Keeping track of changes is usually *very* helpful for diagnosing the specific problem you are having.

16

How Forgetful Are *You*? Evaluating Your Own Memory

> *THERAPIST:* How often do you have sex?
> *ALVIN:* Hardly ever. Maybe three times a week.
> *ANNIE:* Constantly. I'd say three times a week.
> —ANNIE HALL (1977)

As ALVIN AND Annie illustrate, even if you can objectively estimate your memory ability, you may still not think it is very good. If you passed the tests in Chapter 15, then chances are good that you do not have a dangerous brain disease that is causing memory loss. But even if you don't think you have a brain disease, you may still think your memory is quite abnormal.

It is very difficult to evaluate our own memories. We never give ourselves credit for what we *do* remember, instead we fixate on what we forget! I don't notice having remembered the names of twenty-four people today. I only remember that I forgot the name of my wife's favorite great-uncle. (She reminded me of this one!) And if you have a busy life, you have more opportunities for forgetting, and more opportunities to blame your memory.

How you feel about your memory is a separate issue that we'll discuss later (see Chapter 20). Here, we will try to give you a better sense of how good or bad your memory actually is, through the questions that follow. We will try to get at your memory strengths—and weaknesses—by finding out how often and under what circumstances you have memory problems.

Please keep in mind that, with memory, there is a wide range of what is considered a "normal" frequency. The answers that have been **bolded** are the **averages** determined in one study. But the range across different groups is almost certainly enormous, and the range across individuals even wider. Also, this type of frequency scale has at least one glaring problem: the busier you are, the worse your memory will look, because you have more opportunities to forget. So use these questions more to get a flavor for the range and pattern of your memory, rather than as any absolute guide to how good or bad your memory actually is.

FORGETTING FREQUENCY QUESTIONNAIRE
(When two answers are bolded, the average in the study used as reference was somewhere between them.)

1. How often do you forget where you have put things?
   (a) Not within the last six months
   (b) Once or twice in the last six months
   (c) About once a month
   (d) About once a week
   (e) Daily
   (f) More than once a day

Where you think you put it.   **Where you really put it.**

2. How often do you fail to recognize places where you have been before?
   (a) Not within the last six months
   (b) Once or twice in the last six months
   (c) About once a month
   (d) About once a week
   (e) Daily
   (f) More than once a day

3. How often do you find television or movie plots difficult to follow?
   (a) Not within the last six months
   (b) Once or twice in the last six months
   (c) About once a month
   (d) About once a week
   (e) Daily

(f) More than once a day

4. How often do you forget that your daily routine has changed? You forget where you normally keep something, or your forget the time something normally happens? (Your clue may be that you followed your old routine by mistake.)
    (a) Not within the last six months
    (b) Once or twice in the last six months
    (c) About once a month
    (d) About once a week
    (e) Daily
    (f) More than once a day

5. How often have you had to recheck whether you have done something that you meant to do, such as lock the door, turn on the lights, or turn off the oven?
    (a) Not within the last six months
    (b) Once or twice in the last six months
    (c) About once a month
    (d) About once a week
    (e) Daily
    (f) More than once a day

6. How often have you forgotten *when* something happened, such as whether a particular event occurred yesterday or last week?
    (a) Not within the last six months
    (b) Once or twice in the last six months
    (c) About once a month
    (d) About once a week
    (e) Daily
    (f) More than once a day

Reprinted with special permission of King Features Syndicate

7. How often have you completely forgotten something you were supposed to do, such as take things with you? An example would be, forgetting your keys until you got to the car?

(a) Not within the last six months
(b) Once or twice in the last six months
(c) About once a month
(d) About once a week
(e) Daily
(f) More than once a day

8. How often do you forget something that you were told yesterday or a few days ago, and had to be reminded about it?
(a) Not within the last six months
(b) Once or twice in the last six months
(c) About once a month
(d) About once a week
(e) Daily
(f) More than once a day

9. How often have you begun to read something such as a book or a magazine or newspaper article without realizing that you have read it before?
(a) Not within the last six months
(b) Once or twice in the last six months
(c) About once a month
(d) About once a week
(e) Daily
(f) More than once a day

10. How often do you let yourself ramble on about unimportant things?
(a) Not within the last six months
(b) Once or twice in the last six months
(c) About once a month
(d) About once a week
(e) Daily
(f) More than once a day

11. How often have you failed to recognize close relatives or close friends? (Not recognize by sight, *not* forgetting their names.)
(a) Not within the last six months
(b) Once or twice in the last six months
(c) About once a month
(d) About once a week
(e) Daily
(f) More than once a day

12. How often do you find that a word or a name is "on the tip of your tongue", but you just can't remember it when you need to?
    (a) Not within the last six months
    (b) Once or twice in the last six months
    (c) About once a month
    (d) About once a week
    (e) Daily
    (f) More than once a day
13. How often have you completely forgotten to do something you said you would do or that you planned to do?
    (a) Not within the last six months
    (b) Once or twice in the last six months
    (c) About once a month
    (d) About once a week
    (e) Daily
    (f) More than once a day
14. How often have you forgotten important details of what you did or what happened to you just *the day before?*
    (a) Not within the last six months
    (b) Once or twice in the last six months
    (c) About once a month
    (d) About once a week
    (e) Daily
    (f) More than once a day
15. When talking to someone, how often do you forget what you were just talking about? How often have you had to ask, "Where was I?"
    (a) Not within the last six months
    (b) Once or twice in the last six months
    (c) About once a month
    (d) About once a week
    (e) Daily
    (f) More than once a day
16. How often have you forgotten to tell somebody something important? Forgotten to pass on a message? Forgotten to remind somebody of something?
    (a) Not within the last six months
    (b) Once or twice in the last six months
    (c) About once a month
    (d) About once a week
    (e) Daily

(f) More than once a day

17. How often have you mixed up the details of what someone has told you?

(a) Not within the last six months

(b) Once or twice in the last six months

(c) About once a month

(d) About once a week

(e) Daily

(f) More than once a day

18. How often do you tell someone a story or joke that you have already told them?

... BUT YOU DON'T TURN THERE, IT'LL BE THE FOURTH TRAFFIC LIGHT, AND YOU DON'T REALLY TURN LEFT, YOU JUST BEAR LEFT.

No matter how hard you try, or how slowly they talk, as soon as you roll up the window you'll forget everything.

Real Life Adventures © GarLanCo. Reprinted with permission of Universal Press Syndicate. All rights reserved.

(a) Not within the last six months

(b) Once or twice in the last six months

(c) About once a month

(d) About once a week

(e) Daily

(f) More than once a day

19. How often do you get lost or take a wrong turn on an otherwise familiar route?

(a) Not within the last six months

(b) Once or twice in the last six months

(c) About once a month

(d) About once a week

(e) Daily

(f) More than once a day

20. How often do you forget that you have already done something routine, such as brush your teeth or make coffee, and start to do them all over again?

(a) Not within the last six months

(b) Once or twice in the last six months

(c) About once a month

(d) About once a week

(e) Daily

17

It's On the Tip of My Tongue!—Remembering and Forgetting Names and Faces

BOB, ED... DOROTHY?

WISE/ALDRICH

Another victim of name-retention-center dysfunction.

ASK ANYONE WHAT kind of memory lapse bothers them the most, and you will undoubtedly hear, "Forgetting people's names and faces!"

It is a common enough problem. You know it happens to just about everybody, but that does not make it any less troublesome. Sometimes merely awkward, sometimes downright embarrassing, forgetting a name or forgetting a face is ALWAYS frustrating.

Despite the fact that most of us will do perfectly well on the names and faces of at least 1,000 aquaintances, it is the one we cannot recall the moment we need it that throws us into a panic.

But just how normal is it to forget the name of someone you know? And why do we do it?

Here is your chance to find out. This chapter will give you an opportunity to compare your memory for names and faces to that of others. You will be comparing your abilities to those of average people who voluntarily participated in various memory studies.

First, compare yourself to the 22 people who participated in a memory study. The comparison between *you* and these people can not be very exact: all of the people in the study were between 20 and 40 years old; most were students at a university; and all lived in England. You are likely to be different from them in a number of ways, and you didn't keep a detailed diary of your problems and errors in recognizing other people, for eight weeks straight. But these subjects did. So we know how well memory really worked—or didn't work—in the everyday life of these normal people. As a result, you can use their data as some basis for comparing how well your memory should do.

Each numbered section is a different type of problem that these people experienced. Some of their actual experiences come first, followed by the question about whether you have experienced the same type of problem. In the list of possible answers, the **bold** type indicates the average number of times a problem occurred, as in the previous chapters. (If two answers are bolded, the average was somewhere between the two.)

I have also shown the *range* of their experiences in *italics*, to give you a sense of how much individual abilities can differ and still be considered normal—even in this fairly homogeneous group! The comment after each question tells you more exactly how frequently and how infrequently the 22 people in this group experienced the particular type of problem.

1.   "I was going through the doors . . . when a friend said, 'Hello'. I first ignored him, thinking that he must have been talking to the person behind me."

How often have you failed to recognize a person who is familiar to you?
(a) Not within the last six months
(b) Once or twice within the last six months
(c) About once a month
(d) About once a week
(e) Daily
(f) More than once a day

One person in this study never failed to recognize a familiar person (or at least never reported doing so). At the other extreme, one person in the study failed to recognize a familiar person two times each a week, on average.

2. "I was waiting for the phone. A lot of people were walking past. I thought one of them was my boyfriend."

"I was outside my house, gardening and looking after the baby. I saw a person who lives near me, but I thought it was someone who *used to* live nearby until I remembered the person didn't live nearby any longer."

How often have you mistaken one person for another?
(a) Not within the last six months
(b) Once or twice within the last six months
(c) About once a month
(d) About once a week
(e) Daily
(f) More than once a day

Every one of the 22 people reported that this had happened to them in the last eight weeks. The person who reported the lowest number of such incidents still had it happen twice in the prior eight weeks. The one with the highest number had it happen 38 times, or an average of about once every other day!

3. "I was walking along the street, when I saw a person who looked familiar. At first, she was only familiar. [But] then I thought she was an assistant in the library. ... I wasn't sure [at first]. Gradually I became convinced she was [the woman from the library]"

"I was at the theatre when I saw someone in the audience I thought I knew. I didn't know who she was until I saw her with her sister and parents, who I know better."

"I didn't recognize her until she spoke; then I recognized the voice as familiar. I have no idea who she was."

"I saw a woman about 25 years old, perhaps ten yards away. I thought she looked familiar. I realized on looking more closely that I didn't know her, but that she looked like [a famous pop singer]."

"I just thought the person looked familiar as she waved, and I thought it was at me. I waved back, then realized I didn't know her. She was waving at someone else."

How often have you thought that something about a

person's appearance, name, voice or other feature was familiar, but you couldn't initially remember anything else about the person?

(a) Not within the last six months

(b) Once or twice within the last six months

(c) *About once a month*

(d) About once a week

(e) *Daily*

(f) More than once a day

Every one of the 22 had an experience like this in the prior eight weeks. At the low end, one person reported only one such experience in those eight weeks. At the high end, one person reported 22 examples, an average of three times a week!

4. "I saw another student walking past, but I couldn't remember his name, even though I had been talking about him only a few days ago. Someone had to tell me [his name]."

"I heard Barry Manilow [the singer] on the radio. I knew who it was, and one of the records he had made, but I couldn't remember his name or what he looked like for about a minute. I got his appearance first, then [his] name."

"I had gone to meet him, but I couldn't remember his name! I got very annoyed with myself, but didn't ask because it had been mentioned a few minutes before."

How often did you know more about the person than just the feeling they were familiar, but still couldn't remember details about them, such as their name?

(a) *Not within the last six months*

(b) *Once or twice within the last six months*

(c) *About once a month*

(d) About once a week

(e) *Daily*

(f) More than once a day

Three people of the 22 had never had this happen to them in the prior eight weeks. But one person had it happen 34 times, more often than every other day! Usually, what people couldn't remember was the name. Often, despite not remembering the name, they could still recall their person's occupation, where they had seen the person, their voice, and sometimes even their appearance. But the *name* still eluded them.

5. "I was on my way to a lecture. I saw someone I knew who was a member of the staff, ...but I became unsure and thought I might have mistaken him for another person in the same department."

    How often have you been unsure whether the person you saw was a particular person or not?

    (a) Not within the last six months

    (b) Once or twice within the last six months

    (c) About once a month

    (d) About once a week

    (e) Daily

    (f) More than once a day

    Ten people never had this happen to them at all in the prior eight weeks. But, at the other extreme, one person in the study had it happen six times, an average of about once a week.

6. "I was shopping in the Town Center, when I saw a person who I thought looked like a girl who works in the bank. For about five seconds I didn't think it was her, but a close resemblance...[Then I realized it was her!]"

    How often have you seen a person, initially thought they weren't someone you knew, they only looked like them—and then discovered that they actually were person that you knew!?

    (a) Not within the last six months

    (b) Once or twice within the last six months

    (c) About once a month

    (d) About once a week

    (e) Daily

    (f) More than once a day

    This was rare—it happened to only three people in all. Still, it did happen even in these normal people. The person it happened to the most often had been embarrassed by this about once a month, on average.

7. How often have you given the wrong name to a person?

    (a) Not within the last six months

    (b) Once or twice within the last six months

    (c) About once a month

    (d) About once a week

    (e) Daily

    (f) More than once a day

This didn't happen often, but four people had noted it occurred to them in the prior eight weeks. The person who reported it most often had it happen to him about once a month.

FACES FROM THE PAST

The questions above give us a sense of how *often* we can expect our memory to fail us on names and faces—if we are normal, very often! But how *good* should it be? What is our memory's batting average for remembering names and faces? And what happens to it over time?

Most of the time, it is hard to answer these questions rigorously. After all, who usually measures how well we learned names and faces in the first place? Who tests such memories over spans of many years? But several rigorous studies *have* been done. One was of memory for high-school classmates, measured in different classes over intervals ranging from 2 weeks to 57 *years*. Such studies give us an idea how much we can—or can't—expect from our memories, on the average.

Three months after graduation from high school, people were about 90 percent correct in deciding that the *pictures* of their former classmates were *familiar*. Notice that they were not asked the names—only whether the person in the picture looked familiar to them or not. This memory for familiarity held up well over decades. Almost five decades after graduation, people were about 70 percent correct in their judgments of familiarity.

But remembering the *name* from the picture was a different story altogether. Three months after graduation, people could recall about 70 percent of their classmate's names from their pictures—already worse performance than their ability to recognize the pictures as familiar. But after 48 years, name recall was *much* worse—people could only recall about 20 percent of the names.

This figure may impress you or horrify you. That we remember names at all over such an interval is impressive. The amount of forgetting we have is also impressive. And keep in mind that these are just averages. *Your* memory may be far worse—or even far better—and still be very normal.

ABSENT-MINDED PROFESSORS?

High school classmates are somewhat special. Whether you liked your classmates or not, you had probably been with them off and on for

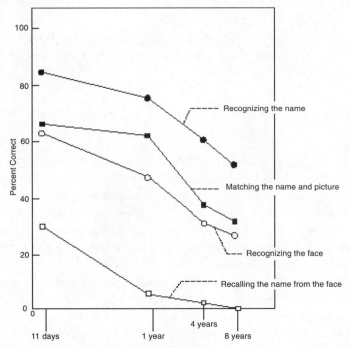

Figure 19: The memory of college teachers for the faces and the names of their former students. The time scale has been compressed. (Adapted with permission from H.P. Bahrick, *Memory for People*, in J.E. Harris and P.E. Morris (Eds.) *Everyday Memory, Actions, and Absent-Mindedness*, Academic Press, New York, 1984).

fairly long periods of time. How about memory for names and faces in more commonplace settings, when the exposure to people is briefer, and they mean less to you?

Under these circumstances, memory is *much* worse. One set of data comes from a study of the memory of college professors for their students. Eleven days after the semester ended, they were 85 percent accurate in recognizing the names of their students from a list. So they had at least learned the names of their students. But even after 11 days, they were only 35 percent accurate in recalling the students' names when shown their pictures. See Figure 19.

After a year, memory for names fades even more. Professors who were tested then were only about 6 percent correct in recalling the name from the face. After that, memory for student names *really* plummets. Eight years after they had taught a class, professors looked at pictures of the students from that class—and could not recall *ANY* names at all! Again, there is almost certainly great individual variation. It is likely that some professors forget everyone much sooner, and some may never have forgotten! But as a group, and on the average, these figures show us such memories are not very durable.

I Never Forget a Face!

What these studies confirm is what we know intuitively: for most people, faces are much easier to remember than names. Part of this difference is accidental: you are asking your memory to work much harder when you ask it to *recall* a name, as opposed to *recognize* a face. *Recall* is always a harder job than *recognition*, whether you are dealing with names or faces. To recall a name, you have to actually produce it, while to recognize it, you can just look at a list of names, let them all wash over your stored memories, and just feel whether any trigger a feeling of familiarity. (These differences were discussed in Chapter 5, page 30.) Imagine trying to recall a face—visualizing it in your mind, or sketching it on paper—as you would recall a name!

But part of the superiority of faces over names is very real. Faces are remembered as *visual* memories, names as *verbal* memories. As human beings, we have tremendous visual memory abilities. You can show people as many as 10,000 pictures, and later they will be able to visually recognize most of them. We are naturally better at remembering visual information—such as someone's face. And there may be reasons our memory for faces is particularly good. Faces are very important to us, and there may even be specialized areas of the brain that deal with memory for faces.

This is not to say that recognizing a face is necessarily easy. We do see a *great many* faces. And there are only so many variations you can have of a face. So faces can get somewhat confused in our minds, and they can be forgotten.

And what I have talked about on the average is not true for everyone. There are some people whose visual memories are much worse than the average. (This is probably because some aspect of their *vision*—their capacity to imagine visual scenes, for example—is much worse than the average.) Some of these people will be good at verbal memory, some will be average. Regardless, these people will have particular difficulty with remembering people's names—*because they cannot remember the face!* But for most people, this is not the problem. Remembering the name is.

Why We Forget Names

Why is our memory for names so poor? It turns out that there are many reasons which, together, make it so hard to remember names.

First of all, names are just plain hard to *learn* in the first place. In experiments where people have been given short biographies that included hobbies, occupations, and even the names of places, recall of the name of the person was worse than recall of any other type of information. This is true even when the name of the person was identical to his occupation, such as Charles Baker, who owns a bakery, and Jim Potter, who makes clay pots. It is much harder to remember that a person's surname is Baker than to remember that he is a baker. One reason this is the case is that names, by themselves, do not *mean* anything. They are not easy to picture, they are arbitrary, and unless they are recognizably ethnic, they don't describe the person. When you try to learn them, they don't necessarily trigger any helpful associations that can lead you back to them later. Meaning, visualization, and connections are all what make things easier to learn and to recall. A name has very little of these, so it is neither easy to learn nor to recall.

Another problem with recalling names is that so many of them are alike. Also, people typically need to recall not just one but two words to get a name (the first and last names). If both the first name and surname are common words (*John Doyle*), then the resulting name is easier to recall than if both are relatively rare words (*Sian Pidgeon*). But it is still not easy! (It becomes a little easier if the first name is common and the surname rare (*Mark Quach*), or if the first name is rare and the surname common (*Blossom Smith*). Then, the combination becomes a little more distinctive, and a little easier to remember.)

No Alternate Routes

But perhaps the most important reason names are hard to recall is that recall of proper names cannot work quite the same way as recall of other kinds of information.

The process of remembering a name—any name—starts the same way. You start with *knowing something* about what it is that you want to say. Thought comes before language; meaning comes before the word itself. Take what happens in your mind, for example, when you have the thought of a TABLE, and want to say it out loud. Thinking about a TABLE automatically activates a whole network of related thoughts: how it supports things, has a flat top, four legs, is usually made of wood, and so forth. From any of these notions, the mental activation can travel to the word "table." Even if any one connection is weak, or if one takes you off on a tangent, there are still many other correct ones being activated. From any of these pathways, activation can converge on the word "table" and let you say it out loud.

Normally, this system of finding similarities, activating connections, and converging on the "right" answer is one of the great strengths of our memories, as I discussed in Chapter 3, starting on page 21. But with proper names, there are problems.

One problem is caused by the fact that proper names are *unique*. You can know many things about a person, you can know many aspects of their face—but there is only *one* name for them that is correct. So only one chain of activation can be the correct one. Approximate is not good enough for proper names. But because there is only one chain of connections, all of our memory for that name rests on that particular chain.

Other kinds of memories rely upon dense webs of connections. Even if each strand is thin and weak, the combination becomes extremely strong. But memory for a proper name is only as strong as the one connection itself. And the strength of this link in the direction we want—*from* the information, *to* the name to say out loud—is often not as strong as we would like. If we have not practiced saying the name out loud, if we have only seen it or heard it, then we have strengthened the link in the *opposite* direction —going in rather than coming out—and this is not the direction we need when we try to get the name out.

There is another problem. Our memory system automatically tries to find similarities, and activates a whole web of connections in the expectation that they will converge on the one memory we want. This normally works very well (although it does give us Freudian slips and other errors that may confuse us!). But for proper names, all this connectivity creates a problem.

Mr. Adam Smith, the person you want to name, may have a *moustache* and be an *accountant*. But you know many people who look a bit like Adam Smith, many people with moustaches, and many accountants. So even when you see the right Mr. Smith, your mind automatically activates *all* the connections you have to people who look like Adam Smith, to "men with moustaches," and to "accountants." It then activates all the connections from those connections, and then *all* of *their* connections ... until the activation dies away. Even when you finally activate the name, "Adam" and "Smith," being activated, awaken in your mind all the *other* Adams and Smiths that you know. Soon the activation for the *right* name finds itself in the middle of a competition against all the *other* names sparked by the original thought or face of Mr. Adam Smith. Only the most activated name will be said out loud. And, if you've have a recent experience with accountants, or just dealt with someone else with a moustache, the correct name may have quite a fight to make itself heard!

Most of the time, this competition seems to be below the level of consciousness. All we are aware of is that we can't say the name, and may have only the fuzziest notion of what it is like. Sometimes, the wrong name wins the competition and enters our consciousness as an interloper. Most of the time, we can suppress them at that stage. But once in a while, out they pop—and we realize we have goofed! When they enter your consciousness, you can even get a sense of what stage was the site of the main battle. If the names are related by meaning (that is, out comes another *accountant*'s name), then the competition was at the meaning level. If the wrong one differs from the right one by sound alone ("*Amadeus*" instead of "*Adam*"), then the competition was played out at almost the very last stage, where the sounds of entire words are selected.

These are the reasons why names are so hard to recall. They also explain why we are prone to calling people by the wrong names. I once had a particularly galling experience with this. I have two brothers who are identical twins. I have never had any problems telling them apart. I can tell them apart in baby pictures, from the back, in the distance. So why, when we were all up on stage once, should I have called the brother walking toward me by his twin brother's name? Because my brain was working correctly (although he may disagree!). It had activated almost all the right information, and almost all the right pathways. His name fit almost all the facts, fit almost all the connections. My brain couldn't help it there was just one small difference between the two names: the tiny details of the face of one brother that set him apart from his identical twin. Being almost exactly right is good enough, as far as the brain is concerned. But not for people's names!

LOST—AND FOUND

As I have hinted, the special mental requirements for naming are the cause of some familiar, yet frustrating experiences. We have all experienced the tip-of-the-tongue phenomenon, blocks, interlopers, and pop-ups. You may experience them again as you try to answer these questions. Pay particular attention to how you feel when you *cannot* get an answer, or get the wrong one:

1.   He played Hawkeye on *M*A*S*H*.
2.   He danced and sang as the star of *Singin' in the Rain*.
3.   Played Moses and Ben Hur.

4. The *French Lieutenant's Woman* in the movie.
5. Actress known for both her serious acting and for her portrayal of Mrs. Emma Peel in *The Avengers*.
6. Actress and Princess of Monaco.
7. The actor whom we remember for having told Sam to play it again.
8. The way she said "Why don't you come on up and see me sometime" made her even more famous.

Answers:

1. Alan Alda
2. Gene Kelly
3. Charlton Heston
4. Meryl Streep
5. Diana Rigg
6. Grace Kelly
7. Humphrey Bogart
8. Mae West

Chances are you *almost* had the answer for some of these questions—but you felt it was somehow blocked. Or perhaps it was not quite blocked, but you still couldn't say it: it was right on the tip of your tongue!

Memory blocks and the tip-of-the-tongue phenomena can occur for any word, but they happen for nouns more than for other words, and for proper nouns—people's names—*far* more often than for anything else. Blocking on names is so common, in fact, that at least *77 percent of all memory blocks are for proper names*, rather than for any other kind of information, according to one study.

It may be surprising, but people tend to block the names of people they know, rather than names they use less often. Subjects in one study recorded all the name blocks they experienced over a two-week period. Over the course of the two weeks:

- 68 percent of the blocks were for names of friends and acquaintances
- 17 percent were for names of famous people
- 8 percent were for proper names such as brand names, book titles and musical groups
- 7 percent were for names of places

What *do* you know when you get into a tip-of-the-tongue state? You "know" the meaning of what you were trying to say—even though you can't say it. If it is a person, then you will almost always know something

about the person himself: who he is, what he does, some distinguish-
ing characteristic. And even though you won't know the name itself,
you will know *something* about the name: perhaps its number of syllables, its first letter, its nationality, or even just the feeling it gives you.
"The rhythm of a lost word may be there without a sound to clothe it;
the evanescent sense of [it]...may mock us fitfully, without growing more
distinct," as William James observed in 1890.

Then there are the "interlopers," or blockers—all the incorrect names
that crowd your mind while you are trying to recall that one stubborn
one. You just can't get them out of your mind. So you stop thinking about
the name you want and move on. Then, when you least expect it, the
name suddenly leaps to mind. That's known as a "pop-up."

The reason for such blocks, tip-of-the-tongue states, interlopers, and
pop-ups is all the same: you know enough about the person to *almost*
activate the right name, but not *quite* enough to do so. That is why the
name you are trying so hard to call up seems like "a sort of wraith of a
name," as William James put it—often, a ghostly outline is all your
memory could conjure up. If you cannot activate any part of the name,
you have a block. If your memory can just tickle the name, you have a
tip-of-the-tongue. And if you activate the *wrong* name, you get an interloper popping into your mind!

Why should your memory be unable to activate the right name? It
may be that it really *is* too weak—you just don't know the person or
their name very well. But, because most of these states occur with people and names that are really familiar to us, another explanation is
more often correct. You do have a good memory for the person and
name that you want to recall—but you also have *other* memories, of
other people and names, that compete. The result is a free-for-all in
your mind, of which you get only a glimpse—sounds floating, names
popping up, everything but the name you want!

What Makes It Worse

Studies have confirmed, for the most part, what we know from everyday experience. Some people are just prone to name blocking and the
tip-of-the-tongue state. These are common occurrences for them; for
other people, they are much rarer.

People are more likely to have memory blocks and tip-of-the-tongue
states if they are tired, stressed or ill. This is because name recall is at
the end of a long chain of activations in your memory. If anything
weakens along the chain, or if the balance of activations among

competing chains is off, the activation we want will not happen properly. So activation of proper names is very sensitive to anything going
wrong with the brain, because it is the chain of processing with the
most and the weakest links.

Older people tend to experience more memory blocks than do
younger ones. And older subjects tend to experience a *complete* mental
blank whenever they block a name. In contrast, younger subjects more
commonly report "interlopers": a related but incorrect name. You try
to think of "Kevin," but all that comes to mind is "Ken."

Why this difference with aging? At least two possible reasons. With
age, the memory system is more overloaded to begin with—you have
more names to remember than when you were younger. And with age,
the neural machinery may also not be working quite so well—it may be
a little slower, a little noisier than when you were young. This combination may be why people notice naming problems as one of the big
indicators of their getting older.

Brain disease—strokes, for example, which damage parts of the brain,
or Alzheimer's disease, which damages wider areas—very frequently
causes problems with getting names out. In these cases, memory activations have been damaged at any of a number of places along the
chain from thought to the spoken name. But there are also cases of
people who have had relatively small strokes, and then lost their ability
to say proper names. These people could say other names, including
the names of cities and towns, perfectly well. They just could not say
proper names. In these cases, the brain seems to have been damaged
at just the point where names are generated. Proper names, being more
susceptible to getting cut off than other names, showed the most severe disruption.

DON'T WORRY, YOU'LL GET IT

What can you do about a name block? Relax, for one thing—it's natural, and very common. It doesn't necessarily mean something is wrong
with your mind. In fact, it's partly a sign that you know the name reasonably well. If you habitually name-block, or have tip-of-the-tongue, it
may even be a sign that you have a rich, healthy, network of connections in your memory, the way you should!

One common and useful strategy is to turn your mind onto something other than the name you are trying to remember. As often as
not, the name you want will just pop out after a while. Why does this
work? Because blocks and the tip-of-the-tongue state often arise

because several memories are too strong. Being too strong, they compete with each other, and block the right one from coming to the surface. If you turn your attention elsewhere, you divert energy from *all* these memories. The correct memory weakens, but the *incorrect* memories weaken *more*, or weaken faster. When the incorrect memories die down, the block evaporates, and the correct activation will be able to pop up into your consciousness.

As most people know from experience, if you think you know the name, you *will* eventually get it out. Your "feeling of knowing" is a sign that the name is probably stored in your memory. The stronger your feeling of knowing, the sooner you will recall the forgotten name. But be patient! In one study, even though most of the blocks proved to be temporary, many of the names took more than an hour to retrieve, and some took several days!

A more direct approach is to try to help your memory along. The problem people usually have is not with knowing about the person—the problem is usually at the level of the name itself. So extra information about the person usually doesn't help. But any part of the name is often enough to trigger the whole answer. So one clever strategy is to quickly run through the alphabet—often, hitting the correct first letter will trigger your memory of the entire name! However well it works, remembering names this way can be slow; it may take practice to work up some speed!

Of course, if all else fails, there is always a time-honored solution to rescue us:

"When I meet a man whose name I cannot remember," Disraeli, the English politician, counseled, "I give myself two minutes, then, if it is a hopeless case, I always say, 'And how is the old complaint?'"

18

How Does Normal Memory Normally Behave?*

He: We met at nine. She: We met at eight.
He: I was on time. She: No, you were late.
He: Ah, yes! I remember it well.
He: We dined with friends. She: We dined alone.
He: A tenor sang. She: A baritone.
He: Ah, yes! I remember it well.
He: That dazzling April moon! She: There was
none that night. And the month was June.
He: That's right! That's right!
She: It warms my heart to know that you remember
still the way you do.
He: Ah, yes! I remember it well...
            —*"I Remember It Well" (from* **Gigi**)

WE MAY SNICKER, but this song nicely illustrates some basic truths about how normal memory works.

WHY MEN AND WOMEN HAVE DIFFERENT MEMORIES

We all have different interests and desires. How well we remember is partly determined by how well we *want* to remember—the greater the interest, the better the memory.

Women do better than men at remembering names and faces, and remembering verbal material ("and Mabel lives on Monument Street"). They also are better at recalling details about such things as dress and appearance ("What was the color of the gown Cindy Crawford wore at the Oscar ceremonies?"). Men do better than women at remembering cars—no surprise!—as well as the position of things in space, and at remembering how gadgets operate.

---

* This chapter by Barry Gordon, M.D., Ph.D, with Rachel Wilder

Some of these differences may be due to differences in the way the brains of men and women work, just by virtue of the fact that they are men or women. This is certainly true in other animals. In animals, sex alone makes a difference in memory. And different sex hormones can alter an animal's ability to learn. In animals, these differences between the sexes are rooted in the very different roles the sexes have. The male lion always protects his pride's territory. The lioness always provides dinner. And something similar may have happened with people.

Reprinted with special permission of King Features Syndicate

Some researchers think that some of the differences between men's memory and women's may have originated in the very different roles that Stone Age men and women played in food-gathering. The division of labor among today's hunter-gatherers is usually quite strict, and probably was similarly strict for our ancestors. Women, who collected most of the food, walked about four or five miles away from the home base each day, gathering fruit, nuts and root vegetables. Remembering the visual details of stationary landmarks was the most efficient strategy for them. For example, to find the way back to the tree with the ripest fruit, they might have remembered that you pass the big termite mound, head towards the acacia tree, walk to the second water hole and then go over the little hill.

In contrast, hunters tracking a wounded warthog had to deal with a moving food source. Even today, men tend to find their way using vectors, a sense of moving in the right direction. They will remember how to drive somewhere by thinking, "go straight ahead for a while, then turn right." They are more likely to navigate using a general map of the area stored in their minds, rather than relying on the recognition of familiar landmarks.

ANCIENT STRATEGIES IN MODERN LIFE

These differences in the memory requirements for our ancestors may still show up in modern men and women. In one study, researchers "tricked" their volunteer subjects by telling them to wait in a cluttered office for a few minutes while they got the testing room ready. The subjects were not told that the waiting period was actually the first part of the study. After they entered the testing room, they were asked to remember what the office looked like. The women did much better than the men at remembering exactly what was in the room and where it was located. Even in the one group that had been told about this question in advance, the women's memories for the placement of objects was far superior to the men's.

In another study, men and women had to find their way through a maze of underground tunnels. Then they had to navigate the same maze on a computer. More women than men got lost when the landmarks were removed from the computerized maze, and more men got lost when the maze's shape was distorted. When subjects were shown pictures of various parts of the tunnel system, women were much better at identifying where in the system the picture was taken.

So there may be some biologic basis for the differences in memory between men and women. That is, some of the differences between men and women *may* be due to genetic differences in the brain, and hormonal differences.

Different Interests, Different Memories

But perhaps the biggest differences between modern men and women are not biological, but cultural. Men and women find themselves in different cultures, and these different cultures generate different levels of *interest* in different things. Women's roles tend to make them more interested in such things as names and faces, in a person's appearance and dress, and in interpersonal relationships. As a result (your wife may know more about your Aunt Gladys than you do!) they'll have a better *memory* for such things because of their greater *interest* in them.

Interest improves memory in at least three ways. You pay more attention. You lock in memories better. And you develop a richer network of memories in which to put new memories. Because men are required to know how things work, how to get from Kalamazoo to Boise and who's who in the world of sports, their greater interest will mean better memory for all of *these* things. The difference is interest, not gender. (Although gender may be the basis for some of the different abilities in the first place.) When experiments have taken interest into account, many of the apparent differences in memory ability between men and women disappear.

The differences in memory ability between men and women—both real and apparent—are just an example of the differences in memory abilities between different people. We all know people who seem to be particularly good at remembering faces and names; perhaps others who are good at remembering numbers or facts. But as we noted in the last chapter, these differences always—or almost always—seem to be due to differences in *ability* and *interest*, not to any differences in memory itself. The individual who can *remember* a picture better does so because he or she actually *sees* it better, and thinks about it harder, not because of having a memory that works better than another person's.

How people get these different abilities is not known. It is clearly a mixture of heredity and environment. The cause of these different abilities—what part is due to heredity, and what part to environment— may even vary in different people. But these differences do exist, and they mean that different people will seem to have different "memory" abilities.

DIFFERENT RULES FOR DIFFERENT TASKS

In the song, the gentleman remembers (or thinks he remembers) the time, eating with friends, the singing, and the dazzling April moon. These are all somewhat different kinds of memories. Memory for names and memory for faces—the focus of Chapter 17—are only two of the many different kinds of memories we possess. Remembering the time something occurred is memory for a fact, a different kind of memory than that involved in remembering a name or a face. Memories of the dazzling moon would be a visual memory, stored as an image, not as words. There is also memory for doing things, with its concomitant forgetfulness for what you were going to do.

This variety of memories is so much a part of being human that we may overlook the fact that all these different kinds of memories involve different types of information we take into our minds, different ways of storing them, and different ways of getting them out. They use different parts of our mind and brain in different ways. Therefore, it shouldn't be surprising when one type of memory works differently than another, or seems to work by different rules—because they do!

ANIMAL VS. HUMAN MEMORIES

It is easier to see these differences in different kinds of memory if we look beyond our own species. The memory capacity of each species—

including man—is very specialized, so that some types of things are remembered with great ease, others with great difficulty, and still others never register in memory at all.

Rats, for example, have an excellent memory for smells (and tastes); however, their memory is terrible for color. If a rat eats something that makes it sick, it will remember the taste and smell of that food, but not the color. Smell means little to birds, however. They rely on vision rather than smell to find food, and they will learn to avoid poisonous berries by remembering the color rather than the smell or taste.

Our memory capacities show their own pattern of strengths, weaknesses, and unique properties. We are *very* visual. And we are *very* verbal (we are the *only* animal that uses words). But while we do have smell and taste, most of us do not have a very good vocabulary for describing smells or tastes. Some of what smell and taste does to us is unconscious, below the surface. We *can* have memories for smells and tastes even if we cannot describe them very well, and even if we are not consciously aware of their effects.

When the man in the song "remembers it well," he talks about verbal facts, a visual image—the dazzling moon—and perhaps a sound—the baritone singing. He never mentions the scent of the night air, the taste of the food—or her scent, for that matter. But that doesn't mean scent didn't make a difference to him. As *she* may have been very aware, her scent may have registered without his realizing it—which may be why he is still sentimental about that night. Human memory for scents turns out to be quite good in some situations—usually situations connected to survival (which means food and bodily scent). But it is not something we talk about—or even *can* talk about—because it is compartmentalized in a different part of our brain, it has a different language, and it works by different rules!

Memory Is Often a Collaboration

The exchange between the man and woman in *Gigi* shows that recollection of memory is often a collaboration. You bring up a fact. Your partner corrects it, and adds to it. This evokes another fact, and so forth. Long-term companions—such as husbands and wives are the clearest example, but it is really true of any friends who often have an implicit pact as to who remembers what. This pact may be based on different abilities, different interests, or just different opportunities (one may have more time to remember). These collaborations let us have a far better "memory" than we could manage on our own.

"Would you excuse me, Miss Arkwright? I just remembered that I promised to forsake all others."

But there is a sad side to this dependence. It means that losing a life partner—to death, separation, or disease—often also means losing the memories you entrusted to the other person.

WHAT WE FORGET CAN BE SURPRISING

Even if your memory is perfectly normal, it may occasionally fail to remember the most extraordinarily unforgettable things. Consider this sampling from my recent reading:

- Two women found themselves chatting at a McDonald's in Fillmore, California. They talked for a number of minutes. They discovered they were both born in London, and amazingly, had even grown up on the same street. Finally, they remembered: They had been friends 50 years before! In fact, one had been the maid of honor at the other's wedding!

- A woman checked out of a hotel room in no obvious hurry. She returned, quite agitated, to report she had forgotten $10,000 cash and left it on the bed. She didn't even leave a tip for the maid who had discovered the money and turned it in, untouched, to her manager.

▶ A professor, in one of my professional publications, noted how he had chanced upon a book chapter on an interesting topic. Only after reading it for a while did he realize that he himself had written it, some years before.

We Remember the Gist, and Forget the Details

The gentleman in the song might be chided for forgetting, but he actually remembered a great deal. He remembered that they met during the spring or early summer, that it was the evening, that they had dinner, and that a singer crooned in the background. True, he forgot the details, or got them wrong—but that is exactly how memory works!

Memory Can Invent New Details

> *It isn't so astonishing, the number of things I can remember, as the number of things I can remember that aren't so.*
>
> —Mark Twain

Special events are often remembered with such apparent intensity and detail that the result has been called the "flashbulb effect." We recall such events in our minds as though we are seeing a photograph, with every detail highlighted. Anyone who lived at the time of President John F. Kennedy's assassination can probably remember what they were doing that day, and how they watched the news, and how they felt about the news. I, myself, have vivid memories, as a seventh grader, of the class being ushered into a room, a TV being turned on and everyone watching in stunned silence while a man I now know to be Walter Cronkite related events and periodically said, "The President has been shot." I think I remember us filing out of the room, going home with my best friend Marc and walking from the bus stop with him, and our asking each other how could this happen.

These memories are very vivid for me, and I have relived them several times. However, I would not be surprised if they were not completely correct—because that inaccuracy has been repeatedly shown to be the case. There may be a flash in the flashbulb effect, but the film we use is still our normal memory, with all its imperfections. So even if the gentleman from *Gigi* had a memorable evening, it is not surprising that the details blurred, combined with others, or even vanished completely. This has been repeatedly verified.

CHALLENGING MEMORY'S ACCURACY

The explosion of the space shuttle Challenger in 1986 gave experimenters a chance to study memory for a dramatic event—and also to study *memory for the memory* of the event. On the morning after the explosion, Ulric Neisser and Nicole Harsch had 106 students fill out a questionnaire. They first wrote a description of how they had heard the news. Then they answered a set of more specific questions about when they heard it, how they heard it, where they were, what they had been doing, how they felt about it and so forth.

Almost three years later, the students were again contacted, but not initially told that their memory of the Challenger explosion would be tested. They were asked to participate in a brief experiment. Forty-four of the original group agreed to do so. They were then told that the study was about memory for the Challenger explosion. They filled out a new questionnaire. The new questionnaire was very much like the old one. They wrote a short essay about how they had heard the news, and then they answered specific questions. In addition, they were asked to rate how confident they were of their answers to the specific questions, whether they were "just guessing" or as much as "absolutely sure." They were also asked whether they had ever filled out a questionnaire about the Challenger explosion before. Finally, some months later, forty of the forty four subjects who had come back the second time were re-interviewed in depth. The interviewer did not know how good the memory of any individual subject had been.

Here is what one student recalled, nearly three years after the event. She was "absolutely certain" about almost all of these points:

> When I first heard about the explosion I was sitting in my freshman dorm room with my roommate and we were watching TV. It came on a news flash and we were both totally shocked. I was really upset and I went upstairs to talk to a friend of mine, and then I called my parents.

But this is what she had written down the day after the explosion:

> I was in my Religion Class and some people walked in and started talking about [it]. I didn't know any details except that it had exploded and the school teacher's students had all been watching, which I thought was so sad. Then after class I went to my room and watched the TV program talking about it and I got all the details from that.

So even though this student was "absolutely confident" of how she had heard the news, she was wrong. She was "absolutely confident" of where she had been, but she was wrong. She was "absolutely confident" of what she had been doing and whom she had been with, but she was wrong. She was even "absolutely confident" of how she had felt, but she described her feelings very differently at the time. She was not quite so confident of what time of day it had been, which was appropriate because she was also incorrect about this (the Challenger exploded at about 11:00 in the morning, and she recalled it happening about 2:00 or 3:00 p.m.).

None of the students was entirely correct, even when comparing their own memories three years later to their answers to virtually the same questions the day after the Challenger explosion. More than one-third of the subjects had grossly incorrect recollections about most of the facts they had put down before. Recall was not all-or-none. Students remembered some facts correctly and others incorrectly. But they were far from perfect in any event.

The students themselves were surprised at their own original responses. As Neisser and Harsch noted, "They found it hard to believe that their memories could be so wrong. As one student exclaimed: 'Whoa! That's totally different from how I remember it.'"

A surprising fact that emerged from the Neisser and Harsch study was that, three years after the explosion, what the students *believed* had happened to them was what they wrote down at that later time. Even seeing what they themselves had written three years before did not jog their memories. Instead, they were simply incredulous about what they themselves had written down the day after the explosion. Their original memories seemed to have disappeared.

She Could Have Been Wrong, Too!

Everyone forgets something. We laugh at the old beau in *Gigi* because he is forgetful—but his former sweetheart may not have remembered correctly either! And certainty alone is no guarantee—even though it is a rough guide—that you remember something correctly. The students interviewed about the Challenger explosion were often certain about details that were completely wrong.

Memory Is Not Forever

We often have the feeling that we lock everything inside our heads—the only problem being, it doesn't always come out. Why is this a common feeling, and why is it a widespread notion? Is it true?

People often find themselves recalling fragments of memories of experiences that seem entirely trivial. Such memories may pop into our minds through tangential associations, apparently accidental meanderings, or sometimes for no apparent reason at all. The fact that such trivial information seems to have been saved may suggest to us that our brains must save almost all events and experiences.

We may believe, as a result, that our inability to recall everything that happened to us is not because it is not inside our heads. Instead, it may seem that all we need to do is to somehow find these past experiences. We look for the proper key, the right pathway, the right state of mind, or the right technique.

Three kinds of techniques in particular have been thought by many to be able to reveal "lost" memories (and by the revelation help prove that we really do have more experiences stored in our heads than we normally can retrieve): Psychotherapy, hypnotism and direct electrical stimulation of the brain.

Not all psychotherapists claim special status in being able to unearth old memories. But some therapists claim that their techniques—free association, scribbling down random thoughts, group therapy sessions—can identify, magnify and sharpen latent memories. Unfortunately, while some memories of real experiences can be retrieved this way, what is often recovered is distorted or, frankly, false. Recovering "memories" of childhood sexual abuse is perhaps the most dramatic example of the use of such techniques, where the results are often known to be false. This is discussed in more detail in Chapter 35.

Hypnotism has also been claimed as a method for bringing out permanent memories. Here is one admiring author in the 1950s, citing an example that he felt was among the irrefutable proofs for both the permanence of all memories and for hypnotism's ability to elicit at least some of them:

> ... a master bricklayer ... had spent considerable time working on the "showcase" locations of [Yale] university's neo-Gothic buildings—interior walls, corners, arches over windows and doorways. Such work ... calls for special bricks which must be matched carefully. Although no two bricks are alike, they must be arranged in esthetically pleasing patterns.
>
> The bricklayer was hypnotized and asked to describe a certain brick in a certain wall he had constructed on a certain date. After a few moments, he came up with an answer.

The brick had been burned a shade too much in the kiln. It was dark in color. A purple pebble was embedded in the clay at the lower left-hand corner. The brick had a "belly," a slight swelling, at the upper right-hand corner which matched the hollow of the brick just above it.

The worker's statement included many other details, and every one of them checked with the facts. He had put the brick in place more than ten years ago. Furthermore, he had probably laid nearly two thousand bricks on that same day. Yet his brain had recorded the impressions of a pebble smaller than the end of your little finger, and he furnished equally accurate descriptions of other bricks in other locations...

— from Pfeiffer, *The Human Brain,* 1955

Sadly, for such an interesting and fairly well-known story—I have had several people tell me they have heard versions of it—it may not be true. (Anyone who can help me trace this story to its original source, please do so!)

More important is that, in general, people do not necessarily remember more accurately under hypnosis—they may remember more true facts, but they are also likely "recall" many *false* "memories" as well. This is one reason why hypnosis is not used in legal cases.

ELICITING TRUE AND FALSE MEMORIES

Direct electrical stimulation of the human brain, even more than psychotherapy or hypnosis, would seem to be a technique which would give far more scientific weight to the possibility of "finding" hidden memories. And in fact, the bricklayer story I relate above has often been told to me by people who attribute the recall to electrical stimulation of the brain. Apparently, this example was not due to electrical stimulation.

The electrical stimulation observations that are usually cited were carried out by Wilder Penfield and his colleagues in Montreal from the 1930s through the 1950s. The patients were typically people who had brain tumors or epilepsy, or some other reason for which part of the brain had to be removed. In an effort to minimize the damage to normal brain tissue, Penfield and his colleagues developed a method of electrically stimulating the brain. This could help identify the regions of the brain that were involved in different functions.

For example, stimulation of a point in the brain might lead to a jerking of a finger. That would identify that brain region as being involved in motor functions, and more specifically, involved in the motor functions of the fingers and perhaps the hand. Stimulation in another part of the same individual's brain might produce a sensation of pins and needles in the same finger. This would then help identify that brain region as one involved in sensation, and more specifically, sensation coming from that particular finger.

But sometimes, Penfield elicited much more dramatic responses. People would report that when the electrical stimulation began, memories would suddenly force themselves into their consciousness. One patient suddenly exclaimed, "Yes, doctor, yes, doctor. Now I hear people laughing—my friends in South Africa." When he was asked if he could recognize who these people were, he replied, "Yes, they are two cousins, Bessie and Ann Wheliaw." He did not know what they were laughing at, but he thought that Bessie and Ann must have been joking.

After the operation to remove brain tissue, he was asked about the experience. To quote Penfield and Jasper's 1954 report (page 137): "He said that it seemed to him that he was with his cousins and that they were all laughing together at something. This was obviously a real experience to him and he was much surprised that he seemed to be with them back in South Africa which he had left about a month previously."

In other patients, electrical stimulation injected songs into their heads; in some cases, they felt as though they were actually listening to the music.

These reports have often been interpreted as evidence that all of our experiences are stored, the mundane along with the important. The electrical stimulation, by accident, would electrically tickle one pattern, and wake it up while others still lay dormant.

The Penfield observations are actually far better evidence for some truths we already know about memory: not all experiences get stored; the ones that do get stored may be stored in altered or fragmentary form. Recollection of a memory can alter it, and a person's mental state—at the time a memory is being recalled—can alter the memory even further.

Elicited memories were relatively rare in Penfield's patients, occurring less than ten percent of the time. And although the retold descriptions tend to be quite dramatic, as in the one I have chosen, most of the self reports were fragmentary and uncertain. Some were even frankly physically impossible, or clearly hallucinatory. When a 12-year-old boy was electrically stimulated, he had the experience that robbers were coming at him with guns, which was similar to the experience he had had with the start of his seizures. Another patient heard a familiar woman calling, and placed the position in a lumber yard—but also noted that she had never been in a lumber yard (Penfield & Jasper's Case 36, page 651).

It should also be remembered that these patients were in the middle of brain operations. Their brains were exposed during the operation. The surgeon had no more than a few hours to map the brain and decide what parts to take out and what parts to leave in. So it is likely that the patients were not feeling their best and were under considerable stress at the same time. In another neurosurgeon's patient, when a very detailed record of goings-on in the operating room was kept, it became clear that the patient's apparent experiences with stimulation were, in fact, quite influenced by the immediate context in the operating room and the immediately preceding thoughts of the patient. These were not memories sparked at random from a permanent memory store.

In these experiments, it was often not clear what was real memory and what was hallucination or misperception. Furthermore, these apparent evoked memories seemed to occur when the stimulating current was also producing seizures. Therefore, it seems unlikely that Penfield's so-called memories could be considered actual finds, diamonds and other stones plucked out of the inner recesses of the mind.

I Just Can't Get That Song Out of My Head

Further reason to believe that the apparent memories that Penfield observed were more products of particular situations than of the human mind itself come from our own experiences at Johns Hopkins, where electrical stimulation of the brain is done for purposes similar to those of Penfield. However, Penfield had to use only the time available during the operation, and only then while the person's brain was exposed, while, at Johns Hopkins and at many other medical centers, similar mapping of seizures and brain function is done using arrays of electrodes implanted over the surface of the brain. The skull is then closed and the array of electrodes is left in for up to two weeks. The patient is free to walk around (carrying a pigtail of wires) and, in general, is completely normal during the time. Stimulation is then done through the electrodes while the patient is awake and comfortable in a hospital room. What we do with the patient, and how the patient responds, is videotaped. In addition, brain electrical activity is monitored through the electrodes almost simultaneously with the electrical stimulation that is applied.

Penfield reported on the results of 1,132 patients. To date, we have studied about 120 at Johns Hopkins. But Penfield could examine only an average of about five sites in the brain per patient, under very rushed conditions in the operating room. We examine, on the average, 32 sites per patient, under much more relaxed conditions in the patient's room. Among all the patients we have tested over the last seven years, only one has had an experience that comes close to meeting the criteria for an evoked memory. This was a patient in whom electrical stimulation in the temporal lobe produced the irresistible sensation of a song being played inside of his head. At first, this patient could not recognize the song. But then he realized it was the jingle for a commercial. The commercial had been popular about ten years before. He had liked the music of the commercial very much at the time, but why it should have been brought out by the electrical stimulation remains unclear.

What is clear is that the brain's record of experience is neither complete nor permanent. Most experiences wash by us, and we are never conscious of missing them. Some do seem to stick in our memories, at least for a time, but even many of these fade and disappear. No lode of hidden memories waits inside our heads to be discovered by the right key or through the right route.

MEMORY IS NOT A SNAPSHOT

Our memories are not complete, perfect, or permanent. We do not take everything into our memories, we do not save everything in original detail, and we do not keep memories forever. And from what we know about how memory is saved by the mind and brain, there is no reason to believe that we should.

The trap that may mislead people into thinking that memory can be both photographic and forever is the analogy that we may have with papers in a file cabinet, or snapshots in a photo album. These are useful analogies—I have used them myself. But they are incorrect and misleading on this particular point. Our minds never take a snapshot of everything.

The kind of picture we take of our experiences in our mind, even while they are happening, is an incomplete one, already affected by our prior memories and expectations, as we have seen. So the "snapshot" is not perfect to begin with. And memories change as they are kept in storage, unlike papers or pictures. It is almost certain that the pieces of information our brains use to store memories are laid down overlapping each other. They are not kept on separate sheets or as separate pictures. Instead, the same letters that go to make up one message are used, in part, to make up another. The same dots on the page that make up one picture, are also used to make up another. An illustration of this was given in Chapter 14 (Figure 18, page 84).

So even if the actual letters or dots themselves were permanent in our memories—and we are not sure that they are—we could still not expect the messages they make up, or the pictures they create, to be really permanent and unchanging. The words will get altered; the pictures will smudge, streak, and melt into each other. A particularly distinctive phrase or sentence, a particularly important picture, may stand out and resist this constant reworking. And such singular memories may mislead us into thinking that *everything* is kept within our heads. But it is not.

Because of these processes alone—the imperfections of our initial record of experience, and the reworking of those memories over time—we should not expect our brains to be a vault of unaltered memories. There can be no magic potion to correct the imperfections of our original record of experience, nor any magic process that can reverse the mixing and churning of memories that takes place within our minds.

19

Truly Amazing Memories. What You Can Learn From Them. Why You Shouldn't Envy Them

IF YOU WORRY about your recollection of names and faces, consider James Farley's talents in this area. Jim Farley was Franklin D. Roosevelt's campaign manager.

> ... [He] possessed a truly compendious memory for faces and names, a total recall that visibly impressed the man who was remembered.
>
> In the campaign of 1932 Mr. Farley was aboard the Roosevelt campaign train when it stopped at a small Western town. "Hello, Jim," a man in the shadow of the depot sang out. Mr. Farley couldn't see the man, but he glanced at the name of the railroad station and shouted, "How are you Frank? Glad to see you."
>
> He explained that some months previously a man named Frank had written him a number of letters, and that he had remembered the name by associating it with the town.
> —*New York Times* (obituary), 1976

There are enough documented feats of memory to make us all feel inadequate. Consider these other memory accomplishments, all verified by careful researchers:

How well do you remember the story "The Ghost Warrior" on Page 54 of Chapter 11? You may have just read it a little while ago. Can you remember its gist? Can you remember it word-for-word? Here is how V.P., a store clerk, remembered it—after *six weeks!*

One night, two young men from Egliac went down to the river to hunt seals. While they were there, it became foggy and calm. Soon they heard the sound of paddles approaching, and they thought: "Maybe it's a war party." They fled ashore and hid behind a log. Soon, one of the ... canoes came ashore, with five men in it, and one of them said: "What you think? Let us go upriver and make war against the people."

"I will not go," said one of the young men. "I might be killed. My family does not know where I have gone. But he," said he, turning to the other young man, "will go with you." So one of the young men returned to village and the other accompanied the party.

The party went upriver to a point beyond Kalama, and when the people saw them approaching, they came down to the river, and they fought. In the heat of the battle, the young man heard somebody say: "Quick, let us go home. That Indian has been wounded."

"They must be ghosts," thought the young man, who felt no pain or injury. However, the party returned, and he walked from the river up to his village, where he lit a fire outside of his hut, and awaited the sunrise.

"We went with a war party to make war on the people upriver," he told his people who had gathered around, "and many were killed on both sides. I was told that I was injured, but I feel alright. Maybe they were ghosts."

He told it all to the villagers. When the sun came up, a contortion came over his face. Something black came out of his mouth, and he fell over.

He was dead.

V.P.'s recollection differed from the original only in a few words, some phrasing, and some punctuation. How well would the average person do? *I* would be happy if—after six weeks—I could remember that the story was about Indian warriors, and have some jumbled recollection of arrows, boats, battles, and ghosts.

Normally, people cannot repeat any more than about seven digits that they hear in sequence. Any more, and the digits just seem to evaporate inside our heads (as you can rapidly prove to yourself if you try to remember a new telephone number). But two extraordinary individuals, S.F. and D.D., had digit spans of *84* and *101* digits, respectively.

Ishihara, a Japanese mnemonist, could memorize lists of over *2,000* digits. He could recall them with 99.7 percent accuracy.

Hideaki Tomoyori broke Rajan Mahadevan's record for memory for *Pi* when he recited *40,000* digits over the course of a little over 17 hours. Rajan had held the record by being able to remember the first *31,811* digits. Some have argued that Rajan still had the more impressive performance: he recalled the digits at an average rate of *3-1/2 digits per second*, while Tomoyori took *0.85 digits per second*.

T.E., an English mnemonist, could remember almost *140* meaningless symbols paired with numbers (for example, ROQ-52) after just *one* learning session.

Professor Aitken was a mathematician with an extraordinary memory for many things. His memory was so good that academic committees often used him as an unofficial record of their conversations. After a single reading of the names and initials of each new class of 35 students, he never had to look at the class list again. As an experiment, he was given a list of 25 words to memorize:

> head, green, water, sing, dead, long, ship, make, woman, friendly, bake, ask, cold, stalk, dance, village, pond, sick, pride, bring, ink, angry, needle, swim, go.

By his fourth repetition, he had them all correct. When retested *15 months* later, he had them all correct and in almost perfect order. *Twenty-seven years later*, with a little bit of thought, he was able to recall the entire list, in the original order.

S., a professional mnemonist studied by A. R. Luria, a famous Russian neuropsychologist, could learn a nonsense mathematical formula with almost 50 elements in seven minutes. He was able to recall it after *15 years*, on a surprise test.

This is just a sampling of the kinds of abilities that have been reported from a fair number of individuals. It is very clear that the human mind can accomplish amazing mnemonic feats. Should we be envious that we missed out on these abilities? What can mnemonists teach those of us with more ordinary memories?

MEMORY ALONE MEANS NOTHING

Before you get too envious, consider what a fabulous memory *doesn't* do for you:

Many people seem to believe that memory is the basis of intelligence.

But it's not. Having an amazing memory does not make you smart. While Professor Aitken was a gifted mathematician, and V.P. was very intelligent (he had an IQ of 136), many other mnemonists have had only average intelligence. And some mnemonists have even been idiot savants, able to remember a few things extremely well, but otherwise profoundly retarded. Having an extraordinary memory does *not* necessarily mean that you have an extraordinary mind. Memory is how well you store information. But intelligence is how well you *use* information. For most people, what limits their intelligence is not what they have in their heads, but how well they use what they have.

Having a superlative memory does not necessarily make you successful, either. It is true that a great memory for names and faces will help make you be a better politician or campaign manager, as Jim Farley was. But it is certain that his memory was not the only talent Jim Farley brought to the job. Self-help books tout a superior memory as a fundamental for success. But the kinds of superior memories these books encourage—rote learning of disconnected facts—do not help most people very much.

Professor Aitken considered his superior memory useful, but hardly necessary for what he did. Frequently, it was something of an annoyance, because people would want to use him as a human tape recorder. V.P., despite his superior memory and high IQ, worked as a store clerk. His position in life seemed satisfying to him, since his real passion was competitive chess. But his job is certainly proof that a good memory is not automatically the secret to worldly success. And S., Luria's famous mnemonist, turned out to be fairly incompetent in everyday life. He tried many jobs, but the only job he could really hold was as a professional mnemonist on the stage.

MNEMONISTS HAVE LIMITATIONS, TOO

Just because someone is a mnemonist—or just because someone has a superior memory—doesn't mean that they can remember *everything* well. In general, memory skills are not transferable from one type of material to another. That is, even if you can remember names and faces extremely well, you may still not remember to take your keys, to find your car in the parking lot, or remember your spouse's birthday. Typically, mnemonists can do amazingly well on random letters, numbers and words. Yet they may not have the practical memory skills required for everyday life. V.P., who remembered the story, "The Ghost Warrior," so perfectly, could not recall telephone numbers he had had

Strange Gifts of Nature

© 1995 Roz Chast from The Cartoon Bank, Inc.

in a prior home. He had forgotten some of the addresses where he had lived. And he failed to recognize the wife of one of the professors studying his memory when she came into his store, even though he had met her socially two or three times. V.P., confronted with this memory lapse, even commented that he thought a *politician* would have made it a point to remember the wife's name, but that was not how *he* used *his* memory.

MEMORY CAN HURT YOU

Having a great memory may not only not be beneficial, it may even cause problems:

It takes time and effort to memorize as well as these mnemonists do—in most cases, an enormous amount of time and effort! You might be able to find better things to do with all that time and energy.

To learn just the mnemonic techniques takes years of practice. T.E., who did so well with the meaningless pairs of letters and numbers, started practicing his mnemonic tricks at age 15 and kept them up assiduously over the years. It took S.F., the individual with the extraordinary digit span, more than 180 hours of practice, spread out over two years, to raise his digit span to 84.

And even after mastering the techniques, it still takes great effort to learn new material. Mnemonists may spend many, many hours studying the materials they are trying to learn. While they are clearly more efficient at studying than any person with a normal memory would be, they may also invest far more time in studying than any normal person would—because normal people give up long before the mnemonists do! Perhaps the people who refused to waste their time on the meaningless pairs of letters and numbers that T.E. learned, were the real winners after all!

Superior mnemonic abilities can be an actual *hindrance*, not a help, for their owners. V.P. thought of his memory as something of a "handicap" (his term). He had learned how to memorize by rote, but he had not learned how to apply what he had memorized. His opinion—shared by many—was that too much memory stifled *understanding*.

S., who could remember a complex mathematical formula so well after 15 years, was a perfect example. Here is the formula he learned:

$$N \cdot \sqrt{d^2 \times \frac{85}{vx}} \cdot \sqrt[3]{\frac{276^2 \cdot 86x}{n^2 v \cdot \pi 264}} \; n^2 b = sv \; \frac{1624}{32^2} \cdot r^2 s$$

Here is how he learned it. This is his description of the associations he used to remember the various parts of the formula; the parts of the formula are in parentheses:

Neiman (N) came out and jabbed at the ground with his cane (.). He looked up at a tall tree which resembled the square-root sign (), and thought to himself: "No wonder the tree has withered and begun to expose its roots. After all, it was here when I built these two houses" (d^2). Once again he poked with his cane (.). Then he said: "The houses are old, I'll have to get rid of them (x);* the sale will bring in far more money." He had originally invested $85,000 in them (85). Then I see the roof of the house detached (___), while down below on the street I see a man playing the Termenvox (vx). He's standing near a mailbox, and on the corner there's a large stone (.) which has been put there to keep carts from crashing up against the houses. Here, then, is the square, over there the large tree () with three jackdaws on it (). I simply put the figure 276 here, and a square box containing cigarettes in the "square" (^{2}). The number 86 is written on the box. (This number was also written on the other side of the box, but since I couldn't see it from where I stood

I omitted it when I recalled the formula.) As for the x, this is a stranger in a black mantle. He is walking toward a fence beyond which is a women's gymnasium. He wants to find some way of getting over the fence (_____); he has a rendezvous with one of the women students (n), an elegant young thing who's wearing a gray dress. He's talking as he tries to kick down the boards in the fence with one foot, while with the other (2)—oh, but the girl he runs into turns out to be a different one. She's ugly—phooey! (v) . . . At this point I'm carried back to Rezhitsa, to my classroom with the big blackboard . . . I see a cord swinging back and forth there and I put a stop to that (.). On the board I see the figure 264, and I write after it n^2b.

Here I'm back in school. My wife has given me a ruler (=). I myself, Solomon-Veniaminovich (sv), am sitting there in the class. I see that a friend of mine has written down the figure . I'm trying to see what else he's written, but behind me are two students, girls (r^2), who are also copying and making noise so that he won't notice them, "Sh," I say. "Quiet!" (s).

S. was so happy with the tricks he used to memorize the "formula" that he failed to make any attempt to *understand* it at all. He understood nothing of the terms in the formula, nothing of what they were supposed to mean, *nothing* of their relationship to each other. S. did not even appreciate that the formula was completely meaningless! For this mnemonist's mind, everything was the same, whether it was gold or dross. S. could not understand even simple statements of everyday physics, because he could not ignore the irrelevant details and see the basics of the problem! Would S. appreciate that this formula —

$$E = mc^2$$

— would have helped win a Nobel Prize, while the formula he memorized was only worthy of a circus sideshow?

A perfect memory may confine our creativity, and shackle our imagination. One of the virtues of normal memories is that they blend, shade, and make creative leaps. If we could remember every detail, every word, every aspect of punctuation of everything that we have ever read or heard, would we ever have a creative thought? Santayana noted that those who do not remember history are condemned to repeat it. But those who remember too well are also condemned to repetition. Memories have to be malleable to be useful. Robin Williams, the comedian and actor, clearly has an extraordinary memory for the elements of modern culture. But what is really amazing about his performances is how he selects these fragments, shapes and trims them, and weaves them together into an hilariously evocative torrent of thoughts.

What Can We Learn From Extraordinary Memories?

What can people with extraordinary memories teach us about our own? At least one very surprising fact: Their elemental memories are not actually better than average! Their basic ability to learn and remember is no better than yours or mine. There is nothing special about their nerve cells or nerve cell connections. In every case in which that has been studied, it does not appear as though their brain cells can actually store memories better. Rather, it seems that the reason they are better at learning and remembering than ordinary people are is because they use the same basic abilities more thoroughly and more efficiently. What creates an extraordinary memory in otherwise ordinary people are *strategies* and *connections*. Mnemonists make their memories—the same memory abilities everyone else has—work much harder and more efficiently. Eliminate their tricks and strategies, and their memories—their ability to learn and to recall—become no better than average, in almost every case. Most mnemonists don't seem to have been born with these strategies; they learned them. So can you.

What are the strategies? J.C., a waiter who could memorize up to twenty complete dinner orders in a normal restaurant setting, shows us something of what they look like. To find out how he remembered orders so well, researchers at the University of Colorado created a restaurant in the laboratory. The artificial "restaurant" offered eight different "meat entrees", five different levels of how well the meat could be done (*rare* to *well done*), five different salad dressings, and three different "vegetables" (baked potato, rice, French fries). The "artificial restaurant" also had tables that could seat from two to eight people. All the different possibilities added up to a total of over 600 different possible orders. J.C. and a set of normal young men and women were tested on how well they could remember the different "orders."

J.C. made virtually no errors in filling the dinner "orders" compared to the others, who made a great many errors. He also needed much less time to learn and recall the orders. How did he do it?

Not by any special, rare ability of his brain, but by basic strategies and tricks. J.C. had worked out a system for *organizing* information as he learned it, and for recalling it in an organized way. He *categorized* the information he got from each table. Instead of remembering each person's order separately, for each table he would put all the entrees together, and all the salad dressings together. Then, for each group—entree, salad dressing or vegetable—he used a mnemonic. For the temperatures of the meats, he used a scale ranging from 1 to 5. He would remember an order of one rare, one medium rare, and one rare as "1-2-4-1." For the salad dressings, he took the initial letters of each dressing and would make up a word. For example, he would remember bleu-cheese, oil-vinegar, and thousand-island as "BOOT." He used short sounds to stand for the vegetables (for example, he remembered rice, baked potato, baked potato and rice as "ABBA"). The position the person was seated in who made the order determined where in the sequence their entry was placed. And each table had its own code. Table A in our example had "1-2-4-1", "BOOT", and "ABBA." The first person at Table A had the first position in the code: "1" (rare), "B" (bleu-cheese), "A" (rice).

It was this scheme that J.C. used to remember "orders" so much more spectacularly than did the students. And it was presumably this scheme, or a version of it, that J.C. used in his real life as a waiter. When J.C. was prevented from using his mnemonic scheme, his ability to remember "orders" dropped closer to that of normal students.

When people have been found to have differences in their memory abilities, in almost every case where it has been studied in detail, strategies such as J.C.'s have been found to be the basis for those memory differences, not any intrinsic differences in memory *abilities*. Chess masters may be able to remember the positions of pieces in dozens of games, *simultaneously*! How? Because they know the game, know the rules, and know how pieces should be related to each other on the board. What the chess master actually remembers is a code, a shorthand for the game on the board at that moment, not the actual location of each piece. If you interfere with that code—move the pieces around, so they could not be a real game—then the chess masters turn out to have quite ordinary memory abilities. They do no better at remembering where the pieces were than anyone else.

So far, no one has actually been *proven* to have an intrinsically better brain capacity than anyone else for remembering things—or, for that matter, an intrinsically worse capacity for remembering things than other people.

ARE ALL MEMORIES CREATED EQUAL?

Does this mean that actual brain differences in memory ability do not exist? No. It is virtually certain that different people have different brain abilities for different things. One of these differences *must* be in memory. But most of the differences in memory abilities that we see in everyday life do not seem to be due to differences in the brains we are born with, but to differences in how well we *use* the brains we are born with. Our brains are probably somewhat like our muscles: everybody is born with different amounts of muscle. And this is probably particularly true of the muscle that is your heart. So it is likely that some people have bigger, stronger hearts than others do at birth. But it is also true that many people can take whatever amount of heart they are born with—large or small—and train themselves up from couch potato to marathon runner. The differences we find in everyday memory probably are comparable. They are probably still mostly based on how much we exercise what we have, not how much memory we are born with.

This is not to minimize the fact that different people *may* be born with different memory abilities. We know or suspect that there are genetically-based differences in brains. Some of the evidence comes from identical twins. Identical twins are almost exactly alike in their genetic composition. And identical twins show remarkably similar intelligence and memory abilities, even when they have been separated at birth and reared by different parents, in different environments. They even show remarkably similar patterns of how those intellectual abilities *develop* in childhood and adolescence. These similarities suggest that there is a genetic program for intelligence and memory, that partly determines the intelligence and memory that we have in later life.

At the brain level, less is actually known about actual individual differences in the brain, and even less is known about individual differences in nerve cell connections. But these also certainly exist. One known example: an area of the cortex of the brain—the gray matter— is the first stop for information coming from the eyes. (The technical term for this area is the *striate cortex*.) This area of the brain is clearly important in vision. Species with good vision have more of it; species that lose their vision (such as some that live in lightless caves) lose this brain region. In humans, on the average, this brain region is three to four times larger than it is in monkeys—some reflection of our superior brain power, we would hope. But we also know that in some *people*, this area can be *three times* larger than it is in *other people*.

We do not know whether these brain differences mean that the people who possess them had different abilities during life. But it seems reasonable to assume that they must have *some* significance. We expect different capabilities of a man weighing 300 pounds than we do of one weighing 100 pounds. And this is the same magnitude of the differences we are finding in the brain!

Notice, incidentally, that bigger does not necessarily mean better. The 100 pound man of our example may be far better suited for some things than the 300 pounder—running, acrobatics, or dancing, for example.

And even if bigger in some brain area does mean better, Nature may not be totally unfair. While some people may have been given more brain power in some areas than others, the differences in *total* brain power between people may be more modest. Since the total size of the brain is perhaps more constant, an exceptionally large area for one function may mean a smaller area of the brain devoted to some other ability. I want to caution you that this encouraging thought is virtually pure speculation on my part!

INFORMATION OVERLOAD AND THE PARADOX OF THE EXPERT

Mnemonists' memories also help us understand a long-standing paradox. We know that memories can interfere with one another, and we know that information overload can take its toll on memory. Since experts know more things about a given topic than anyone else, they should suffer from information overload. But they do not.

Ornithologists, for example, know all there is to know about birds. They know all about beaks—from the long strawlike beak of the hummingbird to the curved hook of the eagle. They know everything about feathers—not the colors of the plumage that a casual observer sees, but facts about its density and function. Does the bird eat insects, worms or seeds? Does it hop, flutter or fly? Ornithologists know all this and more about endless varieties of birds!

Trying to learn all these things as isolated facts would quickly confuse anyone. Without a structure, new information often becomes a muddle. Cramming facts into your head without a frame of reference creates a tangled mess, from which it is very hard to extract anything useful. So if we learn more, should we expect to remember less? The expert, who does learn more, actually remembers it better than the novice. This is "the paradox of the expert."

Why do experts remember better than non-experts? Why don't their heads get too stuffed with facts to function correctly? The expert's secret is *organization*. When you really know a lot about a single subject, you know not only facts, but the relationships between those facts. Experts learning about birds also learn *categories* into which the facts can be grouped, from raptors such as hawks and kestrels to flightless birds such as penguins, ostriches and cassowaries. The ornithologist's knowledge of birds is ordered and outlined. The facts fit into slots; the slots fit into drawers; the drawers fit into cabinets, and all the cabinets fit into different rooms. Using this filing system, experts can learn *more* facts than someone just learning them in isolation. They know more *about* those facts than the strict memorizer knows. Experts can also use these facts better, because they see the connections between the facts that the crammer never learns. Experts integrate information into a web that waits to capture it.

WE ALL BECOME EXPERTS

Many people are not aware of the strengths of their own memories. We may justly marvel at the feats of world-class mnemonists. But many of us probably have some memory capabilities that would astound our friends and neighbors, if we only had an opportunity to show them off. A bank teller may well have an exceptional memory for people's names and faces—perhaps even their bank account numbers or Social Security numbers. A trash collector may remember which houses have which trash cans. Doctors can remember the details patients and their families tell them in an hour. Homemakers remember where each item is located in the supermarket, what days steak goes on sale, and the coupons they have for them. London cabbies learn and remember the best routes to 25,000 different locations in the city. Realtors remember the preferences of buyers and the exact features of the homes available for sale. Chess players remember the positions of the pieces on the board. Waiters remember who ordered what, and how they want it. We have each become experts—mnemonists and more—in what we need to remember. To do so, we probably use many of the same methods professional mnemonists use, that we have unconsciously discovered for ourselves.

Part IV

People With Problems: What Can Make Your Memory Worse

FROM WHAT WE have learned so far, it should be clear that what we mean by *memory* is not a simple or single thing, but instead, a large number of brain and mental functions. Some of these are directly concerned with memory (that is, with storing information, or keeping it stored). But many of the processes involved in our memory are not strictly concerned with memory storage. They are instead the operations necessary for getting information into your head in the first place, putting it into the proper form so that you can learn it, and then getting it out again in the proper form so that you can use the memories that you have. Whether your memory is "good" or "bad" depends not only on whether you can store information well or not, but also on how well you can get it into your head and out again. To have a good memory, it is not enough to have just one function working well—all have to work well, and they all have to work together.

To have a *bad* memory, then, any one of a number of things can go wrong: with memory storage itself; with getting information in; with interpreting or coding information properly; with finding it inside your head; even with recognizing that you have found the right answer—or knowing that you have the wrong one! What follows are cases illustrating some of the types of problems that can occur with memory, that can be bad enough to bring them to a doctor's attention.

20

"I Can't Remember Anything!"—The Worried Well

"I CAN'T REMEMBER anything!"

The 61-year-old school vice-principal, Mrs. V., was angry and tearful at the same time. She couldn't remember her schedule, the names of students, the names of teachers, nor meetings she was supposed to attend. Nor could she remember the meetings she had attended. She couldn't remember if she had bought food for the house, or if she had enough money in the bank, nor if she had paid her bills. She couldn't even remember where she had put the bills.

We were her last hope. Her own doctors had not been able to find anything wrong with her or with her memory. But she knew we could. And if we couldn't, she would go to doctors in Boston, or to the Mayo Clinic.

I tried to get specific examples of what she couldn't remember.

"I told you: everything!" was all she would tell me.

So I tried to start where I usually do, at the beginning. Problems are usually simpler and less pervasive when they first begin.

"When did you first notice something going wrong with your memory? What was wrong then?"

"Oh, it's been like this for twenty or thirty years, only lately it's been getting worse."

At least I could relax a little. This was not a medical emergency.

"Well, how bad was it twenty or thirty years ago when you first noticed the problem?"

"It was terrible, just terrible! But at least then, I could remember the students' names. Now, I forget the lesson plans."

So I asked her to remember back even further than that, to when she was clearly normal. Most people who come to me with memory complaints can think back to a time when they were normal. But Mrs. V. could not be sure she had been normal, ever. So we started with her earliest childhood memories.

161

Since her father had been in the military, and moved a great deal, it had been an eventful childhood. Mrs. V. remembered it all, it seemed to me. I had two pages of notes on where she had gone to school, who her teachers had been, and who of her classmates I might contact about her memory in those days, and we had not even gotten her out of high school yet.

I tried a different tack. I asked her about who she had seen for this problem over the years. As so often happens in such cases, she had prepared a list to make sure she would not omit anybody. The list had the usual names and addresses of her physicians, and the usual statements about what they had told her. As also usual, her list omitted the most important information: what had actually been wrong. What had she been complaining about?

But this was the first such list I had seen that also had the prices of the drugs she had been prescribed. Why had she had put in the price? She thought it was a good way to compare different pharmacies. I asked her how she had taken inflation into account. She pointed out that I had missed seeing her notes about the Consumer Price Index for each year, written in the margin.

"Did you get these figures from any diary that you kept?" I asked.

"No." She was surprised. "I remembered what they were. But that isn't my problem, doctor!"

She went for memory testing while I talked to her son. From the firmness of his handshake and his posture, I knew he was in the military. What did he think of his mother's problems?

"Well, as long as I can remember, she's been complaining about her memory. Now they tell me from the school that her complaints have gotten worse. But I can't really see any difference in the way she acts. She seems to remember everything perfectly well to me."

Her neurologic exam was completely normal. I reviewed the memory and other testing that we had done. Her IQ was above average, as was her memory. Holding the results in front of me, I asked her how she thought she had done.

"Oh, terribly."

That was what I thought she would think.

"And I thought I did particularly badly on that paragraph about the sea lions. I didn't remember the name of that third sea lion pup until just as I was walking out of the room, and your young man here (she glared at the technician sitting uneasily next to me) refused to give me credit!" After a thirty-minute delay, most people remember the sea lions as seals anyway, and nobody remembers the name of the third one, the most insignificant player in the story.

"Ma'am … (I had momentarily forgotten her name, trying to remember the name of that darned sea lion myself) … you won't believe what I am going to tell you. But I want to assure you that I won't be lying to you. It is my job to try to tell whether people have brain disease or not. We see more than 500 patients a year here. I have to give many of them terrible diagnoses. I have to tell them that they have Alzheimer's disease. But sometimes, I can give a person good news. I can tell them that there is nothing wrong with their brain. Often they won't believe me. However, I want to assure you in advance that we are experts at this, and if I had bad news to tell you, I would tell you."

"I can take the bad news, Doctor."

"No, I don't have bad news for you. I have good news! Your brain is fine. Your memory is far better than average. You don't have Alzheimer's disease. There's no other disease affecting your memory. I think you're just a bit anxious about your memory, that's all. Even though you think you're having problems with your memory, your memory is actually working quite well."

"Then why did I do so badly on the tests?"

"You didn't do badly on the tests. Here's how you did. You are way above average. You are way above where I would be on these memory tests. And even if your memory wasn't exactly as good as it once was, the most I could blame that on would be perhaps aging and additional administrative responsibilities. You don't have Alzheimer's disease."

She wasn't very happy when she left, as I had expected. Her son, however, thanked me with obvious sincerity. I told him that I wasn't very satisfied with what I had been able to accomplish.

"Oh, no," he corrected me. "It was just what we needed. No one had ever tested her before, and no one had ever told her right to her face that there was nothing wrong with her brain. Now, whenever she complains, I can remind her that the doctors at Johns Hopkins told her that she was fine. It will be another couple of years at least before she gets fired up enough to try to see another specialist."

I assured her son that I would be happy to see her back again myself. Also, I pointed out to him that there was a good reason to have the testing done by the same group, so that exactly the same tests could be used. That way, there could be a direct comparison of how his mother had been doing over the years.

"No, that won't work. She's going to remember the answers, so you'll have to use a new set of tests anyway."

I never did figure out why Mrs. V. was so unhappy about her memory. Some people are just complainers. Others are just too perfectionistic; they set too high a standard for themselves. People with Mrs. V.'s complaints can be either, or both.

However, Mrs. V.'s complaints did perhaps contain some truths. First, people's memories often *do* get somewhat worse as they get older. We'll discuss that more in Chapter 26. By the time they get to Mrs. V.'s age (61) some people may notice this more than others.

And there is a second reason why Mrs. V.'s complaints may have an element of real truth in them: If you don't leave your mind alone, you interfere with the way it works. If you keep watching everything you do with your memory, always ready to pounce on any problem, then you *will* have problems.

SELF-MONITORING

We call this problem "self-monitoring." It is a problem because mental functions were generally meant to go on automatic. If you try to monitor them too closely, especially while they are happening, you will interfere with their flow. Driving a car is an example. After you have mastered the skill, if you try to pay attention to every aspect of how you drive, you will discover that you interfere with the smooth coordination between your eye, your hand and your foot.

Imagine driving while constantly talking about exactly what you are doing—how you are moving the steering wheel, how you are putting your foot on the brake or gas, how you are shifting, how you are turning. Even just *talking* about what you are doing is very disruptive, because these are functions that really should be done automatically by your brain. If you try to watch yourself perform, if you try to comment on every move you make, you will interfere with these moves, slowing them down, jumbling them, or even blocking them completely. (Having someone else talk about them is also a problem—which is perhaps why backseat drivers are so disruptive!)

Self-monitoring can create a similar problem with memory. Some people create this problem for themselves. They watch their own minds as they perform everyday tasks, remember people's names or read the paper. They will wonder, as they read each word, whether they fully understood its meaning. They will try to remember, as they remember the person's name, whether they know the names of their spouse and children as well, or whether they are pronouncing the name exactly as the person wanted. Are they reading as quickly as they should? Are they understanding as much as they should? Such self-observation can paralyze your mind. And indeed, this is what such people often complain of. They tell us that they can't make toast any more. They can't operate the microwave. They think their memory is terrible, and they have forgotten how to do everything.

So Mrs. V., in her ceaseless attention to her memory, may have actually been making her memory worse. She certainly could not have been making it better!

"Self-monitoring" does not afflict only people with normal memories. People who actually *do* have memory problems due to aging, or sometimes even early Alzheimer's disease, may also become quite aware of their memory. They may self-monitor, and therefore make their memory problems worse. But when this happens, their basic memory problems will usually be evident to other people and clear on testing, not at all like Mrs. V.'s!

The moral: sometimes you should leave your mind alone! Let it do its work, and it will work far better for you.

21

The Man with Too Many Mistresses, and The One With Too Many Telephones —Too Much to Do*

MR. R. WAS A 60-year-old international businessman. His escalating successes were toasted at all his business clubs, but his escalating memory problems he kept to himself. He sometimes could not remember where he was driving to, or what day of the week it was. He forgot details of his business deals. He could not always remember what deals he was doing, what advantages he was trying for, or what prices he had promised. And everything had been getting worse over the past year or so.

Mr. R. had flown into Washington, D.C., a few days before, with his wife and son. Brazilian, they lived in Rio de Janeiro. His wife had found a great deal about the shopping in the Washington area that she had liked, and she was loaded down with shopping bags when they arrived for his afternoon appointment with us. These, I later found out, were gifts for me and the staff.

Mr. R. was slim and perfectly poised. He admitted to being worried about his memory problems, but his recitation of them was organized and detailed. So much so, that it was hard to believe that the man who could tell me so much about his memory problems, in such a clear way, was *suffering* from all those problems. Nonetheless, his wife confirmed that he was having very real problems with his memory. Her husband kept a busy schedule, she explained, as did she. But most nights, he would come home bleary, sluggish, and with very little recollection of what he had been doing that day. Weekends were better times for him, but the rest of the week still seemed to be a blank. No, she didn't think he was depressed. But she did think he was extremely tired.

Mr. R.'s son, whom I interviewed separately, gave me the critical hint. He would not tell me what he thought was wrong, but he suggested I

---

* This chapter by Barry Gordon, M.D., Ph.D., with Rachel Wilder

166

talk to his father again. "Make sure he understands that whatever he may tell you is *very* confidential."

Gradually, the background history came out. Men of his class had always maintained mistresses. There was even an apartment building, centrally located, that made it very convenient for him and his friends. And as he got more successful, it seemed to be expected that he would accommodate the other women who gravitated to him. Up until about a year before his visit, he had a fairly happy equilibrium with just four mistresses. He kept a convenient rotation schedule. Each had a different day, sometimes in the afternoon, sometimes in the evening. He would have a good meal, some wine, and be back at his house by 10 or 11 p.m.

But then, about a year before, he had closed another large deal. He seemed to have acquired another mistress with that territory. But this new mistress was far more demanding of his time. He found himself crisscrossing the city far more often than he had wanted to. And at about this time, business became much more difficult. There was chaos in the currency markets, and panic in commodities. His businesses were in too many time zones. The telephone never stopped ringing. Too many decisions had to be made. But he was just always *so* tired!

When Mr. R. thought about his problems again, he realized that it wasn't just his memory—he was falling asleep all the time! The trip to Johns Hopkins had been a godsend—he had finally caught up on his sleep over the weekend. *That* was why he seemed to be so different from the man his wife and he described to me! And the neurologic examination and neuropsychologic testing of his memory confirmed that exactly.

I could now see several reasons why Mr. R. couldn't remember. He was overstressed, he was drinking a lot, he was physically worn out, he was anxious over his sexual performance—something he could not admit to, but which he hinted to me—and he had many good reasons for not remembering details to tell his wife!

"Mr. R., let me reassure you; your mind is okay. You have to realize that if you wear yourself out, you're not going to remember very well. And you certainly don't have Alzheimer's disease or any other reason why your memory shouldn't be working that we can see. Your memory is working just fine for us up here."

"What should I do?"

"Well, the answer is obvious." It wasn't, actually. However, I have learned that if people think that there is a solution, they are more likely to find one. I did not know what kind of delicate balance Mr. R.

had managed to achieve, but I certainly did not want to be the one to tip it in the wrong direction.

Mr. R.'s face brightened. "I shall reduce my social obligations!" I didn't want to ask what *that* meant.

A year later he called to tell me how things were going. He had cut back to two mistresses, "on doctor's orders." I didn't contradict him on that, but I certainly would not have written a prescription for it, either way. His son had taken over one of the problem areas. His son relished the challenge, and perhaps what went with the territory. Mr. R. said he was resting well, his energy was superb, and his memory excellent. He and his wife were both doing quite well. I could stay with them whenever I came to Rio. If I did, I made a mental note to myself, I would be sure to check with him about whether the night would be convenient or not.

THE MAN WITH TOO MANY TELEPHONES

Mr. A. was 44 and frantic. His memory was going. He had seen it happen to his father; he was terrified that it was now happening to him.

What was the problem?

Mr. A.'s days were busy and stressful. He and his wife ran a successful advertising agency. Lately, Mr. A. was forgetting what people said to him even before they had finished speaking. He was trying to take notes, but he lost them on the top of his desk. He forgot the names of people who called. When they told him their names, he could not remember who they were. He was confusing projects and people. He had sent a printing job to the wrong company. He had forgotten deadlines.

He was forever confusing people and events. He thought he had met one client's wife in the Bahamas. This was news to her husband, because they had never been to the Bahamas together.

On the other hand, Mr. A. said he had no problem dressing himself, eating, ordering food in a restaurant or speaking to people in general (except for his memory). He was neatly dressed. He carried himself well, and his neurologic examination was normal. His internist had already sent me a clean bill of health.

While he was getting memory testing, we interviewed his wife.

Yes, his memory lapses were annoying. Yes, he had really fouled things up on a couple of occasions and she had gotten pretty angry with him. Yes, she had to soothe some clients' feelings. But she thought the answer was obvious: The office had gotten too big and he had too many telephones.

He had started the business ten years before. Before that, he had worked for another advertising agency in town. Initially, it had just been himself, with his wife as his secretary. Then, he had become more and more successful. As he added staff, he added clients and he added more telephone lines. But he never wanted to give up the personal touch in his business. So he answered virtually every call himself. Even when his secretary was around, he would jump on the phone. He had four separate phone lines into his office for business, a separate speaker phone, and two other lines for personal calls.

"Just watch him," his wife said, "and you'll know why he can't remember. The phone interrupts him in the middle of every sentence. He keeps three people on hold at once. The files he needs are always with someone else, so he has to run around the office looking for them. He can't let go of anything!"

Were there ever times when his memory seemed to be normal? Well yes, she thought, some of the time. When they had managed to take a vacation, he had no problems remembering the arrangements for the tickets, where they were supposed to go, or the people he had to contact. It was the one time he didn't let himself get distracted by the office, and she was grateful for that.

Mr. A. had rejoined us by this time. His memory abilities were above average, according to the testing, as was his intelligence. He thought he had done fairly well on the tests.

His wife, of course, had made the diagnosis, but at least I could lend it my authority.

"Mr. A., your real memory is fine. But no one can remember well when they are being interrupted and distracted. The problem is, you have too many telephones. You have too many distractions. Although I don't want to tell you how to run your business, you probably need to delegate more. Let somebody else worry a little bit." I made the usual disclaimer that this was easier advice to give than to take. I was, I confessed, probably guilty of just the same problem.

And what about his father, who had memory problems for the last two years of his life? Should the son have been worried about getting Alzheimer's disease?

His father had had memory problems, it was true. But his father's memory problems had fluctuated. This would not be typical of Alzheimer's disease at all. And it was unlikely that someone in his fifties, as his father had been, would have been afflicted with Alzheimer's disease.

We discovered after a bit of detective work that his father had severe liver disease. His liver damage had not been caused by alcohol, but by hepatitis. The hepatitis—the liver disease—is what had ultimately killed him in his late fifties. Memory and mental status often fluctuate in liver disease. So it was a safe bet that it was the liver disease that had caused the memory problems in his father, not Alzheimer's disease. Mr. A. didn't have any special reason to worry about Alzheimer's.

I called Mr. A.'s office a year later, and his secretary answered the phone. Only after speaking to a number of people and using my "doctor" title was I able to get through to Mr. A. himself. He confirmed that a secretary carefully guarded his time and he now only had the two phone lines that he really needed—one business, and one personal. He still didn't think his memory was as sharp as he'd like it to be, but he certainly thought it was normal.

Then, he asked how many phone lines I had ...

No matter how good your memory is, if you demand more of it than it can handle, it will cause you problems. Mr. R.'s problem was due to a combination of excessive demands and weakening abilities; Mr. A.'s was clearly due to excessive demands.

Demanding too much of our memory can, by itself, cause our memory to malfunction. Suppose your memory is normally a one-fact-a-minute-memory. (I am just making this number up for purposes of the example.) If you overload it—if you try to remember three facts a minute—you just will not be able to. But even worse—your mind won't be able to spend the time it needs for even one of those facts. So your mind, which is perfectly capable of remembering at a one-fact-a-minute rate, will now seem to you as though it cannot remember anything. And you will be right. You will not be able to remember even one of the facts. Your mind and your memory are overloaded, and will not be able to do even what they can normally accomplish.

This problem is frequently compounded, because overload is often accompanied by conditions that weaken our abilities themselves. These include lack of sleep, poor eating habits, and stress. No matter what the cause of different kinds of overload, they all create a similar type of forgetfulness. The examples I gave here both were of men in business. However, busy women with young children at home can be afflicted with a similar combination of overload and fatigue, which some call "mother brain."

Actually, it is probably a fact of everyday life—at least for most of the readers of this book—that we all suffer from some degree of information overload. If you wonder why our memories do not work as well as we need them to, consider this: our brains were not built for the modern world. They were built for the Stone Age world our human ancestors inhabited for most of the last 200,000 years.

In that Stone Age world, the groups we lived in had no more than 20 to 50 people. Those were all the people we needed to know intimately, although we probably knew the names of a few prior generations. Any memory more than that was the province of the tribe's shaman, charged with keeping a verbal record of the past. There were no clocks, no pagers, no news flashes.

Contrast that with what we expect to remember today. Take names alone. We probably are ashamed if we cannot remember hundreds, if not thousands, of people, by face and by name. In a spot check for this book, I found that one New York City businessman had over 1,500 names in his *personal* Rolodex! His business Rolodex was far more extensive!

How much do you ask of your memory? Consider what happens if you move to a new city. Over the course of a few weeks, you walk your dog in the neighborhood and meet at least five of your new neighbors—and you try to learn the names of their spouses, children and dogs—probably about 15 to 20 new names. Then your child starts school. He has 25 classmates, and you begin to meet them, their parents, and some of the teachers. Add about 75 new names. You start your new job; you are lucky to have a small office, but still, there are about 10 key people who you feel would be insulted if you still could not remember their names after a few weeks. So, in addition to all the other stresses of moving—getting lost, trying to find a new bank, dry cleaner, grocery store, and dentist, suddenly you have more than 100 new names to learn! That is about the total number you would have had to learn over an entire lifetime as a hunter-gatherer. But now you have to add those 100 to the 1,500 you already have stored away in your memory and in your Rolodex. And that is only the beginning of your life in this new city. There is the new phone number, and maybe a voice mail number and a fax number, and all the PIN numbers...

There is simply too much information out there, too much that we are trying to get ourselves to remember. We simply were not built to really handle it. We are pushing the limits of what our brains were designed to do. Frequently, we are operating beyond those limits. So it is no surprise that our memories often seem to fall short of our expectations. But the problem is not really with our memories, it is with our world.

22

Amnesia Island—Too Little To Do Can Be Bad, Too!

A 55-YEAR-OLD BUSINESSMAN came to see me, concerned about his memory. It was normal, although he was convinced it was his stressful lifestyle that was the cause of his problems. So he retired to his own tropical island (he was quite successful!), taking along only his wife and secretary.

But then he began *really* having a problem with his memory, he thought. He couldn't remember the date, the day, even the time of day. Without the structure of his everyday life, his memory melted.

He gave up the island, and returned to the workaday world—or at least, his version of it—and his memory, and mental sharpness, returned.

Too *little* to do can also cause forgetfulness. Retire, get laid off from work, become ill. All of these make us lose two things that are vital for memory: structure and motivation.

Everyday events and rhythms help structure your day and your memory. You get up at a certain time, listen to a certain program on the radio driving to work. You meet certain people in the morning, and different people in the afternoon, you have your lunch in the middle. You go home at the end of the day. You have dinner at home five nights of the week; you have dinner out on Saturday night. You have dinner with your parents on Sundays. You watch *Home Improvement* on Tuesdays, *Roseanne* on Wednesdays, and *ER* on Thursdays. Mother's Day is in May, Father's Day in June, Thanksgiving is the fourth Thursday of November, Christmas comes on December 25th and New Years is January 1st.

Mundane, inconsequential, and boring as they may seem, these everyday events and rhythms give us structure to our existence. Without them, we lose the small braces, struts and ropes that tie our memories to events and to other people. Without these markers and minor

172

celebrations of everyday life, morning is the same as afternoon. Days become indistinguishable from one another; evenings are no longer unique. You can watch *Roseanne* any day of the week—if you don't mind watching reruns. For that matter, if you have that much time on your hands, you will quickly discover that even TV no longer anchors you. You can watch Johnny Carson excoriating politicians who have long since left the scene and David Letterman interviewing movie stars touting films released eight years ago. So not only do you lose your supports, anchors and time tags, even the ones you might now have time for undermine your sense of time.

And, of course, if you have time free, or if you are disconnected from the world, then you have no motivation to remember. The bright and buzzing messages of the world may assault your senses, but your mind won't capture them in any way, nor link them with the memories you do have.

One problem with memory loss due to idleness is that it is often not very much of a problem; if you are that idle, you do not *need* that much of a memory. For many people, this is an acceptable equilibrium.

But if you do not want to succumb to a passive forgetfulness, the solution is obvious: get involved and get interested in something.

23

You Never Know It's Enough, Until You've Had Too Much— Alcohol

MRS. E. WAS *REALLY* offended. How *dare* I suggest that her memory problems were due to drinking!

I wasn't suggesting that they were due to drinking. I was *hoping* that they were due to drinking! If they were due to drinking, then her problems would have a chance of getting better if she stopped drinking. At least, they shouldn't get worse. If her problems were not due to drinking, then Mrs. E. might well be suffering from Alzheimer's disease. Not knowing that I was hoping for the best, Mrs. E. was quite offended.

———————————

Memory loss due to alcoholism is well known in medicine. Such alcoholics are typically male. Typically, they have drunk heavily for years. Their memory gets worse and worse over the years, as do most of their mental abilities. Some may develop a profound memory problem suddenly, as the result of a dramatic neurological problem called Wernicke's Syndrome. They go into coma or near-coma, and their eye movements become partly frozen. The lack of Vitamin B1—thiamine— brings on this condition, and giving massive doses of Vitamin B1 may only partly correct it. These alcoholics wake up, and their eyes begin to move again, but they may be permanently left with a staggering gait. And most permanently of all, they may have a profound amnesia. In its purest form, that amnesia looks like the pure amnesia we will describe later (Chapter 28).

Mrs. E.'s situation was nowhere near as florid. She ate well; she didn't go on benders. And the alcohol she drank was hardly rotgut—her favorite was cream sherry. But I was concerned nonetheless. Mrs. E. was a widow with no constraints on her time. No one monitored her, and no one was there to tell her what was bad for her. And unlike the street drunk, Mrs. E.'s drinking was not going to be limited by running out of money. Mrs. E. was not drunk when we saw her—if she had been drunk, we would not have gone ahead with the testing. But the friend who accompanied her confirmed that Mrs. E. was frequently tipsy in the afternoons.

Mrs. E.'s examination did not show any of the stigmata of a chronic alcoholic. There were no scars on her head, relics of past falls. The nerves in her legs, in particular, worked perfectly, undamaged by any effects of alcoholism that I could detect. But her memory was clearly not very good for her age. She could not learn a list of items—a task she thought silly, but which is a good standard we use for comparison nonetheless. Nor was she clear on many details from the past. Drinking by itself could have caused this problem with past memory. After all, if she were drunk, I would hardly expect her to remember what was happening in the world or what was happening to her. But it was worrisome. She might have once known that information, but now be having a problem at getting at it because of damage to her brain.

I explained the situation to Mrs. E. as best as I could. There are many reasons to believe that excessive alcohol can damage the brain. It may do this, not just because of vitamin deficiencies, but also because it may be directly toxic to the brain itself. This is not a proven fact, just a suspicion. However, what is known is that it may be hard to tell what is "excessive" for one person until it is too late. People seem to differ in their tolerance for alcohol, and that may be true of the brain as well. There certainly may be people who can get roaringly drunk on all occasions throughout their lives, and never seem to suffer any ill effects on their brain. But there is no real way to tell what kind of person you are until it may be too late. And if you drink to the point of getting drunk, or even just tipsy, every day, then you are probably into a danger zone of high risk.

Some of the damage that alcohol does to the brain may not be able to heal. This is especially true if it has gotten so bad that a person has suffered from the Wernicke's Syndrome described above. These people may never get their memories back, and may be forced to live out their lives in institutions, under constant care. But milder degrees of damage may be reversible. The only way to know is to stop drinking, and to be re-checked.

24

Prescription Drugs

ALCOHOL IS PERHAPS the most common, and the most clearly known, drug or agent that can cause memory loss. Alcohol is also perhaps one of the more worrisome, because it actually does seem to cause damage to nerve cells. But in truth, anything—alcohol, food or drug—that interferes with the way the brain works can cause problems. Even water, if you drink too much of it, can cause confusion and memory loss. Nothing is *completely* safe.

Alcohol's dangers are well known. Modern-day drugs are a blessing for the conditions they treat. But drugs can also sometimes—relatively rarely—cause problems with memory and mental abilities. Sometimes this is easy to determine. But, unfortunately, sometimes it is not very clear that a medication is causing a problem. Older people may forget to take medications at the right time or in the right amount. Frequently, they may give themselves too little one day and too much the next. This may prevent the body and the brain from adapting to any of the side effects of a particular medication. Or sometimes people simply take too much of the medication altogether. In addition, older people often have slower metabolism. Because they get rid of drugs from their body more slowly than younger people, the same dose of drug may have a greater effect on an older individual.

If you are having a memory problem and are taking *any* drugs, then it is reasonable at least to think of the possibility that the drug (or drugs) is contributing to the problem that you are having. Fortunately, in general, memory loss and confusion caused by medications will disappear if the medication dose is adjusted or if the medicine is stopped.

A note of caution: drugs and substances are on the following list because they are most commonly associated with mental impairment. The reverse association is not necessarily true: These drugs and substances do not necessarily commonly *cause* mental impairment. It is actually uncommon (often less than one chance in a hundred) to experience mental impairments with drugs given as prescribed. And in each person, the possible or actual side effects of a drug need to be weighed against its real or possible benefits. If you are concerned about the possibility of a drug effect on your memory or other mental functions, check with your doctor.

DRUGS MORE COMMONLY ASSOCIATED WITH MENTAL IMPAIRMENT

DRUG/CATEGORY	COMMON NAME	GENERIC NAME
Insulin	—	—
Minor Tranquilizers	Valium	Diazepam
	Dalmane	Flurazepam
	Equagesic	Meprobamate
	Equanil	
	Meprospan	
	Miltown	
	Serax	Oxazepam
Antihypertensives	Aldomet	Methyldopa
	Inderal	Propranolol
Major tranquilizers	Haldol	Haloperidol
	Thorazine	Chlorpromazine
	Mellaril	Thioridazine
Analgesics	Demerol	Meperidine
Anti-acid	Tagamet	Cimetidine
Antidepressants	Elavil	Amitryptyline
	Pamelor	Nortryptyline
	Ascendin	Amoxapine
Anti-Parkinson's disease	(Amantadine)	Amantadine

25

"My Mind is Melting!"— Depression and Anxiety

MRS. P.'S MEMORY PROBLEMS began when she thought she was losing her job. By the time she came to me, she had not worked for three years.

Mrs. P. had worked as a secretary while she was raising her three children. She had done very well for years, as far as she could tell. She had mastered the switch from typewriters to document processors, and then from document processors to computers. She was the de facto director of the secretaries in her area. She enjoyed the work and her authority.

But she started having trouble with her memory. And this was around the same time her company was rumored to be collapsing financially. For six months rumors flew about downsizing, and about whose boss would be kept and whose would be let go. There was talk of secretaries being fired; some said a secretarial pool would be created; it was whispered that some secretaries would have to leave and work in an office on the other side of town.

Mrs. P. found it very difficult to work. She would come home feeling evil-tempered, her head pounding. On Friday nights, she would feel a little better. Saturdays, she would feel fine. But every Sunday evening, the headache would return. She would get a funny feeling in her stomach or fluttering in her chest, and lose her train of thought. She often forgot what she was talking about while talking on the telephone.

In the end, her position was not eliminated. But she decided to quit anyway, because she felt so badly.

Then her problems got even worse. It was hard staying at home. Now that she had given up her paycheck, she had to cut back on just about everything. She started shopping at a cheaper grocery store, even though it was farther away. She stopped using the full-service gasoline pump in an economy move. But she hated the smell. And she constantly forgot which steps came first in trying to pump gas.

It was so difficult for her to do anything! She was so slow, and everything took so much effort. It was hard for her to write checks. She constantly lost the train of her thought. She forgot appointments. She forgot to bring her grocery lists to the store, or she would just forget to look at it. She was constantly running back and forth to the store to pick up the things she had forgotten.

Eventually she became fearful of doing much of anything by herself. She was afraid of the consequences of her forgetting. Mrs. P. became so distressed by her problems that she stopped driving, stopped cooking and refused to go out of the house unless her husband, a friend or a neighbor went with her.

Her husband was despairing. Yet he noted some aspects of her problem that he thought were odd. He felt that her problems seemed to fluctuate a great deal. Some days and some hours her problems were so bad that she would forget her birthday, her social security number and even their own phone number. And then, a few minutes later, she would remember them again! She was often worse in the morning, and got better over the course of the day. Some days—particularly when he took a day trip with her—she seemed back to normal, although the slightest little thing could send her into a panic and make her revert.

Despite all these problems, much of her memory seemed to be better than his. She would remember the faces and the names of the people they met with the same unerring accuracy she had always had. She remembered where everything was kept around the house, where she had put everything, and even where he had put anything. When he misplaced his glasses, as he often did, she was the one who remembered where she had seen him put them. She would forget what she had to buy at the store, but would never forget the price she had seen in the newspaper. Standing in the checkout line, she would watch the register and make sure that the price rung up was the price she had remembered!

And although she could not operate the microwave at all, aimlessly pushing the wrong buttons, she had no problems operating the washer and dryer, and she operated their portable stereo with ease. She loved the music and could quickly switch between CD, tape and radio with an agility that he found amazing, seeing how incompetent she was in front of the much simpler microwave.

When I interviewed Mrs. P., she admitted all this. In fact, she knew exactly what had gone wrong, and when it went wrong. She could think back and recount all the repeat trips she had made to the store that past week, who had driven her, how she had gotten there, and all the meals she had attempted to cook. She admitted to being tense and anxious at times. She also admitted that she felt very "bad." But she thought her feelings were a result of her memory problems—not a possible cause of them.

I tried to find out more specifically why she could not use the microwave.

"I just can't do it! My mind is melting!"

"Well, think of it this way. You walk up to the microwave. What do you do next?"

"I just stand there! I really don't know what to do next!"

"Do you push a button? What's the first thing you try to do?"

"I really don't know."

I decided to try a different strategy. "How about your stereo? How do you work that?"

"Oh, that's different! If I want the radio, I preset it to the stations I want. So I just hit the radio button and then the preset button, and there's the music!"

One of the stations she had listened to had just changed its format from easy listening to seventies hits. I asked her how she had coped with this.

"Oh, that's easy. There was a station I had been hoping I could get on the set but didn't have enough room for. I just changed it to the station, held down the button and there it was!"

Asking about her TV habits brought out a whole other range of abilities. It turned out that she and her husband liked to watch the evening news on TV, but he often came home late from his job. How did she solve the problem?

"Oh, I just tape the show on our VCR."

How did she do that?

"Well, if I'm there when it's starting, I just push the record button. You have to hold down play at the same time."

And if she wasn't there when it was starting?

"Then I just set it to record at the right time."

Did she have VCR Plus or some other simple way of programming the time and station?

"No, our VCR's kind of old. I have to set everything in by hand."

No wonder her husband was surprised that she couldn't use the microwave.

Mrs. P. had begun having menopausal symptoms a few years before, but these had gone away when she began taking estrogen supplements. She took a great many vitamins every day. But all were standard, commercial brands, and none were so excessive that they could have caused any problems. She liked beer, but a six-pack seemed to last them a fairly long time. She had certainly used no illicit drugs.

Mrs. P.'s neurologic exam was striking. She behaved much worse than she had while I was just talking to her. Even the simplest motor functions seemed to take her forever. She had difficulty even imitating how she would comb her hair or brush her teeth. And at every step, she had to be encouraged to even try what I was asking her to do; she seemed to put very little effort into the testing.

Her neuropsychologic testing was also quite revealing: she did terribly. She could barely remember more than one word at a time. Her ability to recognize words and faces was barely above chance—worse than we usually see even in Alzheimer's disease. Her drawing of a complicated figure was inept, and she remembered virtually nothing of it after a short delay. She could not name even some common pictures, such as those of a bridge, a bicycle wheel, or a carrot. And she was extremely slow and labored in her reading.

Yet she had shown no such slowness when she had been talking to me, looking through her purse, or dressing and undressing. I had deliberately come into the room when she was putting on her shoes. She slipped on her pumps with no problem, even though just minutes before, she had trouble holding a pen.

I asked Mrs. P. questions to find out about a possible depression. How was her mood? "Oh, I feel fine. I'm just really worried about this!"

How was her energy? "Well, some days I seem to have more than others. But I think it's pretty good. But why can't I do things, doctor?" I told her we would talk about that later.

What had she been interested in, and what had happened to her interests? "Well, I'm really not interested in much of anything anymore."

Food? "I don't really have an appetite anymore." Had she lost any weight? "No, but I hope I haven't gained any! I just sit around all day."

What had happened to her interest in sex? "Really, doctor, I'm too old to be interested anymore." I interpreted what she told me as evidence that her interest had disappeared.

How was her sleeping? "I have a hard time getting to sleep most nights. I lie awake there, or I just go walking around downstairs." Did she find herself waking up in the middle of the night? "Oh, yes! Many times, 3 o'clock, 4 o'clock in the morning I wake up and I don't know why. I don't remember any bad dreams, but it's just hard to go back to sleep then." So what does she do then? "I go downstairs and just kind of wander around the house. I don't really feel like doing much of anything then."

How did she feel about herself? She looked puzzled. Did she feel worthless, or no good? This got a reaction. "I should never have been born! I'm no good to my family. I should never have been born!"

Had she ever thought of hurting herself? Committing suicide? This took some digging. She had toyed with the idea of suicide, and how things would be if she were gone. But this was mostly a late night thought, when she was up and wandering the house. It had not happened very often. And she had not even thought of how she would do it. She was actually surprised by the question. "Pills, I guess." What pills? "I don't know. Isn't that what everybody uses?"

Stress. Depression. Anxiety. These are often hard to disentangle in the real world. Alone or in combination, they are common causes of memory complaints and of memory problems.

People with depression frequently have complaints about their memory, but they usually complain about far more as well. They feel hopeless or helpless, their energy level is low, they can't get to sleep easily or they wake up in the middle of the night. Their appetite may be poor, their sex drive low, their interest in their normal activities and hobbies gone. They may feel vaguely guilty or blameful, or more explicitly feel that they should be punished for unspecified wrongs or failures. More dramatically, and of more immediate concern, a person who is depressed may feel so low and so worthless that they become suicidal.

Everyone goes through minor bouts of the blues. But if an episode seems to be more profound, or if it lasts more than a few days or weeks, or if it interferes with a person's life, then their family and friends should really encourage them to get professional help. And because depression may not be that obvious to family or friends—let alone to the person themselves—it is something that the healthcare professional has to consider in every case of memory loss.

One positive side of depression is that it leaves no permanent scars on the brain. A patient with profound memory complaints due to severe depression can be transformed into a completely intact, high-functioning individual with proper care. One of the most gratifying examples of this for me was a patient from another country. He came to me complaining of his memory, but it was very clear that he was extremely sad and depressed. It also came to light that he was quite suicidal. He was, therefore, admitted to the Psychiatry Service at Johns Hopkins, so that he could be under close observation while he was being aggressively treated with drugs and counseling. Within two weeks, his spirits were better. Within a month, he felt great. He was delighted with his new-found energy, positive outlook and *joie de vivre*. His memory, which had not been that bad, was restored to normal in the process. We have kept in contact over the years. Depression has never bothered him again. Now he is just concerned about aging!

Everything Mrs. P. had told me, and everything her husband had said, pointed to anxiety and depression, mixed together, as the cause of her problems. I still had to be suspicious that something else was going wrong, though. Sometimes, people *do* have brain problems that only first show themselves as anxiety and depression. Sometimes, people can exaggerate relatively minor or early problems. This can be conscious or unconscious, in an attempt to get attention. And although Mrs. P.'s problems, as we saw them, were mostly due to anxiety, there was always the possibility that she could have both a brain disease and psychological problems together. Being anxious doesn't immunize you against brain disease.

Nevertheless, I could reassure Mrs. P. and her husband that most, if not all of her problems, were caused by her fears, anxiety, and depression. They were not caused by any brain disease that I could detect. Her brain was actually working pretty well. After all, if she could program her VCR, she was doing better than most people already.

Mrs. P. went to a psychologist for counseling. A year later, she felt like a new woman. One of her daughters had a baby, and Mrs. P.'s expertise was urgently needed for baby care. She drove her daughter and granddaughter everywhere with no hint of problems. She never did master the microwave they had, but after repeated attempts trying to do it himself, her husband thought it was broken. A new one caused her no difficulties. And she was now too busy to even bother taping the evening news.

26

"The Socialite Who Spilled Too Many Secrets." Aging. When Your Memory Isn't As Good As It Was

MRS. AMEY WAS AN elegant 75-year-old who had been complaining to her doctors about her memory for some time. She misplaced her keys at least once a day. She forgot what she had planned for dinner in the course of the afternoon. But most distressing to her, she forgot who she had heard gossiping about whom. This was particularly troublesome, because Mrs. Amey was a prominent socialite.

Hearing stories about her friends, neighbors and acquaintances, and passing them on was her principal activity. On the golf course, at the club, and when dining out, she was having trouble keeping her stories straight. She could not remember who did what to whom, or who did what with whom. And most distressing of all, she was having trouble remembering who told her each story, and who had sworn her to keep it a secret.

After several embarrassing episodes of revealing confidences to the wrong people, she decided to once again seek medical attention. Her husband was not very sensitive to her concerns. "She has been like this for years! I don't know why it bothers her! None of her friends can remember anything either!"

Mrs. Amey had insisted on speaking directly to me in making the appointment. She knew exactly what she was concerned about, and what she wanted done for it. "I want tests to show me I don't have Alzheimer's disease."

She showed up promptly for her appointment, and dressed for a Baltimore winter, which was surprising to me, as she lived in a far more sultry climate. I commented on her overcoat. She explained to me that she had anticipated the need, and she always kept a few overcoats in case she ventured North.

Mrs. Amey's problems were mostly in learning new things. She did have some problems recalling the names of old acquaintances and family. Her speech and language were faultless. Her self-care was obviously excellent and she showed an astounding attention to detail. She made it a point to ask the name of everyone she met, and obviously made a point of using the names over again at every opportunity. She asked my staff about their families, so much so that by the end of the session, she knew more about their personal lives than I had ever known.

Testing showed her IQ to be above-average, as we had expected. Her memory was slightly below average. But it was still well above the impaired range.

We followed Mrs. Amey's case for several more years. Repeat testing never showed any change in her memory; if anything, it showed some improvement. But her memory problems remained very annoying to her.

Before we talk about Mrs. Amey's particular problems, we need to consider what happens in aging in general.

When does aging start? Personally, about 10 years from *now*. However, the evidence suggests a more complicated picture. On the average:

- Some drop in memory ability begins to occur in the twenties or thirties.

- Another decline in memory ability begins to occur in the sixties, but it is especially more pronounced in the seventies and eighties.

However, not everyone is affected the same way by aging.

Even before aging begins, each of us starts with a somewhat different bundle of abilities and disabilities. Some will be better at talking; some, at doing; some, at seeing; some, at hearing. Some people will have better memories than others, and in different areas (as we discussed in Chapter 19).

Each of us ages at a different speed. Some 80-year-olds will have the bodies and minds of 65-year-olds; others will be much worse off than others of the same age.

Different parts of our bodies—and our minds—can age at different rates. Perhaps what most people notice most about their aging minds is that their memory seems to be worse. But even then, not all kinds of memory worsen. For example, vocabulary memory can *grow* with aging and experience.

It is possible that the aging process will be somewhat different for different generations. People who are in their eighties now had their most formative years in the 1910s and 1920s. Nutrition was in some way worse than it is now. Infectious diseases were more prevalent. Higher education was less universal, particularly for women. Television, portable telephones, and computers never entered into their upbringing. So both biology and environment may affect the way members of different generations will age.

People in their eighties now may age better than someone just being born, on the average. If you're in your eighties, you're a survivor. You survived all that the 1910s, the 1920s, and the intervening decades could throw at you. So you've proven you're tough. And you learned how to do things with your mind differently than kids being born today will probably do. You learned how to listen to the radio and how to imagine a scene when all you had were the words and sounds to go by. You learned how to memorize, because that is the way you were taught. Some of these skills may be helpful to you as you age, skills that you can use to enhance or replace abilities that aging may dull or take away.

What will aging alone do to our minds? Some of the possibilities are sketched out in Figure 20. There seem to be three possibilities:

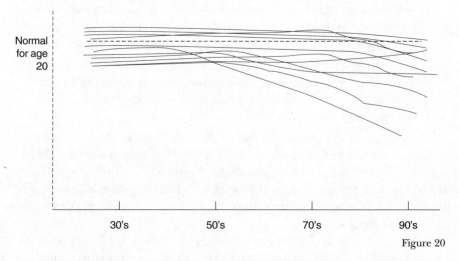

Figure 20

- A very, very small set of individuals will hardly seem to age mentally. Their reflexes will be almost as fast as they were, their minds as sharp, their memory intact.

- Most people will find that their minds seem to be slower, their memory a little worse. The most common mental change with aging is perhaps a *slowing* down of mental functions. The reaction you could make in six-tenths of a second when you were younger, now takes you a second or more.

▶ Some people will find that their minds have considerably more problems with aging than do other people's. In some, this will take the form of marked slowness of their thinking. In others, it will be their memory that will seem to suffer the most. These are the people afflicted by what is called Age-Associated Memory Loss. However, these problems will be a long time developing, and they will only gradually get worse. Most people with this problem will *not* develop Alzheimer's disease, even though their memory may be fairly poor.

Mrs. Amey had memory problems associated with aging, but **not** Alzheimer's disease. We can tell she did not have Alzheimer's disease in several ways. Her memory problems were only mild, and did not really affect anything she did that was critical to her everyday life. She could still remember what she needed to get at the store, and who she had to see for her appointments. Also, her memory problems had been present for a fairly long time, without obvious worsening. People with Alzheimer's usually experience a more rapid decline, eventually apparent from one year to the next, or even faster. And she was otherwise intact mentally. Patients with Alzheimer's disease typically have some other problems with their mental function. They may have problems finding the right words, or problems getting dressed. Or they may lose social awareness. Mrs. Amey most definitely had *not* lost her social awareness.

Because she definitely did have some memory problems, she fit within the broad category doctors call "age-associated memory impairment." This is a somewhat controversial diagnosis. It is not clear what standards should be used to diagnose it, and it is not clear what such a diagnosis really means. As we discussed above, most older people, especially beyond the age of seventy, will show problems with certain types of memory compared to younger people. They will be slower to remember, and have more problems on recall of information. And within this group of older people, there are going to be some people who have worse memories than others.

It is possible that age-associated deterioration in memory is due to a degeneration of nerve cells in the inner temporal regions of the brain—possible, but far from proven. In any event, this degeneration is probably a very different process from the degeneration that occurs in

Alzheimer's disease. Its effects seem to be restricted to memory, and to be milder and slower.

It can be tricky telling age-associated memory impairment apart from Alzheimer's disease in every person's case. Alzheimer's typically seems to begin in the same region of the brain, the inner temporal lobes, and it typically begins by affecting the same kind of memory—the ability to learn new things. So, in the very earliest cases of Alzheimer's, it is hard to tell it apart from normal aging, because they both produce the same kind of memory loss. But the memory loss of Alzheimer's disease is more rapidly progressive. Over the span of a few years, in most cases, family and friends can see the worsening. And the memory loss of Alzheimer's disease also tends to be more severe. The forgetfulness of normal aging is an annoyance, but that of Alzheimer's disease is a definite problem in the person's life. Another way to tell the two apart is that Alzheimer's typically affects other functions of the brain—word finding and the ability to find one's way around or to dress oneself.

An unfortunate problem in trying to tell age-associated memory loss apart from Alzheimer's is that both are very common, and therefore can exist together by chance. That is, an individual might well have age-associated memory loss and then develop Alzheimer's disease, solely by chance, and not because age-associated memory loss is a precursor for Alzheimer's disease.

The best available evidence suggests that if an older person truly has a problem that *only* affects his memory, his chances of developing Alzheimer's disease are relatively low—perhaps lower than 10 percent. But if the same person, with the same memory problem, also has other problems when he is first seen—problems with language, shown for example by problems naming pictures, or problems with visual spatial function, or minor signs of Parkinson's disease—then his chances of having Alzheimer's disease develop in the next few years are much higher, perhaps in the 30 to 50 percent range. Frequently, a repeat examination after one to two years is the only way to tell the two apart. If there has not been much of a decline, then chances are that it is aging and not Alzheimer's disease.

One important recent development in this area has been studies giving evidence that there is a genetic factor that might help predict the risks of developing memory loss with aging, and the risk of that memory loss turning into Alzheimer's disease. As discussed more fully in the next chapter, there are three different genes for a protein in the body called Apolipoprotein: the E2, the E3, and the E4 varieties. Everyone has two genes for this protein (one of each inherited from your mother and your father). The two genes can be of the same type, or of different types. People with memory impairment due to aging, who have the E4 version of the gene, appear to have as much as a four times higher risk of getting Alzheimer's disease within four to five years as those who do not.

It is important to keep in mind that this is a higher *risk*, not an absolute certainty. Many of the individuals with E4 who were studied did *not* develop Alzheimer's. The reasons that E4 seems to give a higher risk of progressive memory loss and Alzheimer's disease are far from clear as yet. Nor is Apolipoprotein-testing for memory loss now a standard clinical test, although many university medical centers do it as part of research into memory loss and Alzheimer's. (Mrs. Amey had it checked as part of our research, but neither she nor I were told the results, to prevent us from becoming biased. Nor would it make a difference—I will follow her the same way in either event, and so far she has not had any appreciable worsening or new problems.) I expect that what I will be able to discuss about the diagnosis of people with age-related memory complaints, such as Mrs. Amey's, will be considerably different in the next few years, as more of these research studies come to fruition.

27

"Everyone Forgets Who Their Children Are!"—Dementia and Alzheimer's Disease

ELEANOR E. WAS a 49-year-old woman who had experienced progressive problems with her memory for three years. Her problems had begun imperceptively, only gradually getting worse. In the previous year though, her problems seemed to have gotten considerably worse. Both Mrs. E. and her husband were aware that she quickly forgot conversations, needed to have things repeated to her frequently, and often wound up doing the same things repeatedly because she had forgotten that she had already done them. Nevertheless, she dressed herself without problems, prepared meals for her family and continued to lead the church choir.

Her neurological examination showed the only abnormality was in her mental abilities. Although she was completely alert and worked very hard, but she had considerable problems understanding and remembering the instructions for what she was supposed to do. Even when she seemed to understand what she was to do, she had many problems trying to do it. Mrs. E. was very aware of her problems and was both embarrassed and intensely frustrated by them. Not everything was wrong. Her speech was quite intact. She had no problems describing complicated pictures or finding the words she needed to do so. She could recognize pictures of famous people quite well. She could hold a pen without difficulty and was able to draw well. However, she could not remember what she had just learned and she quickly forgot having heard words given during the testing, or the simple pictures she had been shown. She had great difficulty even drawing simple pictures. She could not remember anything from a short paragraph that had been read to her an hour before. She also had severe problems understanding a test in which she had to guess the rules the examiner was using.

We diagnosed Mrs. E. as having Alzheimer's disease. Shortly after her diagnosis, Mrs. E. and her husband gladly agreed to have her plight

190

made public for the education of others. She was the Alzheimer's disease patient featured in the 1984 PBS series, *The Brain*.

Mrs. E. continued to worsen following her diagnosis. Although she was able to walk and feed herself, her speech was ultimately reduced to meaningless babbling. Both her husband and her daughter cared for her at home until she passed away. After her death, an autopsy proved that she did, in fact, have Alzheimer's disease.

―――――――――――――

A healthy 60-year-old man had enjoyed a successful career and was looking forward to an early retirement. But he began having trouble driving home, and got into a few accidents. He could not describe what was going wrong or why he did not feel comfortable driving. He also felt that he was having problems speaking. He was not able to find the right words, and he would get off the topic.

While testing of his memory and other functions did not show any abnormalities, a special scan of his brain showed that the flow of blood was decreased in the back regions on both sides of his brain, which helped in diagnosing Alzheimer's disease. Since that diagnosis, his problems have continued to very slowly worsen.

―――――――――――――

A healthy 65-year-old man checked into the hospital for minor surgery. He had been thought to be slightly forgetful at times, but not to any appreciable degree. The night after his surgery, however, his family found him to be extremely agitated and confused. He was not quite sure where he was and didn't remember that he had surgery. He wanted to go home so much that he was found in the parking lot in his hospital gown searching in vain for his car (which was actually at his house, because his family had brought him to the hospital). Sedation helped him get to sleep. In the morning, he seemed to be only a little confused. He still wasn't quite sure of the day or date, but did remember having surgery. After a few days at home, he seemed to be his old self, however, over the next several years, his memory definitely worsened.

―――――――――――――

Mrs. E., and these other patients are only a few examples of a chillingly familiar disease: Alzheimer's disease. They are also examples of how differently Alzheimer's can affect different people.

Many people, particularly those people over the age of 65, are concerned about their memory and most worried that they may have

Alzheimer's disease. This fear is not unfounded. Alzheimer's disease is very common, particularly after age 65; up to 30 to 40 percent of people over the age of 80 will develop it. And there is currently no cure for this debilitating condition, only some treatments that may alleviate certain symptoms and make it easier for the family to cope.

In this chapter, I will give you an overview of the nature of Alzheimer's disease, how it is diagnosed, some of its possible causes, and treatments or medications that might be tried for a person who has the disease.

THE NATURE OF ALZHEIMER'S DISEASE

Alzheimer's disease seems to damage—and ultimately kill—many of the nerve cells in the brain. In the process of damaging or killing these nerve cells, it damages or weakens the connections between them as well. It does not damage nerve cells and connections in every region of the brain, at least not at first. For example, it does not usually first affect the basic sensory or motor pathways of the brain, nor the lower centers that control breathing, heartbeat, chewing, swallowing, eating, or walking and other basic movements. So these will not be affected in a person with Alzheimer's disease in its early stages.

But the damage to nerve cell connections and nerve cells in Alzheimer's disease usually does start first in the regions of the brain involved in memory, in the inner parts of the temporal lobes. As a consequence, in the typical patient with Alzheimer's disease, it begins with memory problems. These memory problems look in some ways like those of pure amnesia (discussed in the next chapter, Chapter 28). The Alzheimer's patient often has trouble learning or remembering anything new. Mrs. E. was a classic example of this. Initially, this memory problem is mild and hard to distinguish from the problems with learning new things that can occur in people with normal memories, or those with age-associated memory loss (as we discussed in the last chapter, Chapter 26).

Usually, the beginning of Alzheimer's disease is almost imperceptible. But then—over the course of a few years—the memory loss becomes more severe. The person forgets his keys, not just once a day, but all the time. He cannot remember why he walked into a room every time he walks into a room. He is introduced to people and cannot remember them a few minutes later. He loses his way while trying to drive to someplace a little new and unfamiliar. There may be a tendency for memories that still are preserved—old memories—to substitute for new ones. So the person with Alzheimer's disease may endlessly repeat conversations and events from the past, or drive to a familiar but incorrect address instead of the new one.

As the disease gets worse, old memories also suffer. The loss of nerve cells and connections begins erasing knowledge of even very well learned things, such as the names of grandchildren, or knowledge of familiar streets and routes. These erasures of old information, combined with the problems learning anything new, may cause sufferers to get lost driving in an otherwise familiar location. Damage in the language regions of the brain frequently results in problems with finding the right words.

In addition to these memory problems, damage occurs in other parts of the brain in early Alzheimer's disease, which creates other kinds of problems. The frontal regions of the brain orchestrate our behaviors and help us regulate and prioritize mental activities and keep some behaviors in check while letting others surface. Damage in those frontal regions shows itself as alterations in behavior. As a result, the patient with Alzheimer's disease may not be able to resist gambling or other vices. They may make inappropriate comments—ones we may normally think, but not normally say out loud.

The frontal lobes are also regions of the brain that seem important in providing motivation and direction. Damage to these areas can cause a patient with Alzheimer's disease to become somewhat apathetic and lose initiative. They will sit all day, uninterested and unmoving.

The mind's ability to find information and to link it together may also be damaged in Alzheimer's disease. The Alzheimer's patient may "not be able to put 2 and 2 together." You may explain to them why they shouldn't leave the gas burners on, and they may *tell* you they know not to leave the burners on—but they do it anyway.

Alzheimer's disease—perhaps in particular the damage in the frontal regions—impairs the mind's ability to monitor its own performance. So the patient with Alzheimer's will typically minimize his problems. You point out to him that he doesn't know his grandchildren's names. "I have so many, I forget. You would too!" You point out to him he doesn't know his *children's* names. "I have so many, I forget. You would too!" But, of course, no one would. Not normally.

Unfortunately, the initially imperceptible changes in memory eventually begin to accelerate. On average, it is generally three years from the time that a family first starts noticing problems to the time when a patient is diagnosed with Alzheimer's disease. In some cases it is the appearance of the more accelerated change that leads to the diagnosis. For example, it may finally become clear to a family that the forgetfulness in father that they witnessed last Thanksgiving is now clearly worse. Father now forgets the names of all of his grandchildren— not just some of them.

Other times, it is a sudden change in behavior or the appearance of certain bizarre behavior that precipitates a visit to the doctor. One patient who came to see me had been thought to be normal when she checked into the hospital for a cataract removal. She seemed fine after the operation, which was done under local anesthesia and which shouldn't have caused her a problem. At 2 a.m. on the morning following her surgery, however, she woke up unable to remember why she was in the hospital. She thought that she was in a strange place and consequently found her way to the parking lot where she was found several hours later looking for her car in her hospital gown. She was bothered because she could not locate her car; the fact that she had a bandage over one eye and it was pitch black outside didn't seem to bother her.

After diagnosis, the typical case of Alzheimer's disease becomes progressively worse. Initially, the change from year to year may not seem too great. But the deterioration eventually begins to accelerate. Typically, patients with Alzheimer's disease live for an average of eight years from the time of diagnosis. Often, it is not Alzheimer's that causes the death of Alzheimer's patients but other illnesses associated with aging—heart attacks, stroke, and cancer.

But about half of the deaths are more directly due to the effects of Alzheimer's disease. The body itself is not directly damaged by Alzheimer's—the disease has no direct effect on the heart, the lungs, the kidneys or other organ systems of the body. It is, however, the poor self-care and lack of movement that causes these patients to become more susceptible to other serious conditions that can lead to death, such as pneumonia. My grandfather, who had Alzheimer's disease for many years, died in his early nineties from complications arising from a hip fracture.

By the time of death, the degeneration in the nerve cell endings and nerve cells in the brain of an Alzheimer's patient has become much more severe and more widespread. The brain as a whole has shrunk from this nerve cell loss, although the damage is still particularly severe in the temporal lobes, the posterior parts of the brain, and in the frontal regions of the brain; that is, the areas where it first began. With a microscope, the neuropathologist can detect in these regions of the brain collections of abnormal protein, called amyloid, surrounded by degenerating and degenerated nerve cells and nerve cell endings. These are the *plaques* of Alzheimer's disease. It is important to note that there are still no proven diagnostic laboratory tests for Alzheimer's disease. So a diagnosis of Alzheimer's disease is done by a process of inclusion and exclusion: determining whether the condition has the characteristics described above (inclusion) and ruling out other diseases and conditions that could cause those same characteristics (exclusion).

Dementia and Alzheimer's Disease

Alzheimer's disease is one of a group of diseases that are called the *dementias.* The term *dementia* literally means "without mentation." Alzheimer's disease is only one of the patterns a dementia can take.

Dementia in older people is most often (about 65 percent of the time) due to Alzheimer's disease. About 15 percent of the time, dementia in an older person is thought to be due to something wrong in the blood vessels of the brain. Years ago, the term "hardening of the arteries" was applied to most people who had dementia. We now know that relatively few cases of dementia are due to problems with the arteries.

About 10 to 15 percent of people with dementia are found to have a combination of Alzheimer's disease and severe blood vessel disease in their brains. Some patients with Parkinson's disease develop a dementia, and in some of these cases, the dementia looks exactly like Alzheimer's disease.

There are a number of other, rarer, diseases that can cause dementia. A few of these are treatable; most, unfortunately, are not. One of the tasks of a physician when evaluating a patient for dementia is to look for any possible diseases that might have caused the dementia and determine whether that other disease might be treatable or reversible.

Alzheimer's Disease in More Detail

The following is a list of the typical criteria used by physicians to diagnose Alzheimer's disease:

- Age of onset between 40 and 90.
- No disturbance of consciousness. Persons suspected of having Alzheimer's disease must be fully conscious and not delirious.
- Problems in two or more areas of mental function, such as memory, speech, or drawing ability.

- Progressive worsening of these mental problems.
- No evidence of other diseases that could account for the progressive worsening.

Let's discuss each of these points.

ONSET AGE 40-90

The youngest reported case of Alzheimer's disease started at age 35, but this is extremely rare. Alzheimer's disease is uncommon before the age of 65, but thereafter the percent of people it affects rises rapidly: from 0.1 percent between the ages of 60 to 65 to 30 to 40 percent by age 80 to 85. The number of people it affects may level out after age 90. Cases of Alzheimer's occurring before the age of 65, particularly those at much younger ages, are more likely to be more clearly due to genetic influences than those that occur later in life.

NO DISORDER OF CONSCIOUSNESS

Alzheimer's disease, when it starts, should not make a person sleepy. And if a person *is* sleepy or drowsy—which can happen because of drugs or disease—then their mental functions will be poor. They may appear as though they have Alzheimer's disease, but do not have to have this condition.

PROBLEMS IN TWO OR MORE AREAS OF MENTAL FUNCTION

Memory is the most common area of mental function that is affected by Alzheimer's disease. Usually, when a patient is first seen, he is having problems both in learning new things and in remembering old information.

Problems finding words are also very common (sometimes, these are the first problem to appear). This type of problem is often labeled a memory problem, although it is a different kind of memory, and a different kind of problem, than involved in memory for new facts.

Some patients begin, not with memory or language problems, but with vision problems or problems with driving or in getting around. Such patients can be very puzzling at first, as in the case of Dr. S., described below.

THE CIRCLING SIGN OF ALZHEIMER'S DISEASE

Dr. S. was frustrated and worried. A 55-year-old scientist, she had lived in Washington, D.C. for the past ten years. The city of Washington is encircled by a busy highway, called the Beltway. She had never had any trouble driving around it to get to work, or circling back and getting off at the right exit to go home. But now she found herself missing her exit. Oddly, it was not happening when she drove to work. It was only happening when she headed home in the evening.

I asked her what she thought was going wrong. She couldn't really understand or explain. She said she did not know it was her exit. "It didn't look right," she told me. And so she would drive on past, and past the next exit. And past the one after that. And so it would go, around the whole Beltway. A 30-mile drive. And then, often as not, she would miss her exit once more.

Her husband was beside himself. They had circled the Beltway several times one Saturday. She would not believe him when he told her which exit was theirs. It was a frustrating and infuriating problem. He had known his wife had a stubborn streak, but he thought this was ridiculous. What had precipitated the visit to me, though, was their feeling of late that her conversations seemed to wander a little bit.

She thought it was the funniest thing. She would be on a thought, and then find herself on another, entirely different one. She thought she could see the connection between the two ideas, but admitted that her husband and her friends often seemed to be lost.

Throughout the interview, I was listening not only to the history she gave, but also the way she told it to me. She jumped all over and moved backwards and forwards in time. Sometimes this is normal—at cocktail parties and on TV talk shows, for example. And, sometimes, this is because the person is nervous. And sometimes it is because the person has just never had training in telling a coherent story. But Dr. S. was an accomplished writer and public speaker, she was not that nervous and she knew it was not a cocktail party.

There was nothing wrong with the way Dr. S. enunciated her words, or with the words she chose. In language problems due to brain disease, there is often a problem with the way people speak. It can sound as though they are trying to talk while they have food in their mouths or after they have just come back from the dentist. Their pronunciation can be a little fuzzy or slurred. Frequently, in aphasia—language problems due to brain diseases such as stroke—people have problems finding the sounds for the words. So instead of being able to say "door", the person with aphasia may say "Oh . . . the way out." Or "exit."

But Dr. S. was not having any problem with her enunciation, with the words themselves, or with the way she strung them together. Her problem was at a higher level, and it really was not within language at all. Her sentences were well constructed; all the phrases fit together well. Her problem was with the thinking that went into directing her sentences. She seemed to have a number of different ideas in her mind at once. All seemed to be fighting for attention at the same time. Her speech just followed whichever idea was foremost in her mind at the moment.

And Dr. S. herself was bewildered by the turns her mind was taking. One of her complaints was how flighty her ideas had become. It was as difficult for her to follow her thinking as it was for me.

A neurologic examination did not show any problems with her vision. There was no sign on my examination of her strength and reflexes that she had had a stroke. The neuropsychologic testing that we did failed to find any problems. Her memory was, in fact, comfortably above average. We did not know how good her memory had been before, of course, so there was always the possibility that she had had a decline. But, as we often put it, "there was no reliable evidence" that this was actually happening.

We obtained more extensive testing of Dr. S.'s vision. Again, there was no problem with her ability to see.

We checked the MRI scan she had already had done. It, too, was normal. MRI scans that are done routinely photographically slice the brain at about one-quarter inch intervals. Sometimes, if a person has a very small stroke or other small hole in the brain tissue, this thick of a scan can miss it or not see it very clearly. So we obtained an MRI where the cuts were much more closely spaced, approximately one-tenth of an inch apart. Still, this found nothing. It was true that Dr. S.'s brain seemed a little shrunken, but some shrinkage of the brain seems to occur with age (because parts of the brain shrink with age, but not because nerve cells are dying).

We also did a brain wave test on Dr. S. Electrodes were put on her scalp, and we observed her brain electrical activity. This proved to be somewhat surprising. Her brain electrical activity was somewhat slower than we expected it should be. It also seemed to be a little bit more chaotic.

The odds were high then that something very real was happening to Dr. S., but there was not enough evidence to identify what it was. In conjunction with Dr. S.'s other doctors, we ran a large number of tests to determine whether anything potentially treatable was affecting her brain. So we looked at her red blood cells to see if she was anemic and if the red blood cells were abnormally large. We also looked at her Vitamin B12 level. Vitamin B12 deficiency can cause a type of dementia, although there are usually many other signs when this occurs. Her B12 level was normal.

We did an HIV test, with Dr. S.'s permission. This was very unlikely in Dr. S.'s case, but infection with the AIDS virus can cause a dementia. We even did a spinal tap to look at the spinal fluid. The spinal fluid flows inside and around the brain. By examining it for signs of inflammation, or for any signs of breakdown of myelin (the covering of nerve cells), we can sometimes pick up signs of damage. For example, patients with multiple sclerosis (MS) frequently have myelin breakdown proteins in their spinal fluid and, especially during the throes of a multiple sclerosis attack, can show signs of inflammation in their spinal fluid. Or, sometimes, diseases that inflame the blood vessels over the brain can show up as inflammation in the spinal fluid. For instance, syphilis can show up on an test done on the spinal fluid. Although dementia from syphilis is rare these days, years ago it used to be a major cause of dementia (Al Capone was syphilitic).

We briefly considered directly examining Dr. S.'s brain, through a biopsy. This would have to have been done through a hole in her skull, large enough to take out a piece of brain tissue and its coverings. This might have given us a diagnosis. But, as we had checked for everything that might be treatable already, we would not have been able to treat anything we would diagnose with the biopsy. Therefore, there was no good reason to do the biopsy.

Since there was nothing further that could be done, we all waited. Sometimes, problems go away.

But Dr. S.'s didn't. After a year, she felt things were about the same as they had been. But Dr. S.'s husband felt that if anything, things had gotten a little worse. They certainly hadn't gotten any better.

So we reexamined Dr. S. Comparing her to how she had been the year before, it was clear her husband was right. Her memory *had* gotten a little worse. Her thinking *was* a little bit more disorganized. Her brain wave test remained abnormal.

So we did a special test on Dr. S. to look at the flow of blood in her brain. This proved to be the clincher: She had Alzheimer's disease. Even when she was at rest, there was decreased flow of blood in the back part of her brain on both sides. These areas, called the temporal and parietal areas, are among the principal areas affected by Alzheimer's disease. Dr. S.'s brain showed this Alzheimer's pattern of decreased blood flow.

Moreover, in Dr. S.'s case, the right side of her brain seemed to be more severely affected than the left. This was perhaps a clue as to why she had had so many problems finding her exit on the Beltway. The region in the back of the brain, on the right side, usually is one of the main areas involved in seeing, in recognizing what we see, and in finding our way around. Malfunction in this area therefore explained—indirectly—why her exit looked strange to her.

Blood flow can be decreased in an area of the brain for many reasons: the person may not be using that particular part of the brain at that time, or not using it very much. Or something could be wrong with the blood vessels going to that part of the brain. Or there could have been a stroke in that area.

But the amount of the impairment, and the circumstances under which we did the test convinced us that what was going wrong in Dr. S. was another possibility. The nerve cells in that region were damaged or dying. As a result, the brain was automatically decreasing the flow of blood to that region, which the blood vessels and brain have mechanisms to do.

Could we have increased the flow of blood to that area, and taken away Dr. S.'s problems? No. The problem was not with the amount of blood that was available, but with how many nerve cells were left. You can open up the throttle all the way on your car's engine, but if three of your six cylinders are bad, there is no way the remaining cylinders can develop as much force as the whole engine once could.

Dr. S.'s disease has progressed slowly. Her thoughts remain disorganized and flighty. She has given up driving. But her condition remains remarkable for what her disease has *not* affected. Her memory has hardly been affected, unlike 80 percent of Alzheimer's patients. Nor has her insight been dulled: she remains very much aware of her own problems. This, too, is unlike most people with Alzheimer's disease.

But we have given her this diagnosis—Alzheimer's disease—despite these atypical features. What we are really saying with this diagnosis is that she has a degenerative disease of the brain—her brain cells are dying, and we cannot find a reason why. Her pattern is not the typical one for Alzheimer's. But Alzheimer's is so common, and its guises so protean, that it remains the most likely diagnosis in her case.

Dr. S. is content with this diagnosis. She participates in several research projects, and has even read books on Alzheimer's disease. And she has stipulated that when she dies her brain will go to Johns Hopkins for analysis. She wants her children, and their children, to have the best possible knowledge of the disease that is slowly robbing her of her mind.

Dr. S.'s case shows how the diagnosis of dementia, and the specific diagnosis of the particular disease causing dementia, often rests on determining just what mental functions are being affected by the disease. Mental functions are complicated. Many are linked to each other and hard to test in isolation. Some, however, can be teased apart from other functions and tested, more-or-less in isolation. By doing so, the results indicate not only your mental abilities on that function, but also indirectly the capabilities of the *brain* regions that are responsible for those functions. The mental functions most commonly tested include the following:

(i)   attention and concentration;
(ii)   language;
(iii) visual perception;
(iv)   motor control;
(v)   memory (both new learning and retrieval of old memories);
(vi)   judgment;
(vii) insight into one's own behavior; and
(viii) mood.

Because of the structure of the brain, certain diseases of the brain can affect one or more of these functions while leaving the other functions in tact.

Most physicians use a *Mental Status Test* to determine whether a patient has suffered a loss of these mental functions. The Mental Status Test is simply a series of basic questions posed to the patient or the patient's family. These questions are designed to evaluate the patient's attention span, language, visual perception and drawing skills, and memory.

Several short forms of these mental status tests have been developed which typically take less than ten minutes to complete. A drawback with these short tests is that they are not very sensitive to mild degrees of dementia. Also, because they have so few items, the scores on these tests can vary considerably from one test session to another, even though the patient's mental status has not actually changed.

Formal neuropsychological tests provide more sensitivity and more accuracy. In my clinic, we use these tests—really, a series of tests which often last as long as two to three hours (or more, if necessary). The different mental functions of the patient are each tested in adequate depth and with good accuracy and repeatability. A patient's performance can then be more accurately compared to the level of performance expected for the patient in light of his or her age, education and sex. These formal tests are also more accurate in comparing the same patient over time.

PROGRESSIVE LOSS

One critical characteristic that distinguishes Alzheimer's disease from many other conditions that can cause memory loss is the rate of progression. In Alzheimer's, the memory loss continues to worsen and this worsening is clearly apparent from one year to the next, in most people.

By contrast, if an individual suffers a stroke, the problem occurs all at once. It does not tend to get worse; if anything, it gradually improves.

In the memory loss due to aging, both the onset and progression are very gradual. They start imperceptibly—as the memory loss due to Alzheimer's does—but, unlike Alzheimer's disease, the progression tends to be much slower. It may take five years or more to see an appreciable change. As a result, the person should show little, if any, change in memory from one year to the next.

If the memory loss is even more rapid, it may be an entirely different condition. Rapid memory loss may be a sign of a rapidly-progressing condition such as a brain tumor, or even a rare, deadly, viral-type disease of the brain called Creutzfeld-Jakob disease.

EXCLUDING OTHER CONDITIONS

In diagnosing Alzheimer's or dementia, there is still debate as to how far to investigate to exclude other conditions that might look like Alzheimer's disease. There is, however, widespread agreement that a review of an individual's history is necessary, to look for obvious possibilities (such as head injury or stroke). A review of his medication is also necessary in order to rule out the possibility that any of the medications may be causing the memory problems. A review of the patient's educational and work history is also useful, to give a sense of how well he had been functioning before the illness began.

A family history is also important because it may indicate whether any other family members have had a similar condition or related condition. Although relatively uncommon, some forms of Alzheimer's disease do run in families, and other conditions that may at times mimic Alzheimer's disease can also run in families. For instance, Huntington's Chorea—the disease that killed Woody Guthrie—sometimes imitates Alzheimer's.

Finally, a general medical exam and basic neurologic exam are important to determine whether the patient has any diseases in the rest of the body that might affect brain function—in particular, disease of the heart, lungs, kidneys or liver. Diseases of these organs can lead to mental dulling.

A person's medical history and physical exam may also hint at problems that *might* be a cause of their dementia. Severe snoring and daytime drowsiness may mean that an individual has *sleep apnea syndrome.* In sleep apnea, the patient stops breathing temporarily because the throat collapses during sleep. Over months or years, it is possible that repeated bouts of low oxygen due to sleep apnea can damage the brain.

Most physicians agree that the next step after a general medical and neurologic examination is an MRI or CT scan. Both the MRI and CT scan look for large strokes, and certain small strokes, and also screen for conditions such as tumors, blood clots, or increased pressure inside the brain (which causes a condition known as hydrocephalus, literally "water brain").

Sometimes a brain wave test (EEG) is useful in diagnosis. In the earlier stages of Alzheimer's, however, the brain wave test will usually be normal. Only in the later stages of Alzheimer's does it become abnormal. So, a brain wave test may be inconclusive in a patient suspected of being in the early stages of Alzheimer's.

Another optional but sometimes useful test is the examination of the spinal fluid or the *lumbar puncture test.* This involves the withdrawal of spinal fluid from the space around the spinal cord. A spinal fluid test can often detect some problems that other tests are not able to reveal. Evidence of inflammation or infection or of breakdown of myelin such as occurs in multiple sclerosis can be shown in a spinal fluid test.

Years ago, before the availability of penicillin to treat syphilis, a lumbar puncture was almost mandatory in any case of dementia since syphilis is a known cause of dementia that can only be detected through the spinal fluid. However, with the availability of penicillin starting in World War II, the generation that is now at risk of dementia has a much lower chance of having had untreated syphilis.

As we used in Dr. S.'s case, an examination of the blood flow in different regions of the brain can also be helpful. The most widely available test for this is called the SPECT. This test uses a compound which is rapidly taken up by the brain, and which emits radiation. How much radiation is given off in different regions of the brain is an index of how much blood is flowing through them. We have found the SPECT scan to be most useful in atypical cases of Alzheimer's disease, as we discussed in conjunction with Dr. S.'s case. A related test, which uses a positron emission tomography, or PET, scanner, has been used for research purposes. PET scanning has been useful in research studies of

Alzheimer's disease, but has not been approved for clinical use in Alzheimer's or related conditions.

Apolipoprotein E (Apo-E) testing is not yet in clinical use in testing for the likelihood of Alzheimer's. This testing is discussed later in this chapter.

POSSIBLE CAUSES OF ALZHEIMER'S DISEASE

The fundamental cause of Alzheimer's disease at the nerve cell level (or perhaps even below the nerve cell level) is not yet known. However, age, genetics, and the environment all seem to play a role.

AGE

The risk of Alzheimer's disease greatly increases with age, as we have discussed. It is very rare before the age of 65, but present in 30 to 40 percent of people aged 80 to 85. A number of plausible mechanisms have been suggested for this dependence upon age, but none have been proven. One is that errors creep into the system responsible for generating energy for the cells of the body, including the nerve cells. This gradual accumulation of errors leads to a gradual reduction in the efficiency of energy production, which eventually shuts the cell down, in much the same way that sludge and wear gradually build up inside a car engine and eventually cause it to freeze. Another, related possibility is that deleterious compounds such as free radicals (hyperactive oxygen compounds), that are normally produced by the cell, gradually wear at the elements within the cell.

GENETICS

Perhaps 1 to 10 percent of cases of Alzheimer's disease have a strongly recognizable genetic component. Often, these familial Alzheimer's disease cases begin earlier in life than the more common ones (often, when people are in their forties or fifties, and sometimes even in the thirties), and produce different problems than the more typical Alzheimer's disease.

However, even Alzheimer's disease occurring later in life also frequently seems to have a genetic component. The risk of Alzheimer's is increased two to three times in first degree relatives (siblings or children of individuals affected by Alzheimer's disease).

An intriguing new clue to the genetics of Alzheimer's disease has come from research done by Dr. Allen Roses and his colleagues at Duke University on an enzyme called Apolipoprotein-E (Apo-E). Everyone has two copies of the gene that makes the Apo-E enzyme, one from each of our parents. This gene comes in one of three versions labelled E2, E3 and E4. The E2 and E3 varieties are the most common. These different varieties of genes make slightly different varieties of the Apo-E enzyme.

People can have any combination of these three varieties; any single person can be E2-E2, E3-E4, E2-E4, and so forth. Combinations involving E2 and E3 are the most common. This is fortunate, because combinations with E4 appear to put you at a much higher risk of developing Alzheimer's disease. If you develop memory loss, and are also found to have a double dose of the E4 gene, then the odds are significantly higher that you will develop Alzheimer's disease. Some evidence even suggests that those people who have a double dose of the E4 gene are at higher risk of developing degenerative brain diseases if they have been unlucky enough to have had head injuries or lead poisoning.

Scientists do not know exactly why having the double dose of this gene causes people to be susceptible to Alzheimer's disease. One intriguing theory is that it is not the E4 gene itself that harms the brain, but rather the *absence* of the E2 and E3 genes. The theory assumes that aging is associated with wearing and tearing of nerve cells and their connections. The E2 and E3 genes produce proteins that may *protect* the brain against this wear and tear; they are, in this theory, akin to additives to the oil that make your engine last longer. So if people do not have both doses of either E2 or E3 (because they have one E4), and particularly if they do not have *any* E2 or E3 (because they have two E4s), their brain engines are left without this protection. Aging then has a greater effect. So do other conditions that damage the brain, such as head injury or lead poisoning.

Many university centers now do testing for the varieties of Apo-E as part of research studies. None yet offer it as a clinical test, because its actual significance is unclear. But a great many researchers are pursuing the leads offered by the Apo-E connection to try to determine why Alzheimer's disease affects the brain, and what might be done to block or minimize its effects.

ENVIRONMENTAL

The only environmental factor that seems to increase the risk of Alzheimer's disease is head injury. Head injury with loss of consciousness probably raises the risk of Alzheimer's by about 1.7 times. Head injury may do this by jarring the nerve cell fibers within the brain, and by breaking up the microscopic tubing within them that carries nutrients and other materials from the body of the nerve cells out to their endings.

Other than head injury, nothing else in the environment has been reliably shown to raise the risk of Alzheimer's disease. This includes aluminum. While aluminum is increased in parts of the brain in some patients with Alzheimer's disease, there is as yet no reliable evidence that the aluminum is actually responsible for the damage seen in Alzheimer's disease. So there is no reason to stop using aluminum cooking utensils (although in most people, aluminum exposure is through antiperspirants, rather than through cooking utensils anyway).

TESTING FOR ALZHEIMER'S DISEASE

At the present time, determining whether someone has Alzheimer's disease requires pulling together information from a number of sources: the history of their mental deterioration; their physical and neurologic exams; mental status or neuropsychologic testing; routine blood tests to check their general health; MRI scan or CT scan; and an EEG, lumbar puncture, and perhaps other tests as we discussed above.

There is no one, single magic test to prove the presence or absence of Alzheimer's disease. And even though some tests seem to be extremely promising, there are many good reasons not to use them in isolation. As a real example, consider the recent report that changes in the pupils with eye drops could tell patients with Alzheimer's apart from those without it. This test was 95 percent accurate in picking up Alzheimer's disease, which would seem to be impressive. But even with 95 percent accuracy, the test missed 1 in 20 cases of Alzheimer's disease.

The eye drop test is a scientifically important finding. But should your doctor use a test with this kind of accuracy and error rate with *you?* Even though the test was 95 percent accurate, that still means that there was a 5 percent chance (one in twenty) that you could have the disease, even if the test said you did not. In real life, in dealing with yourself, you and your physician are rightfully going to demand something closer to 100 percent accuracy. This is one reason that a test may be scientifically useful, but still not appropriate for you. And this is one of the reasons why testing for Alzheimer's still requires multiple sources of information, and not jumping to conclusions from any one of them.

TREATMENT OF ALZHEIMER'S DISEASE

No drug or therapy is currently known to stop Alzheimer's disease. Only one drug on the market is an approved, direct therapy for some aspects of Alzheimer's disease, and that is Cognex (Tacrine HCl). Cognex is a drug that is thought to work by raising levels of acetylcholine, a neurotransmitter, in the brain, by blocking the enzyme that normally is responsible for destroying acetylcholine.

In patients with mild to moderate Alzheimer's disease, Cognex can frequently seem to temporarily halt the progression of the disease, and in some cases it may even seem to improve the patient (often, it seems to make them more alert and more active). Cognex does have some potential side effects that mean its use must be monitored closely by a physician. Several other investigational drugs are now being studied that probably work by much the same mechanism as Cognex, yet which may be more convenient and safer to use.

Cognex has been approved by the Food and Drug Administration for use only in mild to moderately severe Alzheimer's disease. There is no evidence that use of Cognex will *prevent* Alzheimer's disease from beginning in the first place. There is no evidence that Cognex stops the underlying degeneration of nerve cells in Alzheimer's disease (no drug is yet known that does stop the underlying disease). Also, there is no reliable indication yet that this drug offers normal people, or people with the memory loss associated with aging, any specific way to boost their memory ability.

It is clear that Alzheimer's is going to be a very difficult disease to treat directly, since there are so many things going wrong: the nerve cells are dying, their connections are being destroyed, and this is happening throughout the brain.

Many other behavioral problems can occur in Alzheimer's disease. Behavioral treatments as well as drugs may be effective for these problems. For example, the patient with Alzheimer's often gets up and wanders around at night. It may mean that he needs more exercise and activity during the day to get more tired. If the person becomes angry over certain situations, they may be predictable and avoidable. If necessary, though, different drugs may help some of the problems that can occur in Alzheimer's disease: sleeping problems, marked agitation, and hallucinations. These medicines are not universally effective, and also people differ in how well they respond to them. Also, all these drugs can have side effects. Therefore, the physician may have to spend considerable time adjusting the dosage for optimal effect.

PROMINENT PEOPLE WHO HAVE HAD OR HAVE ALZHEIMER'S DISEASE

Dana Andrews—actor
Rudolph Bing—General Manager, Metropolitan Opera

Aaron Copeland—composer
Arlene Francis—actress
Rita Hayworth—actress
Willem de Kooning—painter
Jerry Lester—television talk-show host and comedian
David Niven—actor
Edmond O'Brien—actor
Molly Picon—actress
Ronald Reagan—fortieth president of the United States
Sugar Ray Robinson—boxer
Irving Shulman—novelist and screenwriter (*Rebel Without A Cause*)
E.B. White—writer

28

The Unfinished Baseball Season—Pure Amnesia. Memory Loss from Other Brain Diseases

JOHN *KNEW THERE* was supposed to be a World Series. He *felt* as though it should have happened. But he had no recollection of it. He knew exactly how every team had been doing, exactly where every player stood. But what had *happened* to them?

John knew that the Orioles had a chance for the pennant this year. The recollection of the Toronto Blue Jays only one game ahead pranced around in his memory. He was sure this would be the year that the Orioles squelched the threat from the Blue Jays, and got into the pennant race. But shouldn't that have *happened* by now?

John knew everything about the state of baseball—up until July 14th. But now something was "weird" with his memory, as he put it. Only, he couldn't explain what.

We could. Up until July 14th, John had been a normal, healthy, athletic 17-year-old. He was president of the junior class, and expected to be a candidate in his senior year as well. He ran three miles a day. He was interested in every sport, but especially passionate about baseball. He was a good student and was beginning to think ahead to his college plans.

But on July 14th, while he was near the end of a long run, an electrical signal that should have passed through one route in his heart took a different direction. His heart changed its rate from the 170 beats per minute he had been sustaining for mile after mile, to 250 beats per minute. But at that rate, even his healthy heart could not pump enough blood fast enough to supply all that his body was demanding. His muscles were demanding enormous amounts of blood just then. His blood pressure dropped; his brain, because it is at the highest point of his body, temporarily lost its full supply of blood. His momentum carried him on, but other runners saw him gradually collapse to the ground.

His heart rhythm shifted back into normal. His muscles gradually lessened their demands, and John opened his eyes after another minute. Yes, he reassured the people that had come to check on him, it seemed as though he had blacked out. But he felt fine now.

But in his brain, there was a small region on both sides, just in front of the ears, that had not gone unscathed. Deep inside the front part of the temporal lobe is an area—the hippocampus—where the brain cells seem exceptionally susceptible to loss of blood or oxygen, and these brain cells were damaged. They were the ones that would cause John his problems.

Except for a skinned knee and a bruised shoulder, John seemed otherwise fine. He studied hard that evening for the extra courses he was taking over the summer, and again studied the next day. But when he took the test, the material on it seemed utterly new to him; none of his answers were correct.

Outwardly, John's behavior had not changed. He was still the sociable, cheery fellow everyone knew. He still continued to study and play hard. He still had his wit and his intelligence, and could joke and laugh at jokes. But he could not learn any new jokes. In fact, he could not learn anything new at all.

John could remember everything that had happened up to that moment on July 14th. He even remembered exactly how happy he was with his running time when he had last checked his watch and checked his distance. But after that—nothing.

If any task required him to retain information for more than a minute, he could not learn it, and could not remember any of it. When he left his home in Baltimore for a time, he could not remember where he was. When he went on a family vacation, he could not remember where they had been. He could not even remember that they had left to go on a vacation. He remembered *nothing* that had happened since July 14th.

John is one of the rare examples of a *pure amnesia*. Patients with pure amnesia have damage to the mechanism that locks new information into permanent form. New information circulates for a time within our minds, bouncing within the echo boxes described in Chapter 10. It can even make contact with memories already there. But without this solidifying process, the new information in a patient with pure amnesia will be only temporary. It will fade from consciousness in 15 to

30 seconds unless the patient makes an effort to recirculate it in his head, by conscious rehearsal.

Patients with pure amnesia may also have something of a block in getting at old memories, memories that were already solidified into their brains. Initially, this problem may be quite profound, and they may not be able to retrieve even very old, highly solidified memories. They may not, perhaps, even be able to retrieve their memory for their own name. But this is uncommon and, when it does occur, it usually decreases with time. So in most patients with the pure amnestic syndrome, the problem of getting at old memories ultimately only affects those memories acquired in the few months or few years prior to the start of their amnesia. Access to older, more deeply embedded memories is perfectly normal.

In John's case, his pure amnesia was due to damage to his hippocampus. All it took was a very tiny region of damage, perhaps smaller than a fingertip. In other patients, the pure amnesia may be due to damage within the thalamus (as discussed in Chapter 14), where the damage can be even smaller—perhaps even just a hole the size of a match head.

The damage in these areas does not alter the workings of the rest of the brain. But it does block the permanent formation of new memories, the hardening process we discussed in Chapter 14.

Our everyday notions of memory loss leave us totally unprepared for cases of pure amnesia such as John's. In everyday forgetfulness, we cannot think of the names of people we know. Our father or spouse with Alzheimer's disease is incapable of functioning in everyday life. They are not only forgetful, they ultimately forget how to do arithmetic, how to dress themselves, even how to eat. And in the movies and TV, amnesia is forgetting who you are.

But the patient with pure amnesia due to true brain disease knows exactly who he is. He does not forget the names of friends and acquaintances. He is as good as ever at doing calculations, at dressing and selecting clothes, at feeding himself or cooking, at judging art, listening to music, painting, fixing a car. But any new experiences or facts that enter his brain do not take up permanent residence. The patient with pure amnesia is always just emerging from time travel. His old memories are intact. What has happened to him in the last few seconds is crystal clear—the gap is in between.

As one such patient, a professional musician who developed amnesia after viral inflammation of the brain wrote in his diary: "2/20: Am just regaining consciousness." Five minutes later, he crossed out the

2/20 and wrote 2/25. Five minutes after that, he did the same thing again. And so it went.

A patient of mine with a tumor of the pineal gland, deep in the center of the head, suddenly developed amnesia when the tumor hemorrhaged, and the resulting blood clot pressed against critical areas of the brain. We had been friendly over the years during which I had been following her, but I had never met her family. Admitted to the hospital, with her family visiting, she introduced me to everyone: "Dr. Gordon, this is my mother and father, this is my brother, this is my sister, this is my friend." I was called away for a moment. When I returned, she looked at me with the same excitement: "Dr. Gordon, this is my father and mother, this is my brother, this is my sister, and this is my good friend." She acted *exactly* as she had before—the same delighted surprise, the same intonation, the same words. Her family looked at each other uncomprehendingly. Who could imagine such behavior? But this is how pure amnesia behaves.

Because his mind could get at *old* knowledge, and because his reasoning abilities were still intact, John could pass any IQ test with flying colors. He could recognize all the presidents, all the baseball figures and tell you the standing of every team. But even though John heard of the baseball strike, and tried to follow its developments every day, he could never really learn this new information. Hearing about the baseball strike was always a revelation to him. Whether he was told the players had been on strike for a day, then a week, then a month, he reacted as if hearing the news for the first time. His shock and dismay never varied: "How could they strike? I can't believe it! This'll ruin baseball!"

John also had other problems. He tried going back to school. But he could learn nothing. A new student had transferred from another school, but John could never learn who he was or his name. John's sister left for college. He was always puzzled why she was never in her room at their home.

Pure amnesia is fortunately quite rare. But it is an important condition for medical science because it shows us a very important part of the mechanism for memory in the human brain—the mechanism that consolidates temporary memories.

Such amnesia is seen in purest form in any disease that damages the inner temporal lobe, hippocampus, or thalamus, especially on both sides of the brain. Many diseases of the brain, some of which are described below, can cause damage to the inner parts of the temporal lobe, or to the thalamus, and can therefore interfere with the storage of new memories. In fact, *any* disease, regardless of its nature, that damages these regions will produce the same type of problem with memory. But most of the diseases that can and do affect these regions—including head injury, Alzheimer's disease, stroke, and encephalitis—damage far more of the brain than just the areas responsible for consolidating memories. Typically, these diseases produce problems with brain function that go far beyond memory loss alone.

Some of the more common or more notable conditions that can cause a *pure* amnesia include the following:

- **Surgery of the brain that removes the inner portions of *both* the temporal lobes, where the hippocampi are.** Such operations on *both* sides of the brain are almost never done now. But before their consequences came to be understood (in the early 1950s), several patients had the inner portions of their temporal lobes removed on both sides, to help cure their epilepsy or other diseases. One such patient, Henry M., is now famous for having one of the most profound, persistent, and best-studied examples of pure amnesia. He has had problems learning anything new, ever since his operation in *1953*.

- **Viral inflammations of the brain (viral encephalitis).** A variety of the herpes virus can (rarely) attack the inner regions of the temporal lobes. Many of the patients who survive this have difficulties learning new information. (Because of the more widespread damage, many such patients also have difficulty getting at their *old* information, too, unlike the purer amnestic syndrome. Some of these patients, for example, will have problems getting at their knowledge for very specific *categories* of information, of the type described in Chapter 34.)

- **Strokes.** Blockages of the blood vessels that supply the inner parts of the temporal lobes or thalamus can produce damage that produces pure amnesia. Usually, such strokes only occur on one side of the brain, so the resulting amnesia is not very severe. However, sometimes people do suffer strokes on *both* sides of the brain, in the same region. This may be due to two separate strokes, occurring one after the other, or two strokes happening simultaneously. One peculiarity of the way blood vessels supply the thalamus that often a single stroke can affect the blood vessels going to both sides.

▶ **Migraine.** The initial part of a migraine headache is due to spasm of the blood vessels. When this spasm affects the blood vessels supplying the inner parts of the temporal lobes or the thalamus, then it can cause amnesia. Usually, however, such amnesia is both temporary, and not very severe. The spasm generally resolves without any permanent damage being done. But it is possible, when the spasm happens repeatedly, for the affected area of the brain to suffer longer-lasting damage due to the lack of blood. Fortunately, only a very few people with repeated migraine attacks in this area have persistent problems with their memory.

▶ **Head injury.** Head injury can shake the brain inside the skull so that the inner portions of the temporal lobes bang against the skull. This can impair the function of these regions, and is probably one reason for the memory problems that occur after a concussion. Fortunately, in most people these memory problems disappear after a very short time—minutes to hours. Even when people have been knocked unconscious for up to fifteen minutes, their memory problems usually disappear after a few months. Unfortunately, in some people, some damage may remain even after relatively mild head injuries.

▶ **Missile wounds.** In one unusual case on record, N.A., a young man in the Navy, was having a mock duel with another, using miniature fencing foils. N.A. didn't duck when his opponent lunged. The result was that the foil went into N.A.'s right nostril, and then penetrated the skull at the base of his brain. The damage to his temporal lobe and his thalamus produced a pure amnesia that has lasted since the accident (in 1960), although it did improve gradually over the course of a number of years.

AMNESIA FROM PARTIAL DAMAGE

Sometimes, when the damage to the brain is only on one side, or is less severe, the amnesia is less severe. When this happens, the amnesia behaves strangely, and it may be far harder to detect. This was the case in a patient of mine who for a whole year was thought to have a purely psychiatric problem:

THE JOGGER WITH JUMBLED MEMORIES

Mrs. T. was 40 years old when I first saw her. She worked on an assembly line in a factory. Early every morning, before the kids got up, she went jogging.

One morning, while running, she suddenly developed a slight headache in the back of her head and her vision seemed to be blurred or double.

That morning she had problems finding her way to work. When she got there, things seemed somewhat unfamiliar to her, the people a little strange. She managed to find her place in line. It still felt strange to her, but as pieces began coming down the line, she found that she knew what to do. She bolted them in place and passed them on even though she felt as though she was just awakening from a dream, and she couldn't clear her head.

By the time she got home, her headache was gone and her vision had cleared up. But her husband and her children didn't seem quite right to her. Still, she seemed to be able to do what they expected of her without anybody noticing anything wrong.

After a few weeks of this, she told her husband how strange she felt. A psychologist thought she was depressed, but he asked that she be checked out by a neurologist anyway. A very careful neurologic exam found nothing wrong. An MRI scan of her brain did not show any abnormalities.

Mrs. T. continued in psychotherapy, although her husband still found her to be in a bit of a daze much of the time. She had problems remembering people's names, where she put things and even her bank balance. She was always bouncing checks as a result. She also seemed to have problems with even simple arithmetic facts.

Otherwise, Mrs. T. felt fine. She continued jogging, but had to be careful to stay on roads she knew well. If she tried a new route, she was likely to get lost and it would take her quite awhile to find her way back home.

She came to me a year after her problem began, complaining of memory problems. Her whole life from before that jogging episode still seemed unreal and faraway to her. She had worked out some ways to get around a lot of the problems by the time I saw her. Her husband now managed the household money and did the checkbook. Her children were grown up enough so that they were responsible for their own lunches and clothes and remembering significant events.

She kept a calendar to remind her of birthdays. She made it a point of jotting down people's names she felt she had to remember, and reviewed it daily. She put things only in familiar places so she wouldn't lose them. She drove on familiar streets, but she let her husband drive anywhere else.

Her neurologic exam was completely normal. She could see out of each eye, in every direction. There was no evidence of trouble in the far back of the brain. Despite her history of double vision, I found no problems with the way her eyes moved, affirming what the other neurologists had said almost a year before. Her IQ and her language functions were exactly normal.

But her memory for language-related things was much worse. In fact, she was in the bottom five percent of the population on the memory tests we gave her—not as abnormal as patients with Alzheimer's or pure amnesia can get, but clearly far worse than she had been before.

Mrs. T.'s memory for visual things—for pictures and for faces—was actually above average. There was nothing else wrong with her intellect that we could find. We did try testing her with pictures of famous people, but she admitted to us that she had never really paid much attention to the news anyway, so we all wound up concluding that was not a very good test for her.

It was clear that Mrs. T. had an amnesia, a difficulty with learning new things and, by her story, some problems with remembering older material. Since she was right-handed, and since there was no history of left-handedness, this implied the damage had to be on the left side of her brain. And the most likely problem, given her story of a sudden onset with double vision, was that she had a small stroke involving the blood vessels in the back of the brain.

As we have discussed, there are two areas of the brain where relatively small areas of damage can cause such memory problems—in the hippocampus and in the thalamus, which is a cluster of nerve cells deep in the middle of the brain.

When Mrs. T.'s MRI was repeated, it gave us the answer: Mrs. T. had, in fact, suffered a small stroke. There was a small hole in her thalamus, indicating that a stroke had occurred when Mrs. T. experienced her headache while jogging. And the hole was not just in any part of her thalamus, but in exactly the region of the thalamus that is known to cause memory problems in monkeys. This type of damage is relatively rare in people, but it does result in memory problems.

It was not surprising that the tiny area of the stroke had not shown up on her previous MRI the year before. Even though the brain tissue in that area was probably dead when her first MRI scan was done, it would not yet have been cleared away by the brain. Unlike skin, which heals by scarring, the brain heals by clearing away the dead tissue and opening up a hole. That is why it may take several months for a stroke to show up clearly on an MRI scan or CT scan. The hole in Mrs. T.'s brain would have been too small to see at the time of her first MRI.

Mrs. T. had a work-up to make sure she had no definable reason for having a stroke. None were found. She tried a few techniques to enhance her memory, but most of them she had already discovered for herself. The others seemed to be too much work for what she needed from her memory. A year later, her memory problem was basically unchanged, but because she and her family had found ways to work around it, she was more comfortable with it, and decided to just get on with her life.

TEMPORARY PURE AMNESIA

Some diseases only temporarily damage the regions of the brain responsible for storing new information. Blockage of blood vessels, which can cause a stroke, can be temporary. When it is, the result is called a *transient ischemic attack*, or TIA. When these affect the blood vessels that supply the regions responsible for permanent storage of memories, the result can be a dramatic—but temporary—amnesia. Migraine and head injury are also causes of temporary amnesias. Head injury will be described in Chapter 32, because it is often a more complex problem. But the patient described next was fortunate to have had only temporary amnesia—but unfortunate in that she had it happen several times!

"WHERE AM I AND HOW DID I GET HERE!?"

Mrs. G. thought the man's voice on the telephone was reassuring. The only problem was that she didn't know it was her husband. She didn't know where she was, she didn't know why she was there, and she had no idea who I was either. Outside of that, she felt fine.

This was the third time this kind of thing had happened to Mrs. G. She was a 55-year-old woman who was working as the bookkeeper in the family business.

The first episode had happened four years before. To quote from the published report of the case (by the author of this book and his professor):

"She awoke without incident and drove nearly 40 miles to a routine appointment with a gynecologist at 9:30 a.m. The gynecologist remembered her as acting normally, showing him pictures of her family, and carrying on a normal conversation. She then went to visit an aunt.

"While there, she was asked about her recent grandchild and did not remember the child's name. She then began to get very thirsty. At about 2:30 p.m. she suddenly looked up and said that she could not remember any of the events of the day, and asked what she was doing there.

"She had to be told about the events earlier that day, and even called up her gynecologist to confirm them. Initially, she could not remember events of the previous weekend either, but gradually was able to remember everything between the time she began to drive in the morning to just before looking up in bewilderment. She remembered subsequent events quite well. A later medical evaluation was normal.

"She was well until [three years later]. She planned and started a bridge club meeting at her home at 10:00 a.m., serving her company well, carrying on conversation, and playing a good hand of bridge. In the afternoon, she was telephoned about a grandson's injury. She drove (with a friend) 40 miles to her daughter's residence to be of assistance, but had some difficulty remembering the route and got lost twice. When she arrived, she summoned her husband, and they started back home with one of her grandchildren. While they were driving, at about 4:40 p.m., she suddenly asked why she was on the highway and why her grandson was with them. She seemed somewhat confused, according to her husband, and was again very thirsty for several hours. She had no memory of the day's events until after the time she became thirsty in the car."

Although Mrs. G. felt fine, all of her physicians were worried that something serious was happening, so she was admitted to the hospital. I was one of her doctors there. In the hospital, everything was fine. Her memory was completely normal. She could remember digits forwards and backwards, remember all the objects I gave her, tell me about current events and past presidents, and recall what had happened to her during the day, all with no difficulty.

A CT scan of her brain, which shows the structure of the brain, did not show any abnormalities. And examination of her brain waves, measured through electrodes on her head, did not show any seizures that could have temporarily jumbled her mind and her memory.

But the standard brain wave test is not a perfect test for seizures. Mrs. G. could have had a seizure which left no traces. Or she could have been having seizures so small that the brain wave test could not pick them up. Or the seizures could have been in areas of the brain that were hidden from the electrodes used in the standard brain wave test. To check this last possibility, her brain waves were also examined through special electrodes inserted through her nose, resting against the very top of the back of her throat. In this position, the electrodes record from the bottom of the brain, near the temporal lobes. But these electrodes also failed to show any evidence of seizures.

Mrs. G. presented her own history to the assembled neurologists at Johns Hopkins one morning, and then chose to walk back to her room herself. The route was a complicated one, but Mrs. G. navigated it with ease. But once back in her room, she called for the nurse. She told the nurses she had trouble remembering how she had gotten back. She was examined almost immediately. The only thing wrong was with her memory.

She could not remember anything new. Attempts at making what she was to try to remember more distinctive or more unusual did not help. She was asked, "Imagine that you have in your arms a locomotive, a very heavy locomotive. Can you imagine it? Now, imagine that you are wrapping this enormous and heavy locomotive in newspaper. Can you imagine that?" But fifteen seconds later, she was totally unable to remember not just the locomotive, but even having been asked to remember anything at all.

"Over the course of the examination, [she] did not seem to assimilate any of the new events or exercises, their temporal series, nor the names of the examiners. [She] would ask, in a very polite but stereotyped manner as if it were a new event, 'Excuse me, I know that this is a silly question, but what am I doing here?'

"The examiner made exactly the same reply each time. 'You are in this place because of some trouble with memory which you seem to have. You will be well very soon.' This same conversation took place 15 to 20 times, with the same degree of surprise on the part of the patient. No recollection of it was ever noticed. [She] was repeatedly urged to try to learn the name of the examiner. Rehearsing the name aloud did not help.... Only by the end of the interview was the patient able to remember (incorrectly) a similar sounding name. From that time on she was able to retrieve the incorrect name, but always with effort. And despite correction, it was always incorrect."

Information she must have learned before the episode was unavailable as well. "She did not know the date or the year, where she was or how many days she had been there. When her resident physician returned, she failed to recognize him, although she stated that she felt reassured by his presence. (In a second entrance he was spontaneously called by his name). Family events were vaguely remembered..."

"She did not remember anything of importance about the terms 'Bicentennial year' or 'election year,' [although this was when these events took place]. Although she lived in Washington, D.C., she did not remember the president or his officials. She did not remember the previous president or Watergate [which had happened just a few years before]. She was unable to remember the president whose name began with 'K' (Kennedy). Once reminded of his name, which she recognized immediately, she was not able to remember what happened to him. Although she recalled a 'catastrophe,' she could not remember a detail. Given a choice of four cities as the site, she hesitatingly picked Washington. She could not recall the assassin and the name Oswald was unfamiliar to her. She could not remember who Roosevelt was, although she could explain what Pearl Harbor meant."

".... She was able to enumerate objects within a category normally (furniture, people in uniforms, fruits, means of transportation). Given a set of characteristics of an object, she was able to name the object—that is, television set, microscope. She was able to give a fairly good explanation of how an airplane flies. She explained in detail the rules of contract bridge playing and some strategies."

Within a few more minutes, she seemed to recover completely. She had no memory of having talked about her own case as the conference, but she did recognize the resident physician and knew his name. She was worried that her problem could be psychological.

"The next day the patient recognized the examiner and remembered seeing him some time before ('perhaps a day'). She knew his name, but this had been mentioned inadvertently to her that morning. There was only a very vague recollection of what had been done during the previous day's examination. She could not remember any of the details of the various tasks. She misplaced her position and the examiner's, and misplaced other physicians and their roles. However, she was able perfectly to recall ... information [from before the episode] that she had been unable to remember during the episode."

After this episode ended, Mrs. G. was completely normal. Her memory was fine, except for gaps corresponding to the times she had been in the middle of the episodes themselves. She never had another episode. What probably caused the problem for Mrs. G. were repeated transient ischemic attacks (TIAs), although we could not be sure. Migraine was a possibility, but she had never really had a migraine attack before.

RECOVERY FROM AMNESIA

In most cases of pure amnesia, the amnesia has been permanent, or nearly so. Any improvement has been relatively slight, and often only seen after a number of years.

One of the exceptional—and very fortunate!—aspects of John's amnesia was that it began to improve. Gradually, after some months, John's memory began to return. He began to have a few dim recollections: a doctor at one institution, a friend's visit. Gradually those episodes became more and more frequent, their associated memories more and more definite. After several months during which nothing had seemed to improve, and several more when only the faintest glimmers were present, finally John's memory began to work again.

The difference in John's case from those of other cases of pure amnesia may be due to a number of factors. His brain was young, with a young brain's recuperative powers. He was very intelligent and in a very intelligent and supportive family. If his remaining brain cells could benefit from coaxing, from family involvement and support, his were in a position to do so. And the insult that John suffered to his brain was perhaps less severe than it could have been. In an older individual, the damage could have been due to a complete stoppage of the heart. Or the loss of blood may have been due to a block in the blood vessel itself, with no chance of a swift return. John presumably never completely lost his flow of blood, and his blood vessels remained wide open to move in what little blood was still available, and to move out any toxic products of brain metabolism.

Whatever the reason, the happy result was that John's ability to save memories has been coming back. While probably still not completely normal, it is now working well enough for him to keep track of events, do fairly well in school, and hold down a part-time job. He now knows about the baseball strike—and also that it is now over. However, he is too busy right now catching up with his life to pay much attention to baseball.

29

Temporary "Amnesias" and Everyday "Blackouts"

TEMPORARY "AMNESIAS" AND "gaps" are very common experiences, perhaps for some people more than others. If you are not paying attention to something (for example, in driving) then there are at least two reasons you will not remember what happened: it never got firmly implanted in your mind in the first place (you were not really paying attention), and even if it did circulate in your brain, the locking-in mechanisms of memory (the consolidation system) didn't work because there was no need (what was happening was not interesting enough to you to save permanently). As a result, when you think back to where you had driven, you cannot remember where you had been or what you had been doing. Until downtown Baltimore became more developed, I would occasionally have truckers complain to me that they could not remember passing through the city. Nothing would be wrong with their memory. The city just was not interesting enough to be memorable! (Now, of course, it is unforgettable.)

One other aspect of these gaps: because learning did not occur in the first place, there is no memory to be retrieved. No amount of straining will bring back the memory that was not locked in to begin with. In this sense, these gaps are like the pure amnesia that can occur with brain disease.

These lapses in memory are definitely accentuated by distraction, fatigue, and by alcohol and other drugs which interfere with the normal memory process.

Alcohol is something of an anesthetic. When you are drinking, although you may be awake and functioning, and you think reasonably well, the alcohol is actually blunting your emotional responses and also probably more directly blunting your brain's consolidation process. Therefore, when you are a little bit tipsy, although you may be acting normally, you may not be storing information well. As a result, you may have no memory for the party or not a very good memory for what went on there. And you will not remember people's names or events. Drinkers often experience as a result what is called an alcoholic "blackout." But this particular gap is not due to a true "blacking out"; there is no loss of consciousness. Instead, even though the person is awake, memories were "blacked out" because they were never locked into the person's head in the first place.

30

"This Woman Is Not My Wife!"—Other Memory Problems from Brain Disease

MR. M'S WIFE could barely hold back the tears. Mr. M. himself could not understand what the problem was.

"Lady, do I know you?" Mr. M. asked. *"Should we be uh . . . like this?"*

Mrs. M. quickly dropped his hand, which she had been holding.

Mr. M. did not recognize his own daughter, either. Nor did he know where he was. Outside of that, there was nothing wrong with his brain.

Mr. M. had developed an encephalitis, an inflammation of the brain caused by a viral infection that strikes the nerve cells. The encephalitis's fiercest attack was on Mr. M.'s temporal lobes. The dead nerve cells of his hippocampus could no longer signal him to learn anything new.

But what was even worse, from his family's point of view, was that other nerve cells in his temporal lobe had been damaged. These nerve cells were the repository of his visual memories, and of his memories of sounds and voices. With them gone, even though he could still hear, speak and understand, and even though he was still physically fit at 50 years old, his ability to recognize his family had nearly been wiped out.

Memories of his own identity were also badly damaged. He knew his name, but it took a little prompting, and he said it with a little less certainty than would normally be the case. He could recognize himself in the mirror, but was surprised at how old he looked.

Mr. M. had suffered much more extensive damage to his brain than had John, the young athlete discussed earlier. In John's case, only the hippocampus was damaged. So information that came into the brain could be processed, and existing memories could be retrieved. But in Mr. M.'s case, either the retrieval mechanism for existing memories, or the memories themselves, were damaged. So either he could not get at the memories of who his wife and family were, or these memories had been wiped out altogether. Whatever the actual cause, the net result was the same.

Parts of his memory had not been destroyed by his condition. He could remember some general features of his wife—or of wives in general. He could tell us how attractive she was, how sympathetic she was, what a good wife and mother she had been. He would explain this to the woman sitting across from him, without recognizing who she was at all.

So he was always puzzled when this woman would burst into tears. What was the matter with that woman? Was anything wrong with his wife? Were we keeping anything from him? We assured him that his wife was fine, but of course she was anything but.

HONEY, I KNOW YOUR VOICE BUT NOT YOUR FACE

Mr. F. had also had encephalitis, but not as devastating as Mr. M.'s. Mr. F. actually seemed to do very well after his illness. He tried to go back to work, but had some memory problems that made it difficult for him to follow day-to-day events.

Mr. F. was concealing a larger secret from us: he could no longer recognize his wife by her looks. He only knew her by her voice. He realized this one day when he went to pick her up outside the supermarket and discovered that he could not tell her apart from any other woman standing there. Only when she called out to him did he recognize who she was.

Mr. F.'s encephalitis carved his brain's memories less extensively than Mr. M.'s. The disease destroyed just memories for faces or access to these memories in Mr. F. In keeping with this, Mr. F.'s damage was much worse on the right side of his brain than it was on the left, although he clearly had damage on both sides.

31

"Girl Loses Identity, and Saves the Plot"—How the Media Portrays Amnesia*

Ingrid Bergman and Gregory Peck in *Spellbound*

WE HAVE SEEN cases of pure amnesia in the preceding chapters. Watch the movies or TV, and this is how "amnesia" looks:

> It is Dr. Anthony Edwards' first day on the job as the new director of a small but esteemed psychiatric hospital.
>
> When he arrives, he is whisked off to a formal lunch. There he meets a number of stodgy staff psychiatrists and quickly learns their names. When the hospital's only female psychiatrist, Dr. Constance Peterson, enters the room, their eyes meet, and an atmosphere of anticipation fills the room. It is obvious that Dr. Edwards is immediately entranced with this attractive and competent doctor. The feeling turns out to be mutual. Dr. Peterson and Dr. Edwards fall in love.
>
> However, it is not long before Constance senses that something is amiss. Anthony confesses that he is not Dr. Anthony

---

* This chapter by Rachel Wilder and Barry Gordon, M.D., Ph.D., with Martha P. Trachtenberg

Edwards after all, and not even a doctor. But he has no idea who he really is. "I can't remember anything—except that I love you!" he declares.

Consumed with guilt because he believes he must have killed the real Dr. Edwards, he flees. His only clue to his own lost identity is a silver cigarette case engraved with the initials "J.B."

Dr. Peterson tracks him down in a New York City hotel and proceeds with great determination to help him remember who he is. She eventually helps him figure out that his real name is John Ballantine. The real Dr. Edwards was murdered, but Ballantine is not the killer.

Together Ballantine and Dr. Peterson strive to discover the hidden memory that made him believe he could commit murder—which turns out to be the witnessing of the accidental death of his brother in childhood and the mistaken conviction that it was all his fault. Suddenly he also remembers that the real killer was the doctor whom Dr. Edwards was to replace as head of the hospital.

The murderer is caught. We are left with the sense that John Ballantine and Dr. Constance Peterson will live peacefully and guiltlessly ever after—together.

—plot of Alfred Hitchcock's 1945 thriller, *Spellbound*

What's wrong with this picture?

Movies like *Spellbound* show us what amnesia is *not*. It is a prime example of the Hollywood-ization of amnesia. Though it is a pleasure to watch young Ingrid Bergman and Gregory Peck wend their way through this early on-screen exploration of memory loss, Hitchcock did play fast and lose with the facts in his portrayal of an amnestic's lot. His romanticized version of amnesia is, in many ways, the *opposite* of real amnesia!—the pure amnesia resulting from brain disease.

Movie amnestics like John Ballantine block out their oldest, most ingrained memories—their names. But in pure amnesia due to brain disease, patients lose the ability to remember *new* things. They lose their most recent memories, not their oldest ones. Real amnestics rarely—if ever—forget their own names. What they cannot do is learn new names. They can hardly store any new information at all.

Yet in *Spellbound*, our hero strides confidently into a roomful of strangers on his first day as the new head of the hospital, learns their names with ease, and takes charge. He even asks in a later scene: "How can a man lose his memory, his name, everything he's ever known, and still talk like this, as if he were quite sane?"

Only with the screenwriters' help.

In real life, victims of true amnesia—amnesia from brain injury—find it difficult to retain new information—such as strangers' names—and most would not be up to the task of impersonating anyone else.

In real life, the oldest memories, such as the knowledge of one's identity, are almost always the last to go. Never is somebody perfectly intact *except* for forgetting his identity.

Real-life amnesia differs from its celluloid counterpart in another way, too. Pure amnesia is actually quite rare in real life. Even a neurologist who specializes in memory is not likely to encounter many patients who have pure organic amnesia—at least not without other serious medical conditions.

A PROLIFERATION OF AMNESIA PLOTS

Yet in the movies, soap operas and sitcoms, the disorder appears in epidemic proportions. The radio soap operas of the 1940s would often bring in a juicy case of memory loss, and since then, plots involving amnesia have proliferated (see Sidebar: You Must Remember This....).

Humans have not been the only ones affected by this epidemic of amnesia. Muppets, too, have been stricken.

In the *Muppets Take Manhattan* (1987), Kermit the Frog is hit by a taxi. He wakes up with no memory of who he is. "Your case is hopeless," he is told. "Why don't you just go out and find a nice job and make a new life for yourself?"

In no time, Kermit becomes a successful advertising copywriter, and immediately adapts to life in the fast lane. He quickly picks up the names of his new colleagues—Bill, Jill, Phil, and Will. He has lost none of his judgment or language ability. He has however, lost his entire past, including his memory of his engagement to Miss Piggy.

He is forcefully reminded of this by the ever-forceful Miss Piggy, when they chance to meet. But he is incredulous. "Engaged to *you*—a pig?" exclaims Kermit (heedless of the compromise *she* made in agreeing to marry a frog!).

Kermit's encounter with Miss Piggy also provides a cure for his problem. Insulted, Miss Piggy wallops him across the room. With the blow to his head, his memory suddenly returns. He remembers his commitment, and all is well.

People with real amnesia cannot just make a new life like a Muppet

amnestic can. Most victims of real amnesia have a hard time retaining
new information for any more than a few seconds. Kermit could not
possibly have remembered all those names and become a crackerjack
advertising copywriter overnight. And only in the movies can a blow to
the head *restore* memory! In real life, a second blow to the head often
produces even more damage.

The 1987 movie *Overboard*, with Goldie Hawn and Kurt Russell, provides another classic example of Hollywood-ized amnesia:

> Joanna, a spoiled blond socialite who is very rich and very
> rude, falls off her yacht one evening. She washes ashore, and
> ends up in the hospital of a small Oregon town—with no
> memory of who she is. The doctors say she's suffering from
> temporary amnesia. No one can predict how long it will take
> for her memory to return. Her husband gladly abandons
> her and takes off on the yacht.
>
> Dean, a struggling local carpenter (and single dad) whom
> Joanna had hired and then refused to pay, recognizes her
> picture on the local news and decides to take revenge. He
> goes to the hospital and claims that the amnesia victim is
> really his wife, Annie, the mother of his four unruly sons,
> and she is released. Dean takes her to his ramshackle house
> in the woods, where he demands that she cook, clean and
> care for the delinquent boys.
>
> "Annie," a bit surprised at the hellish quality of her new
> life, nevertheless accepts it as her lot, since she has no mem-
> ory of anything else. With amazing speed and acuity Annie
> picks up the finer points of housekeeping, cooking, mother-
> hood, and even chain saw operation. Despite a few humor-
> ous mishaps, she is soon baking perfect chocolate cream pies
> and teaching her youngest "son" how to read. It is not long
> before Dean begins to appreciate all she has done for his
> family, and they fall in love.
>
> But one day her real husband shows up to reclaim her. In
> a flash, her memory comes back completely. She returns to
> her pampered life on the yacht as Joanna.
>
> But she is not the same. Her amnesia experience has made
> her kinder and gentler. So she decides to leave her buffoon
> of a husband and go "home" to Dean and the boys—who at
> that moment happen to be chasing after the yacht in a Coast
> Guard boat. Annie and Dean both jump into the sea and
> swim into each other's arms, finally reunited.

If *Overboard's* Annie had been a real amnestic rather than a figment of Hollywood's imagination, she would never have been able to learn the names of her new husband and all his children so quickly—if at all. And, of course, she would not have forgotten her own name.

LOSING YOUR IDENTITY: NOT LIKELY!

There are several ways your brain guarantees that your oldest memories, such as who you are, who your parents and brothers and sisters are, who your wife is, will be the most resistant to being wiped out by disease or damage.

One way the brain preserves important memories is by *consolidation.* A sort of hardening process goes on after a memory is laid down—like concrete setting. It is not clear if it is each individual neural connection that gets stronger, or if more neural connections are recruited with time. But the net result of this hardening process is that the memory is more resistant to disruption.

Consolidation is strongest for our memories of our names, the names of our parents, and for our earliest experiences because these are the memories that have been *repeated* the most in our lives. Just think of how often you say and hear your own name over in the course of a lifetime—many thousands of times! All other things being equal, a memory that is repeated will be better ingrained in your memory than one that is not.

With repetition, your memory builds numerous connections or *associations* to your name and similar facts. You hear your name, you see it, you write it, you read it. You may sometimes dread hearing it—as when you are about to be called on in class. And you may sometimes dread producing it—as when you have to sign your income tax return. But all of these repetitions count for memory. This multitude of situations and contexts builds up a dense web of connections to your name in your memory. This web gives you numerous ways to get at the memory of your name, and to get it out as you need it. Even if many strands of this web are cut—by disease—you will still have many alternate routes leading to your name.

The simple fact that your name is *important* also strengthens the memory of it. The importance of your name to you drives your brain to make the consolidation stronger, the web more extensive, its connections firmer, than for just about anything else. To your brain, nothing is as significant as your name.

Finally, you learn your name *early* in life, before you have many competing memories. Your name can stake out prime open space in your mind and brain. Things may get cluttered later, but your name (and some other early memories) will probably enjoy this special advantage.

What this all means is that the memory of one's identity is so deeply embedded nothing short of tearing apart the brain wipes it out. That happens in very, very few conditions.

WHEN AMNESIA'S ALL IN THE MIND BUT NOT IN THE BRAIN

If our oldest, most ingrained memories are the last to go, how do experts explain those who claim they have forgotten their names but otherwise seem to be alert, able to take in and remember new information, and are perfectly able to get through the day? And why do such stories seem to be so common?

Most of these cases are not due to brain disease. Their brains are working just fine. So there is no *organic* cause for their memory loss. What's wrong does not come from brain disease, but from a mind problem. Its cause is *nonorganic.* Nonorganic amnesia is the kind most often portrayed in the movies.

Nonorganic amnesias come in two varieties—conscious and unconscious.

Conscious, or feigned amnesia—also known as faking or malingering— is often incited by the need to escape a crime, financial problem or unhappy relationship. Many such cases wind up in the newspapers, where they are presented as mysterious problems. Only later is the truth revealed. One such example from my own experience turned out to be a gamblin' man who had been unlucky that evening. "I don't know who I am, but I feel fine otherwise," he told me. His story was a bit suspicious from the start.

"John Doe" didn't know his name any more than we did. He had been brought to the hospital after he had been found by the police, wandering around without reason or explanation. He had no more than a day's growth of beard, and his work shirt and jeans were no more rumpled than the clothes of the interns who saw him. So he couldn't have been wandering for long. He had no wallet or keys.

He had no alcohol on his breath, and none in his blood. His medical and neurologic exams were completely normal. All his blood tests came back normal, an MRI of his brain was normal, and a brain wave test did not show any abnormal electrical rhythms in the brain. There was nothing to suggest a brain disease. Could he be faking?

The residents were fairly certain that his amnesia was not due to anything wrong in his brain, but they asked me to see him anyway. I found Mr. Doe sitting on the edge of his bed watching TV. He was very interested in daytime TV. He told me he had never seen such shows before (and this seemed plausible).

He had no problem speaking or understanding what was said to him. He told me the last thing he remembered was walking through the neighborhood where the police found him, at night. He denied having any knowledge of his name, his age, brothers, sisters or parents. He said he did not know where he had grown up or where he lived. He said he had no idea what he did for a living or where he worked.

I could not trick him on anything. No matter what I tried, I could not get him to talk about a memory from before the time he had been picked up. Not news events, not sports, not the economy, not crime, not even the weather.

So, in desperation, I began going over details of the neighborhood where he had been found. It happened to be an area I had driven through on occasion over the past fifteen years. He had a very good memory of the same street corners. After all, he reminded me, he had walked around them many times on the evening he was found.

Then, completely by accident, I found the key into his old memories—because of my bad one. I misremembered one of the buildings as having been a library.

"Oh no", he corrected me. "It was a library once, but they shut it down last year. They ran out of money."

I decided to play amnestic myself (which wasn't hard).

"What about that Chinese restaurant?" I asked.

"Oh," he corrected me. "You must mean the pizza parlor. The Chinese restaurant went bankrupt. The food was terrible."

We both agreed on that. So we had similar standards in Chinese food, but more importantly, he had several memories that went back to before the time of his alleged amnesia.

What was striking about Mr. Doe—although not unusual for this kind of patient—is that he did not show the slightest trace of anxiety about his condition or what we were doing for it. Either he was incredibly macho, had hysterical memory loss, or he was a malingerer.

We reassured Mr. Doe that although his memory loss was unusual, it was not unknown to medical science. We told him (as was true) that we expected him to make a full recovery. And we told him (as was also true) that often these recoveries happen very quickly, within minutes or hours. We also told him the police were making some progress in tracking down who he was.

"Police!" He was quite startled, and for the first time he looked worried. "Why do you need the police? I'm sick! You don't need the police!"

I told him the police had to be involved because he did not know his own identity, and he might have been listed as a missing person. We were able to tell him, in fact, that with the clues about his neighborhood that he had provided, the police thought they had found a woman who thought she might know of him.

Mr. Doe seemed to be mulling this over when we left the room. A few hours later, his memory was back. And he had a tale to tell, albeit somewhat sheepishly.

He had gotten paid that Friday afternoon and was taking the money home to his wife. But he passed a store that sold Instant Jackpot tickets on the way, in that very same neighborhood that he and I both knew. He had a good premonition about a number, and he decided to increase his odds of winning by putting all of his money down on it.

When he did not win, he was afraid to go home. We did not press him on what had been going through his mind in the next few hours after that. But he was relieved to get the story off his chest, his wife was relieved to find him safe, and he went home with a better appreciation of daytime television.

In faked amnesia, the person's memory is actually quite good for anything new. He says that the past is completely closed to him; usually, he is not very worried about this. In fact, these are often the people who insist they should not be in the hospital. They get quite nervous when we begin asking questions and try to track down their real identities.

Men fake amnesia more than women. They have no knowledge of their prior life at all, they claim. Yet, like amnestics in the movies, they can remember new information perfectly well, and they are willing to learn a new job. They are often very nervous about memory testing—not surprisingly, since they do not know what answers are "right" or "wrong." They often give approximate answers even for things they should know, or make ridiculous mistakes: "7" and "5" is "11." "2" plus "3" is "6." "10" plus "15" is "1015." A "real" amnestic would not give bizarre answers. A real amnestic would either know the answer or not, and tell the examiner exactly that. If a real amnestic were to "guess," the guess, like a normal person's, would not be completely wild; it would look like a reasonable error.

I'll sign my brother-in-law's name till I get my memory back.

Feigning patients often will not try to find out about their past. Frequently, they will even try to check out of the hospital when they discover their past is being investigated. Sometimes, you can persuade them to have "miraculous" recoveries. Often, it turns out that they have committed some crime, are escaping debts, or have left the wife and children, and are "starting over."

Unlike the case of the "gamblin' man," newspaper accounts of people found wandering around with no memory of who they are, or how they got to be where they are, with no evidence of any physical injury—often turn out to be *unconscious, nonorganic amnesia* (also called *hysterical* amnesia). Often the victim is a woman who has had a strong emotional trauma: a death in the family, a traumatic separation, a revelation of a husband's infidelity. One such case was widely reported in 1981:

"It was a strange situation."

So said Sgt. George Schueler, the policeman who led the search in the spring of 1981 for the identity of a woman found in a Florida park, naked, near starvation, and suffering from almost complete amnesia.

He was referring, however, to the way she had lived before she lost her memory.

Cheryl Ann Tomiczek had left her home in Chicago as a young woman, in the company of a man twenty years her senior. They moved to Florida, where she led an increasingly reclusive existence, culminating in his boarding up all the windows of their home. Schueler said "I think he was very, very protective of her....She was a prisoner of love."

How she went from the love prison to the woods was never established.

A national missing persons search followed her discovery, until the Tomiczeks stepped forward. They had last heard from her seven years before, and they flew to Florida immediately. They recognized her immediately, but Cheryl had to be convinced that she was part of the family; she didn't know them at all. Her doctor observed that "only in the annals of movie script writing do we have a meeting of this kind and instant recognition."

Women like Cheryl Ann Tomiczek are not consciously "faking it." Those who seem to have this kind of unconscious, nonorganic amnesia typically lose their knowledge of their identities, and of any other information directly related to themselves. They nonetheless also have completely intact intelligence and the ability to learn anything new. Frequently, they are not very worried about their memory loss. But they do try hard on memory testing. They usually show a good knowledge of past events so long as those events don't involve memories of *themselves*. Such people may be able to describe Kennedy's assassination, but not tell you what they themselves were doing then. This is *very* unusual in *organic* amnesia, the amnesia due to brain disease.

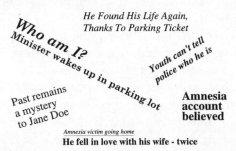

As with malingered amnesia, in unconscious, nonorganic amnesia, memories tend to come back suddenly, in a flood. Often, the sudden recovery of memories is triggered by the appearance of relatives, who recognize pictures of the amnestic in the newspapers, show up to claim her and tell what they know of her story. When the amnesias reported in the newspapers are not blatantly fake, they are more likely to be of this unconscious, non organic form. The following stories were adapted from newspaper accounts in the early 1980s:

"Hi, honey, I'm home."

Picture it. Christmas morning, 1985, in Larchmont, New York. Mrs. James McDonnell was in her kitchen, having just returned from church, when the doorbell rang. When she opened it, she saw the husband who had vanished fifteen years before.

"He had a beard and looked like Santa Claus," Anne McDonnell said. "I thought it was a joke, then I recognized him."

James McDonnell attributed his fifteen year blackout to a series of four head injuries. He said that after the last, a car accident, he had stepped out to clear his head with fresh air, and "The next thing I knew, I was in Philadelphia." He had no wallet and could only remember his first name, so he borrowed "Peters" from a nearby sign, and it was as Jim Peters that he became a short order cook, a position he held until another whack on the head restored his memory.

In the meantime, Mrs. McDonnell had him declared dead and had collected his life insurance money. Still, she was thrilled to have him back. "It's like a fairy tale," she said.

As of last report, she was planning to have him declared legally alive, and he wanted his post office job back.

"License and registration, please."

A routine traffic ticket turned into something a bit more unusual for Officer Mike Kaulfuss of Minneapolis one cold December day in 1980. When he checked the license plate of Jim Cossan's car, there were three warrants from the county, and his dispatcher said "There's something strange about this guy. Bring him in."

Upon their arrival, they received a report via teletype that Jim was a missing person from Florida, the son of Frank and Frances Cosson.

It seems that he had found himself in Los Angeles International Airport two years before, with no idea who he was.

In his pockets, he found a smudged crew list from a merchant marine vessel, with the name "Jim Coss-n" at the top. A private detective he hired assumed the missing letter was an "a", and shortly thereafter informed Jim that his entire family had drowned when Hurricane Camille hit New Orleans in 1969.

As it turned out, Mr. Cossan was actually Mr. Cosson. He had indeed lost his family, but not to a hurricane. Upon his return from a job at sea, a little while before he found himself in the LA airport, his wife told him that she was leaving him and taking the children. The shock of the divorce led to a two-year loss of memory. During this period of "amnesia," Mr. Cosson moved to Minneapolis, fell in love, and got married. He never did get around to telling his second wife that he couldn't recall a thing about his past.

After the happy discovery, he flew to Florida to be reintroduced to his folks, and then returned to his new family in Minneapolis to prepare for the "greatest Christmas of our lives."

"The first thing I thought was, 'Where am I?' Then I saw a sign that read Sheraton Houston. Then I was scared."

The owners of the Sheraton would doubtless find that reaction surprising, but in Rev. John C. Hartman's case, there was good reason for apprehension. He did not know who he was.

In the summer of 1981, Rev. Hartman disappeared for six days after a boating trip near his home in Tennessee. Police dragged the river for his body after his empty boat was found trapped in some trees. Imagine their surprise when he turned up alive and well in Texas, with not a clue as to how he had gotten there. When he "came to" in a parking lot, he walked into a hotel lobby, tidied up in their rest room, and headed for the police station. Within hours, he was identified, and had a tearful telephone reunion with his wife.

Upon his return home, however, he found his congregation split between those who believed his tale of amnesia, and those of little faith. Two years later, he had given up his pastorship, gotten a divorce, surrendered his credentials as a minister, and found a job with a road-building equipment company.

As Reverend Hartman's case illustrates, it may be very hard to tell an unconscious, hysterical amnesia from a faked one.

Why unconscious, nonorganic amnesias occur is still a mystery. Emotional trauma can sometimes trigger a mild form of retrograde amnesia for the specific event, but usually not enough to suppress memory of the event completely. And certainly the suppression caused by an emotional event does not extend to the person's identity and *all* other personal memories, especially not without touching other memories from around the same times in the past.

The "amnesias" described in this section are either fake or hysterical. There is nothing physically wrong with the brain. There are some amnesias that are truly bizarre, but where the brain is clearly at fault. There are other amnesias that are bizarre, but it is hard to tell if they are real or fake. Some more amnesias—and their causes—are described in the next several chapters.

YOU MUST REMEMBER THIS . . .

Amnesia, plot device supreme. It's been a favorite of screenwriters for the last fifty years, and for good reason; it opens up a world of possibilities. Here's a sample of Hollywood's take on memory, decade by decade:

1920s

The Gold Rush, 1925

1930s

As You Desire Me, 1932
Hallelujah, I'm a Bum, 1933
Remember Last Night?, 1935
The Walking Dead, 1936
The Man Who Lived Again, 1936
Two in the Dark, 1936
Ticket to Paradise, 1936
Dangerous Intrigue, 1936
Charlie Chan at the Opera, 1936
Missing, Believed Married, 1937
Strange Experiment, 1937
Rascals, 1938
Remember?, 1939

1940s

Lost on the West Front, 1940
The Great Dictator, 1940
I Love You Again, 1940
Street of Memories, 1940
A Chump at Oxford, 1940
Sullivan's Travels, 1941
Missing Ten Days, 1941
Random Harvest, 1942
Street of Chance, 1942
Dangerously They Live, 1942
Crossroads, 1942
Crime Doctor, 1943
Hangover Square, 1944
The Brighton Strangler, 1945
Identity Unknown, 1945
Two O'Clock Courage, 1945
Without Love, 1945
Spellbound, 1945
Love Letters, 1945

Power of the Whistler, 1945
Black Angel, 1946
Somewhere in the Night, 1946
Crime Doctor's Man Hunt, 1946
The Unknown, 1946
Crack-Up, 1946
Black Angel, 1946
The October Moon, 1947
A Double Life, 1947
Lost Honeymoon, 1947
While I Live, 1947
Singapore, 1947
Possessed, 1947
Girl in the Painting, 1948
The Crooked Way, 1949
The Clay Pigeon, 1949

1950s

A Tale of Five Women, 1951
Her Panelled Door, 1951
Beware, My Lovely, 1952
Home at Seven, 1952
Man in the Dark, 1953
The Long Wait, 1954
Blackout, 1954
The Stranger Came Home, 1954
The Constant Husband, 1955
Anastasia, 1956
Istanbul, 1957
The Haunted Strangler, 1958
Female Fiends, 1958

1960s

Forger of London, 1961
Sundays & Cybéle, 1962
The Manchurian Candidate, 1962
Mr. Arkadin, 1962
Trauma, 1962
The Double, 1963

The Ipcress File, 1965
Mirage, 1965
The Third Day, 1965
Mister Buddwing, 1966
Moment to Moment, 1966
Project X, 1968
Jigsaw, 1968
Run a Crooked Mile, 1969
Sunflower, 1969

1970s

Lady in the Car with Glasses
    and a Gun, 1970
The Private Life of Sherlock
    Holmes, 1970
Someone Behind the Door, 1971
The Groundstar Conspiracy, 1972
The Man with the Transplanted
    Brain, 1972
The Man Called Noon, 1973
Richie Brockelman: The Missing
    24 Hours, 1976

1980s

Double Negative, 1980
Simon, 1980
I Am the Cheese, 1983
Jane Doe, 1983
Brainwaves, 1983
The Man with Two Brains, 1983
American Dreamer, 1984
Paris, Texas, 1984
The Muppets Take Manhattan,
    1984
Captive, 1985
The Return of the Soldier, 1985
Desperately Seeking Susan, 1985
D.A.R.Y.L., 1985
Blackout, 1985

The Morning After, 1986
Stranger in My Bed, 1986
The Stranger, 1987
Overboard, 1987
The Bourne Identity, 1988
Patty Hearst, 1988
They Live, 1988
Street of Chance, 1989
Murder by Night, 1989
Secret Wedding, 1989

1990s

March Comes in Like a Lion, 1990
Memories of Murder, 1990
False Identity, 1990
Total Recall, 1990
Regarding Henry, 1991
Shattered, 1991
Dead Again, 1991
Time Bomb, 1991
The Addams Family, 1991
Landslide, 1992
Bed & Breakfast, 1992
Final Analysis, 1992
Secret Friends, 1992
Desire and Hell at the Sunset
    Motel, 1992
Clean Slate, 1994
The Last Kiss Goodnight, 1995

32

Head Injury—Real and Imagined

MR. B. WAS knocked unconscious in the car accident. He had the cut on his forehead to show where his head had hit. He woke up after a minute or so. He was certainly awake by the time the ambulance crew arrived. But the fact that he had been in a car accident didn't seem to register, even though they told him that repeatedly. He could tell them his name, even though he couldn't give many more details; they got those from his wallet. He was kept for observation in the hospital.

Initially, he seemed to be unable to learn anything new at all. This seemed to get better rapidly, but he had problems for a few days in remembering what had happened from one day to the next. Initially, his memories from before the accident were very confused and patchy. But eventually, he could remember up to just about the time when the light had turned green and he had started his car across the intersection.

For a few months after the accident, Mr. B. thought that his thinking was a little slowed, and his memory not quite as good as it had been before. He noted in particular that he was having problems juggling as many things as he had once done, or learning without effort the way he had once done. He had been also bothered by daily, aching headaches which he had not had before the accident, but these were also getting better.

Six months later, Mr. B. was almost back to normal. His headaches were rare. His memory was fine. He had other problems to worry about, so we left his return visit open-ended.

Unconsciousness of the kind suffered by Mr. B.—for only a few minutes or less—would be classified under a *mild* head injury. Even mild head injuries can have complicated and quite varied effects on the brain. But at the risk of some simplification, we can describe them this way:

The effects of a head injury on the nerve cells of the brain can show itself through a concussion—variously defined as a momentary problem with your brain's function, or even as much of a problem as loss of consciousness. The parts of the brain that are responsible for consciousness are deep in the center, so it is possible for them to be damaged by a head injury—and for you to suffer a brief loss of consciousness—without any other real damage occurring.

(Because the areas responsible for consciousness are deep in the center of the brain, and because of the way the brain is constructed, they are affected most by twisting or turning motions of the head. This is why being hit on the top of the head may not knock somebody out, while being hit with a glancing blow on the jaw—which twists the whole head violently, may knock them instantly unconscious. Boxers have noted this fact for years. Jack Dempsey reportedly trained with a cannon ball tied to a rope around his neck, to strengthen his neck muscles so that he could resist blows to his chin.)

Head injuries can interfere with the function of the brain by direct damage to nerve cells. This is particularly likely to occur in areas where the brain will be bounced or banged against the side of the skull. The inner part of the temporal lobes is one area where this seems to be particularly likely to occur. Head injuries can also cause nerve cell dysfunction by stretching or even tearing the connections between nerve cells. This may be due to the twisting that a head injury can cause, or because of shock waves that a head injury sends through the Jell-O-like material of the brain.

For the most part, the damage that head injuries produces is worst at the initial time of the injury. After that, people tend to recover. Studies have shown that the vast majority of people appear to recover completely from the relatively brief periods of unconsciousness caused by mild head injuries. Within a few weeks to months after such a head injury, most people seem to get back to normal.

Some people do seem to have longer lasting or even quite persistent problems. Often, in such cases, whether the problems are real or psychological it is sometimes very easy to tell, as in the case presented below. But often, it is not so easy to tell the real from the psychological. The injury may have been different than what we inferred. Or the person may be more susceptible to the effects of an injury. Something about their nerve cells or nerve cell connections may cause the person to suffer more damage than someone else's might have.

There is also some evidence, at least in some cases, that the effects of a mild head injury on the brain may not completely disappear. Nerve cells that have been destroyed will not regrow; connections that are torn will not reconnect. And even nerve fibers that have been stretched may have suffered damage to the delicate network of microscopic tubules and other parts of the machinery that keep nerve cells healthy. Perhaps for these reasons, a second head injury may cause more effects on an individual than it would have had there not been a prior head injury, even one from which the individual had seemingly recovered. And the subtle damage caused by head injury may be one reason that having a significant head injury appears to somewhat raise the risk of developing Alzheimer's disease late in life.

Even mild head injuries are sufficiently complex that it is difficult to summarize what their effects can be. Moderate and severe head injuries are vastly more complex. I would also caution the reader that the memory problems caused by more severe head injuries are much more complicated than a book like this can begin to deal with. People with such severe head injuries frequently have problems with their attention and concentration. They may have very specific problems with processing certain types of information, too. These, and other problems, may all add together to create much more severe difficulties with memory than would be caused by any one of these problems alone. Diagnosis and attempt at treatment of these kinds of problems cannot be captured by a short clinical vignette.

Even though mild head injuries can cause different problems in different people, there are certain kinds of problems they do not cause. So there are times I can be very sure that, whatever the cause of the person's problems, they were not caused by the head injury. Perhaps the most dramatic example of this for me came from a woman who claimed to have suffered permanent damage to her brain when she was hit by a small, cardboard, Christmas tree:

"I've been hit on the head and I can't do anything anymore!"

A cardboard Christmas tree fell off the shelf at a grocery store and struck Mrs. J. on the head and shoulder. The cardboard tree was less than two feet high and must have weighed less than a pound. It had no metal pieces, only cardboard. The tree survived the fall well.

Not so Mrs. J. She had let out a yelp, and the assistant store manager had rushed to her aid. Mrs. J. was startled. But she did not feel dazed, see stars, or lose consciousness. She had not been knocked down. Her head never hurt her.

But, Mrs. J. now insists, she was never the same. She got both a doctor and an attorney, and began the process which, a year later, led her to us.

Her lawyer assured me that several prominent neurologists had seen her, and were certain that something was going wrong. However, their records had not arrived by the time she came in for an appointment. Sitting in my office, Mrs. J. looked haggard and depressed. Her speech was slow and stuttering and her whole demeanor seemed to suck energy out of me.

What had gone wrong since the accident?

"Everything!" she told me.

She said she could no longer read properly. Words seemed to make no sense to her. She couldn't understand what people were saying to her. She could barely keep the words in her mind, and then she couldn't understand what they meant. She couldn't plan, she couldn't remember what they needed around the house. She couldn't prepare meals. She couldn't remember how to drive anymore, she couldn't remember how to ride a bike, she couldn't remember how to swim. But these are the skills you really never forget. So did she really have a problem "remembering" how to drive, ride a bike, or swim?

What had she been able to do before the accident? "Everything!" She was a wife and the mother of a teenager. She had been running a small business out of her house, editing books for a small press. She was skilled on a word processor and an accomplished speller. She was also a fitness enthusiast. She bicycled wherever she could, and swam avidly in the summer.

I needed more details.

"How long have you been riding a bicycle?" I asked.

"Oh, since I was a kid."

"What kind of bike?"

"All kinds, you know, the three-speed bikes they had when we were kids, and now the 18-gear mountain bikes."

"And what about swimming?"

"Oh, I've loved swimming since I was a kid. I used to swim competitively. Before this accident, I used to do twenty laps a day at the pool."

"What else did you do before the accident?

"I used to love to cook. I was a very good cook, too."

"What about now?"

"I can't cook at all. I forget the steps and I get mixed up. When I try to look at my recipe book, I can't understand what is written there. I get mixed up when I try to do the simplest steps. I leave things out. I do them in the wrong order. My family is disgusted with me."

Despite her hopeless looks, she denied feeling sad. Her neurologic examination was normal, but it took a great deal of effort to test her strength. While she was sitting on the edge of the table, I asked her to push out with her foot. I could hold back her whole leg with my little finger. Despite my entreaties to Mrs. J. to push as hard as she could, that was the best she could do. In testing almost every one of her muscles, they just seemed to give way.

Yet she could get off the table with no sign of weakness in either leg. She had no trouble opening the bathroom door, even though the doorknob was difficult to turn and the door was heavy and on stiff springs. Those hindrances in my office area were not intentional, but they did show that she had far more strength and dexterity than she showed when I tried to test her directly.

Her neuropsychologic testing had bizarre results. She could read words quite well, even unusual words such as "scintilla." But she said it was more of an effort for her than it used to be. We then asked her to give word definitions. She could define "oxymoron." But she had trouble defining "ball."

"You know, it's that thing you bounce."

"Anything else about it?"

"Well, it's usually made out of rubber."

"Anything else?"

"No."

"What about its shape?"

"Oh, it's round—no, not round, it's a sphere."

She confidently told us she could not remember things. When we tested this by giving her a list of fifteen words to recall for us, and even though we kept repeating the list, she could only recall a few of them. But one half hour later, she was able to recognize every one of the words she had been shown before, even with other words mixed in to make the test accurate.

I called up her attorney.

"I don't see any evidence that Mrs. J. has brain disease. I wouldn't have expected any from the kind of injury she's supposed to have gotten. The kinds of problems she reports are not the kinds of problems that can occur with mild head injury. It looks like she is consciously trying to appear weaker and worse off in her memory than she actually is. It is also suspicious that she didn't have any complaints about her strength, yet she is weaker than a baby when I test her. She might have something wrong with her neurologically, but I can't see it through all this."

I continued, "I think her problem is mental. I think she is depressed, but I can't be sure. And if she had any brain injury at all, it is *not* from that cardboard Christmas tree."

There was a pause while her lawyer gathered up his thoughts. "Did I not tell you, Dr. Gordon, that several other neurologists have found her to have significant problems?"

"I don't deny that she has significant problems, I am just telling you they are not with her brain."

Another pause. I heard him exhale. "Well, actually, that's what the other doctors said too. I just wanted to make sure I got your independent opinion."

I wish this story had a happy ending. Usually, when depression causes memory loss, it can be treated, or it may even lift by itself, and the patient recovers completely. Because a disease like depression leaves the basic brain structure intact, the story often has a happier ending than if the memory loss is due to a hard-to-treat, progressive disease like Alzheimer's disease.

Insofar as I know, this was not to happen in Mrs. J.'s case. For a long time, she steadfastly refused any psychiatric intervention. The problem, she insisted, was due to "that Christmas tree." All she wanted was to be vindicated in court. The last I had heard, her husband had left her. Her attorney was in the process of leaving her. He called me up to see if I could recommend another psychiatrist, one who might finally be able to make a personal connection with her. I hope that Mrs. J. got the help she needed, no matter what she blamed for her ills. Whatever caused her problem, it wasn't the cardboard Christmas tree.

PERFORMANCE AND ABILITY

Mrs. J. illustrates the problem that how badly a person *performs* on a test is not necessarily a direct indication of badly their *brain* is working. The reason is simple. Regardless of the state of your brain, to get any score on a test where you have to participate, you have to expend some effort. You have to be able to understand the instructions, know what is being asked of you, and motivate yourself to try to do it as best as you can. If there is anything wrong with any of these steps, you can get a miserable score on a test of memory—or of any other mental function—and have nothing at all wrong with your brain. That is because unless you put out the effort, your brain may be functioning perfectly well, but you will do poorly anyway.

Testing of your strength is something of an example. Your muscles are what they are. They may be as massive as Schwarzenegger's or barely visible. But up to that maximum limit set by your muscles, how much you can do depends upon your effort. If you don't want to, you won't even be able to pick up your hand. So if I try to test your strength and you barely budge, you might be weak. But you might also not want to do it.

When I, as a neurologist, test muscle strength, I have a number of ways to determine whether the problem is in the muscle or in the mind. I can look for whether the person shows any other signs of effort. Usually, you move more than one muscle at a time, or, in order to tense one muscle, you have to lock other muscles as well. If this does not happen naturally, I can make this happen by seeming accident.

For example, I can test the person's biceps, but not support the rest of their arm or wrist. So actually, I am then testing the shoulder and wrist together. I can feel how much strength can actually be developed. Frequently, when people do not try, they initially resist the movement and then they relax—they give up. This "giving way" is a sure sign of lack of effort. I then rely on the peak force to tell me how strong the person actually is.

Another way I have of telling a person's true strength is watching them move when they think I am not testing their abilities. It is surprising how many people who claim that they cannot push out with their leg hardly at all, can nonetheless squat down on the floor and stand up again, an action which requires exactly the same muscle, but supporting all the dozens of pounds of a person's weight. Finally, for muscles I can test more directly: by using an electroshock to stimulate the nerve or the muscle itself and see whether the muscle would be capable of responding adequately.

Unfortunately, for most mental functions, it is harder to tell. But some of the same principles apply. If a person can remember something perfectly well under one occasion, but seems to have problems learning it on another, then I can reasonably conclude that their problem is not in the brain. The problem is with the situation. I can ask a person to do something which they do not necessarily realize involves the mental function I am trying to test. In this way, I can see them acting naturally, when they may be off guard. And sometimes, I can test them with even harder material and discover that they do perfectly well. An unusual fact is that people may put less effort into easy materials, but then rise to the challenge of something difficult and perform it perfectly well. This is another sure sign that it is interest and motivation that is the problem, not the person's brain.

These problems with interest and motivation need not be conscious. The patient need not be trying to consciously fake or malinger. But by knowing that the problem is with the person's desires and cooperation, rather than with their brain itself, is usually the important first step in deciding where such a problem originates.

33

"Forever Fourteen" "An Affair to Forget"—Amnesia and Emotional Trauma

FOREVER FOURTEEN

When he was found on his kitchen floor in December of 1984, clutching a part from the electric oven he'd been trying to fix, the 53-year-old man known as J. was awake, but not talking. The next day, in the hospital, he was able to give his name, age, location and the date.

The catch was that he was 40 years and a few thousand miles off.

He thought the year was 1945, that he was 14 years old, and in his old hometown. He was no longer able to recognize his wife, his teenage children, or the family dog. He was mystified by the VCR, and said the cars of the 1980s looked like "space cars."

"Where are my mother and father? Why aren't they here?" he kept asking.

In fact, his father had died 11 years earlier, and his mother lived thousands of miles away.

J. was suffering from an unusual case of retrograde amnesia, an inability to recall large chunks of the past. He knew his name, but the last life event he remembers clearly is being hit in the head with a baseball bat at age 14. He did not remember any of the personal or public events that occurred between August-September 1945 and 1984—not the bombing of Hiroshima, not the assassination of John F. Kennedy, not the Korean or Vietnam wars.

J.'s oldest memories—those of childhood events that took place before his fourteenth year, the people and places he knew then—are crystal clear. He remembers teachers, classmates and events up through 7th grade. He remembers the colors of the license plates in his home state in 1945, even though these colors were used only for a brief period

248

of time. He remembers the streets and stores of his hometown remarkably well—just as they were in 1945—despite the fact that when he had visited it in the 1980s, fully 89 percent of those downtown businesses had moved away.

His voice and accent have even taken on a childish quality, his handwriting has gone back to its boyish form. He acts much like a 14-year-old in other ways, too, skipping and giggling when the mood strikes him. He says "sir" or "ma'am" to people 20 or 30 years younger than he is; he complains of having "no one to play with," and is very embarrassed at the mention of sex and girls. J. feels that his own children, who were 15 and 17 at the onset of his amnesia, are older than he is.

J.'s period of amnesia abruptly ends after 1984. He cannot identify people who made headlines in 1984, at the end of his forgotten period, but he has no trouble identifying famous people from 1985. For example, in 1986, when he was shown photographs from Life magazine's "The Year in Pictures" for 1984, he did not recognize Walter Mondale, Geraldine Ferraro, or Olympic star Mary Lou Retton. But he could easily identify people from the 1985 issue, including Dr. Ruth Westheimer, Sylvester Stallone's movie character Rambo, and William "the Refrigerator" Perry of the Chicago Bears.

Since his accident, he has struggled to learn about his lost years. Unlike H.M., the severe amnesic who cannot retain new knowledge, J. has learned that he is 63, married and a father. He has learned again how to shave, to drive a car, and to operate electrical appliances, all of which were new to him when he came home from the hospital. But whenever he passes a mirror, the image is disturbing, as the 14-year-old within waits in vain to see his true, youthful reflection.

What actually happened to J.'s brain? Tests revealed no evidence of neurological damage. But cases such as J.'s show us that memory works (or fails to work) in strange ways.

J. may have had a rare type of psychological amnesia—an amnesia *not* due to brain disease—caused by a psychological need to block out certain highly emotional life events. My colleagues Michael McCloskey, Molly Treadway, and Neal Cohen, who studied J. (a study in which I had a small part), discovered that the 39-year span of time J. forgot was indeed framed by emotionally unpleasant changes in his life. From their studies of people with memory lapses such as J.'s, these memory researchers suggest that we may organize and store clusters of memories around the important events in our lives. These become the anchors for our memories.

When psychological problems block memories, the breaks in our memories may respect these natural anchor points.

McCloskey and his colleagues note that we have all had the experience of hearing a long-forgotten song that suddenly triggers a surge of memories about our lives at the time. If merely hearing a song can bring back whole "constellations" of memories, McCloskey and his colleagues suggest, then perhaps the powerful emotions engendered by specific life events actually determine how our brain stores memories. Our brains may use these emotional signposts as another way to categorize and demarcate memories. As McCloskey and his colleagues wrote:

"For example, for people whose lives were directly affected by World War II—by having served in battle, having lost friends or family members in the conflict, having suffered through rationing of food and materials, and so forth—the war would be an obvious life context, and the beginning and end of the war would constitute landmark events associated with a contextual change. Memories of events occurring during the war years (whether or not they had anything to do with the war itself), as well as memories of subsequent events shaped by the outcome of the war, would likely be tied together and less loosely tied to memories organized around other life contexts.

"To apply this idea to J., we would need to posit ... significant landmark events that ushered in a change in life context near the beginning of the forgotten period (around 1945). This would serve to produce distinct constellations of memories for the periods before and after the landmark events. On this account, J.'s post-1945 memories were organized separately from his pre-1945 memories..."

Did J. have some emotional trauma in 1945, and then another in 1984 that could have framed his period of amnesia?

J. did experience some significant life changes in the mid- to late 1940s. First, his grandmother (with whom he had a close relationship) died. Then, he switched to a new school where he was much less happy. In 1946, J.'s family moved to a farm, so he had to switch schools again. They had put a large amount of money into the farm and house. Then, in the late 40s, the house burned down. It was uninsured, and the family suffered considerable hardship as a result. J. has always had a cause for guilt over this. He had disobeyed his parents by storing his chemistry set in his closet at the house. But even though no one knows what actually caused the fire, and no one blames J. for it, he has always blamed himself for starting the fire that hurt his family.

Things were not going well for J. at the time of his accident in 1984, either. His marriage was in trouble, for one thing. He had failed in a number of business ventures, apparently because he got jobs for which he was not qualified by embellishing his resume with advanced degrees he did not have. Just before his episode, he had received some negative evaluations. He was so stressed out about work, in fact, that he developed a nervous condition with chest pains, restricted breathing and speech problems, and had taken disability leave. His leave was just about to end around the time of the accident.

Although a physical trauma—an electric shock—may have triggered J.'s amnesia, perhaps it was not by chance that the period of the amnesia extended back to the baseball bat incident when J. was fourteen. Did the amnesia represent an attempt to return to the last time in J.'s life when he was relatively happy? Could the brain have a mechanism for "motivated forgetting" of painful situations? These questions remain unanswered for now. But J.'s is not the only case that raises these questions.

AN AFFAIR TO FORGET

S., a 39-year-old mother of four children, was in the bank one day in 1976 when she suddenly "felt as though her head was going to explode." She went home to rest, and when her husband arrived, he found her confused and incoherent. He took her to the hospital. Five days later she underwent surgery for a double carotid artery aneurysm and a large blood clot in the left temporal lobe of her brain.

When she woke up, she thought the year was 1960, and that she was 23 years old. She and her husband had just moved into a new house with their three young children, whom S. thought were between the ages of 2 and 5. Somehow, she had lost 16 years.

At the time of her stroke, her youngest—and fourth—child, whom she did not recognize at all, was 14. S. lost not only the knowledge of what had happened in her own life between 1960 and 1976, but also her memory of world events and technological advances. She did not remember Martin Luther King Jr.'s assassination in 1968 or recognize a picture of Patty Hearst from 1974. She did not know how to operate the dishwasher in her house.

We also showed her a picture that usually stimulates a description of the Watergate scandal. It shows a Marine holding a portrait of Richard Nixon under his arm, walking in front of a wall on which hangs a portrait of Gerald Ford. S. gave the following description to researcher Molly Treadway:

S: There's Ford, the klutz. And a picture of Richard Nixon.

MT: Okay, so what do you think this is all about? What's going on here?

S: Um, that means Nixon's no longer president, and Ford is.

MT: Why is Nixon no longer president?

S: I know that one. Uh, he did something. Oh, what did he do? He did, oh, the tapes, tapes.

MT: What was the name of that?

S: Oh, God, this was just on TV not too long ago. Um, Nixon and the, um, um, he bleeped the tapes...

MT: Do you remember any of the other people who were involved?

S: Agnew. How's that? Agnew. He used to be the governor of Maryland...

MT: Okay, and under what conditions did Nixon leave office? Was he impeached, or—

S: You know, everything I've seen on TV, I can't understand that either...the only thing that they had on TV was that somebody else did something, I don't know who it was—but, other people did something, they broke into a building. And he had nothing to do with it.

———————————————————

Michael McCloskey and his colleagues included the unusual story of how and why S. "lost" these 16 years of her life in their paper on landmark life events:

"Our research revealed that...a salient emotional event had occurred in S.'s life shortly after the beginning of the period for which she is now amnesic. Specifically, we were informed by what we consider to be reliable sources that S. had an affair of uncertain duration with a neighbor, and that her fourth child (whom she did not remember after the onset of her amnesia) resulted from this affair. Although no genetic tests have been conducted to determine with certainty the paternity of the fourth child, the available information suggests that S. believed the neighbor to be the father of this child. Both S. and the neighbor were married at the time of this affair.

"As with J., a stressful situation appears to have arisen shortly before the onset of S.'s amnesia, as well. Several months before the onset of amnesia in 1976, S. had discovered that one of her daughters, who was then an unmarried teenager, had just had an abortion. S. was extremely shocked and upset by this information and refused to speak to the daughter for a long period of time. After the onset of amnesia, S. remembered nothing about this incident.

"...The question that arises is why the amnesia extended back to the specific landmark event of 1960, and not to some other landmark...[One] possibility is that the boundaries of the amnesic period is related to the significant parallels between the events occurring in the patients' lives at the beginning of the forgotten time period...The pregnancy of S.'s unmarried daughter parallels in obvious ways the events in S.'s life shortly after the beginning of the period she has forgotten. Thus, the events occurring shortly before the onset of amnesia may have re-aroused the unpleasant memories from the earlier time period."

As the researchers point out, S.'s case, like J.'s, was most unusual in that she forgot more than just autobiographical events, the events of her own life. In both cases, their impairment extended to skills (such as operating a VCR) and memory for world events. Typically, people with amnesia that is considered to be psychological in origin forget personal, autobiographical memories, regardless of the time in which they were acquired. S.'s and J.'s impairments showed the opposite pattern: It was "informationally-general" and "temporally-specific" rather than "informationally-specific" and "temporally-general." In other words, their memory loss encompassed all information—autobiographical events, world events, facts and skills —acquired during a very specific span of time.

These two cases have challenged some of the current assumptions about how the brain normally organizes memory. Patients like J. and S. may be atypical, but their cases help show that emotional factors can play a more important role in the organization of normal memory than was once thought.

34

"A Shark Has Four Legs, Doesn't It?" A Bizarre—But Real—Form of Memory Loss, and the Brain's Odd Filing System

"A shark has four legs, doesn't it?"

K.R., a 70-year-old retired librarian, was having trouble concentrating and remembering things, although she seemed to be in good health. As part of the routine testing we do for those problems, we showed her drawings of many different things and asked her to name them. She *did* have trouble naming some of the pictures—but not just random trouble. Her problem was quite specific—and very, very odd.

No matter what we tried, K.R. just could not come up with the names of the animals we showed her, even though she was able to name almost everything else she saw correctly. But when it came to animals, she could not write down their names or even tell us what they were called. She had the problem regardless of how we tried to coax an answer from her.

Over the next several months, we tested K.R. more intensively. The tests she graciously agreed to take were designed by Dr. John Hart, who with other colleagues had already described a patient who could not name fruits or vegetables. He had been thinking about such problems for over four years, so he knew what to do.

He found that K.R. definitely could not name animals—not if she saw their pictures and not if she heard the noises that they made. Though she could instantly recognize the sound of a vacuum cleaner or typewriter, she could not say that a duck was what made the "quack", or a bee the "buzz."

Without a picture, she could not describe the physical features of animals, either. She could say that parsley was green, but she could not

254

say what color a frog was. When asked "What color is a rooster?" she answered, "gray." She thought that a shark had four legs. She could not really say whether a mouse was small.

Her problem was not in vision itself. She could identify all the pieces of very complicated scenes. She could even assemble pieces of cut up animal drawings into their proper form, just as if she were doing a jigsaw puzzle. But then she could not tell us the name of the animal that she had put together.

Yet if she saw a picture of an elephant, she could recognize what the proper color of the animal was. She could choose the card with the gray elephant, but she still could not say that the elephant was gray without the card in front of her. She could also tell us that a horse with the head of an elephant was "not right." She knew whether animals were edible or not. She could tell us whether they were pets. Her understanding, in fact, of these aspects of animals was astounding—considering how little else she knew about them.

For example, when shown the picture of a dolphin like Flipper, she could not tell us that it was a dolphin. But she could tell us it was the kind of fish you are not supposed to eat! She went on to tell us that there was another kind of fish with the same name that you could eat. She clearly knew what she was talking about, but she couldn't give us the name of it either.

K.R. passed away three months after the testing ended. On examination, her brain showed a mild inflammation of the nerve cells throughout her cortex, including both her temporal lobes. We surmised that the antibodies to a tumor elsewhere in her body caused patchy damage to the nerve cells in her temporal lobes, although the tumor was never found at autopsy.

———————————

Bizarre cases like K.R.'s show that the brain is full of surprises, and that people with unusual memory problems can sometimes give us important clues about how the normal brain stores and retrieves everyday information.

K.R.'s case suggests that the brain packages and stores information in ways that are different from what we might expect. It keeps what we think is the same information in different places, and it divvies up that information in odd ways.

For example, K.R. helps illustrate that what you know through your eyes is kept separately in your brain from what you know through your ears. Artists and writers have long known this (although perhaps they have not told each other!). The visual scene of a cat on a mat is *different*—in some ways more, in some ways less—than the knowledge our minds extract from the words, "cat on a mat.." K.R.'s case helps show this. The description of animals in *language* is stored in a different place in the brain than the knowledge of animals in *vision*.

So K.R. was able to visually recognize that an orange elephant "did not look right," because she could use her visual knowledge, which was intact. But she could not *say* that an elephant should be "gray," because her language system was partly cut off from her visual system. Cut off from her image of an elephant, her language system had to guess what the color of an elephant was, and it came up with its own strange answer: peach-colored.

But the strangeness of the brain's filing system does not stop with vision and language. *Within* these big files, there are many smaller files, but they are organized differently than any filing system we might care to use ourself. Some of the smaller files look like the ones we would use: "Animals," "Cows," "Parts of a Cow," "Horns," "Udder." But some do not seem to. Instead of having one big "colors" category, for example, the brain seems to have many completely separate storage bins for the colors of things: "colors of animals" and "colors of inanimate objects," "colors of food," and so on.

Another case studied by Dr. Hart, a woman who had suffered a viral infection of the brain, helps show this. She could not remember the names of any small household objects, like scissors or irons. Strangely enough, she could easily remember the names of large ones like refrigerators or stoves. So in her case, it looked like her brain had created a category of "small household objects," that somehow had been erased.

It is not just the existence of this bizarre filing system that is strange. What is perhaps even stranger is how damage to a file in one area can block access to other files, and to the information within those other files. You might have thought that your knowledge of "grandmotherness" was separate from your knowledge of your own grandmother. After all, you knew her before you even knew what "grandmother" meant! You know her voice, her looks, her scent, where she lives, her children. You know something of her life. The fact that she is your parent's mother seems fairly incidental to some of this. But block the notion of "grandmother" by brain damage, and you may not be able to call up your grandmother's image in your mind!

Why would the brain work like this? Why not just throw all information about animals, or household objects, into a big, all-purpose storage bin? Why make all the bins depend upon each other so much?

The answer is not really known. It may be that having so many bins, and so many different types of bins, is actually a more efficient way for our brains to store things (as opposed to for our computers or for ourselves). What for us would be difficult—breaking up information into so many ways, and cross-referencing it so much—for the brain may be easy and natural. For eons, our brains and their precursors have had to live in a real world, where everything may be connected. A quickly-glimpsed pattern of stripes might have been nothing more than branches making a pattern from the sun—or they may have been the stripes on a crouching tiger. The brains that survived were the ones that made those connections, and were sensitive to those possibilities. So we may have inherited this dense interdependency of categories and items because that was the mechanism that worked best, to come up with information fastest.

This is only a partial explanation. And it cannot be completely right. But at the very least, patients like K.R. force us to go back to the drawing boards of our theories. They do show us that the brain has its own way of making sense out of what William James called the "blooming, buzzing confusion" of the world. And they show us that our brain does not always work the way our mind thinks it should.

35

"I Raped My Children, But I Don't Remember It!"—The Unreliability of Recovered "Memories"

PAUL INGRAM, A deputy sheriff in Olympia, Washington, chairman of the local Republican party, father of five, and regular church-goer, confessed to having repeatedly raped one of his daughters, beginning when she was five. He confessed to sodomizing his own sons, and allowing his children—both boys and girls—to be raped and sodomized by his poker buddies. He confessed to being a member of a satanic cult that engaged in ritual sacrifice and dismemberment of babies. But he initially had no memory of having done any of this!

Nor is there any real evidence that the "crimes" he confessed to actually occurred! The original impetus for the accusations against him came from one of his daughters, who had "recovered" alleged memories of sexual abuse by her father. But this daughter did not show any physical signs of the repeated penetrations and stabbings that she claimed she had suffered since she was five years old. Nor was any evidence of a satanic cult, of ritual murders, or of abducted babies ever discovered.

And Paul Ingram also confessed, with the same fervor and the same certainty, to a story of sexual abuse that was *known* to be completely false. Richard Ofshe, a psychologist called by the prosecution, had become suspicious of the reality of Ingram's confessions. So he told Ingram of an episode—completely made up—in which Ingram had encouraged and participated in the sexual abuse of two of his own children. At first, Ingram could not remember this happening, just as he had not at first "remembered" any of the other episodes.

But the psychologist urged him to try to visualize the scene happening, as Ingram had been asked to try to remember the other events, too. Ingram first began to get some images; over a few more hours, he began to "remember" vivid details. He wrote a detailed three-page "confession" to the event—that had never happened! Ingram ultimately recanted all of his confessions, but too late to save him from jail, and his family from dissolution.

<hr />

The passions raised by the specter of childhood sexual abuse, and the understandable rage of those falsely accused, have obscured some basic facts about memory which are essential to understanding the debate. The facts are these:

Most traumatic experiences—such as childhood sexual abuse—are *not* forgotten.

BUT—Real experiences, even "unforgettable," traumatic ones, *can* be forgotten.

Forgotten memories *may* be brought back or restored through a variety of means—re-exposure to a person, place, smell, or scene, hints, repeated questioning, guided imagery, dream interpretation, hypnosis, and group therapeutic sessions.

BUT—ALL memories—recalled normally, or "recovered" by any means—can be incorrect, misleading, or even totally wrong!

Most of us realize that even what we feel is a "memory" can be inaccurate, misleading, or even totally false. It should be obvious that "memories" that we don't even know that we have, have an even higher chance of being inaccurate or totally false.

No one knows how likely it is that "recovered" memories are false. But they clearly *have been* and *can be* false.

How strongly we "remember" a memory is *usually* a guide to how certain we can be that the remembered event actually occurred.

BUT—How strongly or vividly we "remember" a memory that has been "recovered" or "restored" is NOT a good measure of whether the remembered event actually occurred. This is because the process used to "recover" memories actually implants its own memories. No wonder these newly-implanted memories are strongly "remembered:" they have been thoroughly, and recently, pounded into our brains.

And all this leads us to the main point: recovered "memories" are too unreliable to be used as evidence for anything as serious as alleged childhood sexual abuse. Even *if* these "recovered memories" *were* 95 percent accurate, the fact that they would then be *wrong* at least 5 percent of the time probably means that *MANY PEOPLE BEING ACCUSED*

BECAUSE OF "RECOVERED MEMORIES" ARE INNOCENT. And in the far more likely case that recovered "memories" are much less accurate than 95 percent, and far more likely than 5 percent to be false, more *innocent* people than guilty ones are being accused of childhood sexual abuse. In real life, "recovered memories" of childhood sexual abuse are probably almost worthless as evidence that such abuse actually occurred. The people who "recover" these "memories" may be convinced they are true. But they probably are NOT.

The knowledge behind these facts bears elaboration: when childhood sexual abuse does occur, it is usually remembered all *too* well. Memories may be colored by youth, ignorance, and fear, but the majority of people *will* remember such traumatic events from their childhood. The evidence comes partly from knowledge of the memory of other traumatic events in childhood, and partly from data on memory for childhood sexual abuse itself.

In July 1976, twenty-five children were kidnapped at gunpoint. The kidnappers drove them around for eleven hours in two blackened vans, and then buried them alive in the vans for sixteen hours. The children were between the ages of approximately eight and twelve at the time of the kidnapping. Four years after the kidnapping, every child who could still be located could give a fully detailed account of the kidnapping and its circumstances. Not one child forgot or "repressed" this traumatic, fear-provoking event in their lives.

In other traumas—concentration camps, torture, violence—forgetting is also relatively uncommon. The victims w*ish* they would forget, but they cannot.

Since childhood sexual abuse is often covert, it has been hard to directly measure how often it is remembered. Linda Williams, a researcher at the University of New Hampshire, interviewed women who had a previously documented history of sexual victimization—ranging from touching and fondling to penetration—about 17 years earlier, when they had been children. Sixty-two percent of these women remembered these earlier episodes. (It should be noted that the thrust of Williams' article was not how often the women reme*mbered*, but how often they did *not*. This will be discussed below.)

It is not clear that *repression* of memories occurs—in the sense of submergence of otherwise intact memories—separately from normal mechanisms of forgetting and loss of memory. Researchers in the field argue over just how to define repression, and just how to prove whether it exists or not. But what *is* clear is that, whether it is called repression or forgetting, even traumatic events may not be remembered consciously, at least for a time. Even tremendously painful, traumatic events *can* be *forgotten.*

Williams' data, cited above, provides one estimate of 38 percent for the chances of a woman with a documented history of childhood sexual abuse not recalling the abuse years later. In Williams' study, as many as 47 percent of the women she interviewed had periods when they could not recall the abuse.

In early childhood (before the age of three) forgetting is common. Almost no one remembers events of any kind from before the age of about three. At such an early age, the memory is probably not imprinted very well, and the memories that get stored are relatively easily erased, overwritten, or overlayered by subsequent memories.

The forgetting from early childhood is more complete than the forgetting that adults can have. But even adults can forget very significant life events, at least at first. Physicians such as myself constantly confront this. We ask patients to tell us of any medical problems they have. A fair number of people will initially forget to mention heart attacks, strokes, and operations. So many people forget such things, in fact, that doctors use a method—called the "review of systems"—to help jog people's memories. Basically, this means asking them specific questions. The same people who say they have been fine all their life will remember having been hospitalized for a month when specifically asked, or when you point out their scars.

Studies have confirmed this forgetfulness. Fourteen percent of people, who had been in a motor vehicle accident in which they were hurt, did not remember the accident a year later. More than 25 percent of people, who had been in the hospital, did not remember the hospitalization within the next year.

Whether remembered or "recovered," *no* "memory" can be trusted completely. This is just common sense, repeatedly confirmed by scientific study. Investigators have looked at memory for events that actually happened, such as the *Challenger* explosion (as discussed in Chapter 18), and confirmed how misleading recollections can be.

The *Challenger* explosion might be considered something impersonal. What about traumatic events that are more personally experienced? Unfortunately, memory for such personal experiences has not been shown to be any more accurate.

A famous example of memory of a well-documented, personally traumatic event comes from baseball. Jack Hamilton was a pitcher with the California Angels. He threw a fast ball that crushed the face of the outfielder Tony Conigliario. This accident haunted Hamilton throughout his life. He thought he remembered it perfectly, in horrifying detail. Yet many of his specific recollections were completely incorrect!

"Memory" can invent traumas that never happened! Complete, but *totally false*, memories *can* be injected by suggestion. "Recollection" of these false memories can be as vivid and as certain as real memory for real events. Some children, who were interviewed about a sniper attack in an elementary school playground, reported recollections of the attack and what they were doing at the time—even though they could not have been there!

Elizabeth Loftus and her colleagues have shown that it is possible to get children to "remember" a completely made-up "memory" of a fearful event. They invented a scenario of the children being lost in a mall when they were five years old. Here is Jim, a 25-year-old, telling both his 14-year-old younger brother Chris and his mother a made-up story about how Chris had been lost in a shopping mall. Jim is telling this story as part of the study, to test his brother and his mother:

"It was 1981 or 1982. I remember that Chris was 5. We had gone shopping at the University City Shopping Mall in Spokane. After some panic, we found Chris being led down the mall by a tall, oldish man (I think he was wearing a flannel shirt). Chris was crying and holding the man's hand. The man explained that he had found Chris walking around crying his eyes out just a few minutes before and was trying to help him find his parents."

Chris' mother never came to "remember" this event, despite five days of trying. "I feel very badly about it, but I just cannot remember anything like this ever happening." This was what you might expect—the "event" had been totally made-up!

But Chris himself not only began to "remember" the event, but he began to remember his "fears" and specific "details":

"That day I was so scared that I would never see my family again. I knew that I was in trouble. I remember Mom telling me never to do that again. I also remember that old man's flannel shirt. I sort of remember the stores. I remember the man asking me if I was lost."

By a few weeks later, Chris had an extremely detailed "memory" of what had "happened": "I was with you guys for a second and I think I went over to look at the toy store, the Kay-bee toy and uh, we got lost and I was looking around and I thought, 'Uh-oh. I'm in trouble now.' You know. And then I . . . I thought I was never going to see my family again. I was really scared you know. And then this old man, I think he was wearing a blue flannel, came up to me . . . he was kind of old. He was kind of bald on top . . . he had a ring of gray hair . . . and he had glasses."

Chris was surprised to find out that the entire story of having been lost was false. *"Really? I thought I remembered being lost . . . and looking around for you guys. I do remember that. And then crying. And Mom coming up and saying 'Where were you. Don't you . . . Don't you ever do that again.'"*

Loftus and Coan's experimental implantation of a false memory of a traumatic childhood event helps establish that questioning itself can implant the memory of a traumatic event. Being lost in a mall may not be an exact analogy of childhood sexual abuse—but it is a very traumatic event for a child, and it was as far as they thought they could go, ethically, in testing this possibility experimentally. And the example of Paul Ingram given at the beginning of this chapter is evidence that false memories of childhood sexual abuse can be implanted not only in suggestible children, but even in adults who had many reasons to resist the implications of those "memories."

"Recovered memories" of childhood sexual abuse have been pr*oven* to be incorrect—and totally wrong—in some cases. This may be because they were incorrect recollections of actual experiences, or because they were implanted or suggested in some way through the questioning and the process that it took to "recover" them. How often—what percentage of the time—such memories are wrong is not known for certain. But what *is* certain is that they *have* been wrong—with terrible consequences for those falsely accused because of them.

Just because a memory is strongly believed, and just because a memory *feels* real to the person having it, is no guarantee that it *is* real. People can have extraordinarily passionate and secure convictions about events that *never* happened. That is just the way memory works. And this is true even though the trauma may be vividly remembered, with great certainty. Vividness and certainty are not guarantees of accuracy! When Ingram was told by the psychologist that the abuse of his children that he had pictured in his mind and "confessed" to was entirely false—that it had, in fact, been invented by the psychologist as a test—Ingram protested, "It's just as real to me as anything else."

There are many reasons why a "recovered" thought of childhood sexual abuse may be "remembered" with vividness and certainty, even if it never actually occurred. You probably brought the thought back into your mind several times, in the course of trying to "remember" it fully. When that thought is saved as a memory—and such saving is automatic—it will be saved with all the strength of recent memories. Repeated recollection and saving of the "memory" will make it even stronger. The thought may have been accompanied by images, another known way to make a "memory"—real or not—stronger. Emotions—

fear, loathing—are another guaranteed way to more deeply embed a "memory." And if these "memories" were linked to actual childhood events in any way—a remembered trip or family function, for example—then it will be very hard for your mind to separate the false part of the memories from the real part. The false memories will actually gain strength and veracity from being linked to real memories from your childhood!

What is also well-known: the more digging that must be done to get at a "memory," the greater the chances of altering the memory, or creating a completely false one. In one well-known episode in which a high school football player went into cardiac arrest, witnesses in the stands were interviewed six years later about this traumatic event. After they were given a suggestion that there had been blood on the player's jersey, nearly one-quarter of the witnesses "remembered" this, even though it had never happened, and even though the only "clue" about this blood was the one brought up by the interviewer—six years later.

This brings us to our main point. Why so much concern over the chance that a memory may not be accurate? Because this chance, taken together with the chances of childhood sexual abuse actually happening, critically determine how useful *any* memory—remembered or recovered—is going to be as valid evidence. The basic problem is the following: a memory can be 95 percent accurate, but still correct less than half the time! This apparent paradox can be best understood by thinking about memory as you would a laboratory test. You do a test to see if a person has the problem, the disease, that the test measures for. There are two basic facts to keep in mind: no test is perfect. And if you are doing the test in the first place, then you must be assuming that some of the people you test will *not* have the problem you are testing for—in fact, most of the people you test may not have the problem. These facts are critical, but they seem to have been overlooked by many of the enthusiasts of the recovered "memory" movement. So let us consider what these facts are, and what they mean.

Tests are inevitably imperfect in two ways. One is that even if a person has a disease, a test may not always show this. This is called a *false negative*. That is, the test comes out negative, but it is falsely negative. The person really *does* have the disease. In the tests doctors have come to rely upon, false negatives are relatively uncommon. For example, typically doctors rely on tests that are 80 or 90 or 95 percent accurate in picking up a condition in people who actually do have it.

But the more invidious problem that all tests have is being *falsely positive*. That is, the test result indicates the person has the problem, even though they do not. Because false positivity is such a worry—if *you* are the one falsely identified—most good tests are designed so that it is relatively uncommon—perhaps 5 percent or less frequent. But it is important to realize that false positivity still does happen, inevitably. It is just a question of how frequently it happens, for any given test.

So let us now take a test that would be an excellent, highly accurate test by medical standards: 95 percent accurate in picking up a disease when it is present and with only a 5 percent chance of falsely reporting that a disease is present when it is not. Let us apply the test for this disease to a healthy population, where only one person in a thousand has the disease. How well will this test do in picking up people with the disease in this population?

Let us use this test on a million people. Of the million people, one in a thousand has the disease. The test will accurately pick up 95 percent of them, so the test will accurately show 950 of the thousand people who have the disease. This is its 95 percent accuracy rate. But the test will falsely indicate that one person out of twenty has the disease, when they, in fact, do not. In our population, this means that almost 50,000 people will be stigmatized as having the condition, even though they don't. That is, even though this test is 95 percent accurate, it will falsely "accuse" five times as many people of having the disease as it does identify those people who actually do have the disease.

Any use of memory has exactly the same problem as this hypothetical medical test. A memory has some chance of being accurate, and some—let us hope—smaller chance of being inaccurate, of being falsely positive. Proponents of "recovered memories" may claim that the chance of a "recovered memory" being inaccurate is relatively low. *But so long as it is not zero, and so long as innocent people exist, then such "recovered memories" have a risk of falsely implicating innocent people.* As Lindsay and Read, two psychologists who have studied this problem, have pointed out, even if we accept the statistics that advocates of "recovered memories" have suggested are accurate, there is a good chance that any single instance of recovered memory is likely to falsely accuse a perfectly innocent person!

If we accept statistics which are only slightly more realistic, then "recovered memories" become no better at "identifying" a truly guilty person than the toss of a coin! And if we believe that "repressed" memories are actually unusual—if they exist at all—and that a significant proportion of "recovered memories" are false, then many more people are being falsely accused by "recovered memories" than are being discovered through them. "Recovered memories" will rarely be correct; it is a mistake to rely on them at all, for so serious a matter.

Childhood sexual abuse *does* occur, with shocking frequency. But not everyone accused of it is necessarily guilty. There *can* be amnesia for traumatic events. But this does not mean that every "recovered memory" of childhood sexual abuse is accurate. By all available evidence, such "memories" will falsely implicate more innocent people than they identify guilty ones—probably far more. Do we want our judgments about such terrible crimes to be determined by real evidence, or by prejudice? No one wants to see true perpetrators of childhood sexual abuse remain undetected and unpunished, but we should also abhor innocent people being pilloried, humiliated, and destroyed by fanaticism fueled by misguided imaginations.

Part V

Improving Your Memory

36

What Doesn't Really Work, or Why It Isn't Known to Work

> I have tried green algae potion and it made my memory better. Isn't this proof enough that it works?

> I read of a study somewhere that showed something that improved memory in ten people. Why won't my doctors believe it?

WE ARE CONSTANTLY bombarded with claims for how we can develop super memory abilities of some kind. Effortless learning, amazing recall — the ads promise them all. You may need to take a course —an easy one, naturally. Or perhaps a food. Or a vitamin. Or a combination. Whatever you take or do, success is guaranteed.

Believe it or not, success *is* guaranteed with almost anything that you try. Almost *anything* people do to *try* to improve their memory *will* improve it. Just *hoping* that your memory will improve *will* improve your memory by about 10 to 20 percent or more, on the average.

The bad news, though, is that these improvements are not likely to be terribly significant or lasting. And, before we can discuss realistic attempts at improving our memories, we need to clear up some misconceptions about what works and what doesn't work.

THE PLACEBO EFFECT

Surprisingly, people actually feel that their mental ability improves when they are given a placebo, that is, a sugar pill. Even more surprisingly, their mental abilities *can* improve with a placebo.

The placebo effect has been very powerful. It can even boost the memory of people who have major problems with their memory. When patients with Alzheimer's disease participate in research studies of possible new treatments, they often show a slight improvement even when

269

they are getting a placebo. The effect is very individual, and while some people may not be affected, others may show dramatic "improvements."

The placebo effect is tricky, however, and we still do not know fully why or how it works. We do know, though, that some people believe that if they are given a pill, even if only a placebo, they will feel better. In the memory area, this means that these people often expect to see an improvement in their memory which gives them a boost in their confidence. The placebo effect is something of a "mind over matter" dilemma, since it is the expectation that improvement is or will be occurring, not any medication, that actually causes the memory improvement.

All of this is not to say that the placebo effect should be dismissed. Clearly, a placebo can make some people better, although most people are really looking for an actual drug to improve their memory — not a placebo.

DRUGS AND HERBS: NOT PROVEN

Drugs and herbs are often what people have in mind when they ask about ways of improving memory. Some of the drugs and herbs advertised to improve memory do contain some form of a stimulant. For example, certain compounds found in plants often mimic neurotransmittors and, in the right dosages and at the right times, can have beneficial effects that humans can tolerate or even enjoy. For example, the leaves of the tobacco plant produce nicotine. Nicotine acts through the cholinergic nervous system as a strong stimulant. In low doses, this stimulates our nervous systems pleasantly. In higher doses, it is very poisonous. Caffeine is another nervous system stimulant.

It is no surprise that stimulants such as nicotine, caffeine, and the caffeine-like compounds in chocolate (not to mention the sugar and fat!) can improve people's memory performance. These stimulants, in low doses, stimulate our nervous systems and in so doing they improve attention and make you feel more alert. As a result, your ability to learn and to remember may improve.

What is not clear, though, is whether any available "drugs" or herbs contain any compounds beyond such natural stimulants that can actually boost raw memory power. Most of the purported herbs, foods, and food additives have not been proven to help memory at all. Nor do we expect them to do so. The chemicals and chemical balances in our brains are kept highly regulated by nature. Our brain tissue itself is kept highly isolated even from the rest of our bodies, because of a blood-brain barrier that lets relatively little in the way of foreign materials, such as medications, through. And the body has additional defenses that cushion the impact of much of what we take in. So it would be unusual to find a compound out in nature that would not only be able to get into our brains, but which once there would help us rather than harm us.

PROOF IS DIFFICULT

Because individuals are all so different, memory research usually requires at least one hundred people to determine whether a drug or other treatment actually works. In studies in Alzheimer's disease, for example, long experience has shown that about 200-300 subjects or more are needed to ascertain a drug's effect. And, because of the placebo effect, it is usually necessary to have such a research study done *double blind.* That is, neither the researchers nor the subjects can know who is getting the actual drug and who is getting a placebo. These studies cost millions of dollars, so that most of the over-the-counter drugs and herbs do not undergo this rigorous testing. Consequently, all that can really be said of these drugs and herbs is the Scottish verdict, "Not Proven."

37

What Really Works

A TESTED, TRUE chemical approach to memory improvement is likely to become a reality within the next decade, and it will be a blessing for people who develop seriously troubling memory problems. But for most of us, very satisfying and sufficient memory improvement can be obtained from special techniques—some of which have been known for 2,500 years or more. Researchers—such as a group sponsored by the Charles A. Dana Foundation—are searching for newer, more efficient and more sophisticated methods of improving memory, but certain basic principles are likely to remain eternal.

The techniques described in the large number of books designed to improve memory really can work. With a reasonable amount of effort, you could probably improve your memory by 30 or 40 percent. And if you *really* want to, you could probably improve your memory power in specific areas manyfold. For example, you could conceivably improve your memory for names to such a degree that you could stand outside a small auditorium and remember the name of everyone who walks in the door.

The techniques for reaching these higher levels of performance are very specialized. I reference several books that elaborate on these techniques in the Appendix, and I recommend these books and methods for the serious mnemonist. As with everything else, however, it takes serious concentrated effort to reach the best results, and serious training to avoid misusing these techniques.

But, if you are simply seeking a better daily performance by your memory, here are some basic steps to follow. These steps fall into three categories: general tune-up; deciding what you really need from your memory and whether you can find shortcuts that don't rely on memory; and steps that actually boost your memory power. There is reasonably good evidence that all of these techniques, alone or in combination, actually work to help improve memory performance.

GENERAL TUNE-UP

1) Build up your cardiovascular endurance. In other words, exercise. Exercise can improve some mental abilities by an average of 20 to 30 percent. (Remember to obtain your doctor's consent before embarking on a new exercise program).

2) Make sure you are hearing and seeing properly. It is amazing to me how many people ignore this obvious aid. It should not be a surprise to anyone that not being able to hear well or to see well can cause problems with your memory. So if you need hearing or vision aids, obtain them. These aids can reduce the number of times you may have to do a double take or ask people to repeat themselves. And, it will help you focus on what is being said to you or shown to you from the very start.

3) Consult with your doctor and review all of the medications you are taking. Some may dull your mind or your memory. Sometimes, though, this is a necessary evil, and you will have to make do. However, you may be able to eliminate the

medications that interfere with your memory (See Chapter 24.) And, if you are a heavy social drinker — you may be able to improve your memory by reducing your alcohol intake (See Chapter 23).

DECIDING WHAT YOU REALLY NEED

Memory training takes considerable time and effort. And, memory training only works on the specific area of memory being trained. You cannot develop a general memory strength, so you have to ration your efforts.

1) *First, decide what you really need to remember the most.* People's names and faces? Things to do? Long-range plans? Everyday things, like where you put your keys or where you parked the car?

   Determine what you really need to remember, because you do not want to waste your time and effort trying to improve your memory for areas that you rarely use.

   To make sure you have a good sense of what you really need to remember, write down the things you think you should remember better on a list and then carry the list around with you for a week or more. After a few days or a few weeks, it should become clear to you what things you really need to remember. So now, review your list and pick out the most important item on the list. Work on the most important and after you have mastered the most important, you can then work on other areas.

2) *Determine when you need this type of memory.* This will help you determine how you can best try to learn the things you need to know and how you can best cue yourself to remember them. For example, a list of things to do is best kept as a list that you expand as things come up and that you refer to when needed.

   On the other hand, it is impractical to pull out a list of people's names at a party. You can, however, make up a list of the people's names that you expect to see at a party and review it *before* you go.

3) *Find ways to avoid using your memory.* Have a memory place — a spot where you put things. And have an alternate. For example, put a hook by the door and always place your keys on the hook. Your alternate place for keys may be a basket by the door, and by using this system, you'll know that if your

Unfortunately there's more to getting organized than getting a filing cabinet.

keys are not on the hook, they must be in the basket by the door. Park your car at work in the same spot each day. Similarly, park in the same aisle or space when going to places that you routinely visit, such as the grocery store, cleaners, pharmacy or doctor's office. Why be creative, when it strains your memory and wastes your time?

Are there any tricks you can use short of actually making your memory work harder? If you can jot down a clue to what you need to remember, do so. Carry some 3 x 5 cards in your pocket for this purpose — and make sure you have a pen! I use a little digital voice recorder — it is light, unobtrusive, and instantaneous — and, as is often the case with memory aids, after I use it, I remember what I said into it anyway, without its help. So, although I don't have to use it much anymore, keeping it around is reassuring.

IMPROVING YOUR MEMORY POWER

To improve your memory itself, focus on what you need to remember and boost your memory with the following techniques:

1) **PAY ATTENTION!** You will not remember something if you do not hear it or if you are thinking of something else. For example, if you simply read an article or story, at most, you will remember perhaps 10 percent of it. If, however, you read it intently, your retention can go up to 90 percent or more.

Attention is the key both for registering information in your head in the first place and for locking it in more permanently. If you really want to remember something, you must concentrate.

For example, upon being introduced to someone new, make certain you hear the person's name correctly and then repeat the name either in conversation with the person or later to yourself. Also, look at your new acquaintance and try to memorize his or her facial features. By using your new acquaintance's name as soon as possible, you stand a better chance of locking this information in so you do not later forget it. If you let everything go by you, you can't expect to have a good memory for it.

When you park your car, look around to see where you have parked it. What are the landmarks? Note the landmarks on your parking ticket, if you have been given one. Or do as I do, and always park in the same general spot in the parking garage at work. That way I don't have to pay attention to where I park.

2) **MAKE LEARNING CONSCIOUS AND DELIBERATE**. Make it a point to think to yourself that you want to remember something. Make it a point to repeat those things to yourself. This will help force your brain to lock this information in.

3) **PACE YOUR MEMORIZATION EFFORTS.** You will learn better if you try to learn only in small chunks spread over time, rather than in one large lump all at once.

"Can't you remember your number?"

4) **USE MEMORY AIDS**. There is no shame in using a little pocket notebook, a watch buzzer, or a voice-it recorder. And an added benefit to using a memory aid, you can then free your mind for other things.

One thing you probably will discover is that the more you use a memory aid, the less you will seem to need it. Just the conscious act of remembering to write something down will often engrave it in your memory such that you do not have to look at it again. Or, the fact that it is written down will give your brain a marker to search for it. You know where you can retrieve the information and often can retrieve it without ever looking at the paper.

5) **REMEMBER YOUR MOST IMPORTANT MEMORY AID: YOUR MEMORY PARTNER**. Don't try to remember everything yourself. The most intelligent memory aid you can ever use is another person. Different people have different interests and different memory abilities. What you forget, someone else can remind you of. What you remember can also prod someone else's memory.

This same kind of memory dialog, and the bouncing back and forth that you can do inside your head, is often done with your spouse. We see this very commonly in married couples, when they ask each other for the name of people, inquire about events, and carry on a conversation that is actually a memory recall session. (This is one other reason why the death of a spouse can be so devastating. In addition to all the other losses, the remaining partner has now lost part of his or her memory. Important dates, people and connections that the spouse could remind them of are now lost.)

If you have a person in a position to be a "memory partner" like this, you probably already use him or her for your memory. There are ways of making the partnership work better. Remember, though, that if your memory partner resents being used as a Rolodex, then the system will not provide you maximum efficiency. Also, if the memory partner does not know what you want them to remember, they will not pay attention. So find out how they feel about this partnership to iron out any differences. And, let them know when you are going to need their memory services in advance, so they can do a better job of trying to learn what you need. (And do a better job yourself of rewarding them—don't ask your wife to remind you about Valentines Day!).

6) **BE CONSISTENT IN HOW YOU USE YOUR MEMORY AIDS**. This way you will be able to build on the strength of habit and pre-existing structure.

   The biggest problem with memory aids is remembering to use them! Make sure yours is accessible all the time, kept in the same place. Use it religiously. After a while, your memory will get stronger just from this exercise alone, and you will be able to ease back.

   If you have a little notepad and pen, put it in the same place each time. If you tend to forget your car keys, put them in exactly the same spot each time. If you forget where you parked your car, make note of the spot before you leave each time the same way. At first, forming these habits will take some mental effort and discipline. But after a while they will be effortless, and you won't have to waste time or energy hunting for your notepad.

7) **MAKE WHAT YOU NEED TO REMEMBER MORE INTER-ESTING, MORE CONNECTED, AND MORE MEANING-FUL**. This is the basis of many of the best-known mnemonic techniques. Details can be found in any of the books listed in Appendix ii. As an example: if there is a name you have to remember, try to associate it with another name, a face, a song, or anything that works for you. The more interest you have for something, the more it will be engraved on your memory. The more ways you can try to remember it, the better your system of retrieval can be.

8) **DON'T BE AFRAID OF MEMORY FAILURES**. Accept that memory is not perfect, and isn't expected to be. Worrying about it will make it worse. The less you worry about memory lapses, the less likely you are to have them.

   For instance, if you do not remember someone's name at a party, ask them for their name and apologize. Don't make yourself miserable and lose out on the fun by spending all of your time trying to remember.

   Most people forget from time to time. You may have forgotten an acquaintance's name, but there is a good chance that he has forgotten yours as well. If you can laugh about your limitations, people will laugh with you about theirs. And remember what we have learned in previous chapters: you haven't actually forgotten, you've just blocked. At a party recently, the hostess forgot the name of her oldest and dearest friend when introducing her to another person. The hostess, under considerable stress, looked at her friend, but could only shake her head and laugh. The friend picked up on the clue, and introduced herself. Everyone laughed, and went on enjoying themselves.

9) **REMEMBER THAT THE MEMORY YOU REALLY NEED CAN COME NATURALLY**. Most of us do not need memory for isolated facts or faces. We need memory for connections between facts and between names and faces. Fortunately, *this* type of memory does not have to be painful to acquire. If you read things that you are interested in, do things that you enjoy and talk about things you want to talk about, you will learn *both* the facts *and* the connections, without having to work at it. And, these combinations are the kinds of the memories most worth having anyway.

Finally, and most important,

10) **IT TAKES MORE THAN A GOOD MEMORY TO HAVE GOOD MEMORIES**. (*Anonymous*)

Appendices

i. Further reading

This is a guide, not an endorsement. There are a great many books on memory and memory training techniques. Some useful starting points:

Superb general references, generally written at the lay level, by experts in the field:
    Baddeley, A. *Your Memory: A User's Guide.* London: Prion, 1993.
    Squire, L.R. *Memory and Brain.* New York: Oxford, 1987.

Written for professionals:
    Dudai, Y. *The Neurobiology of Memory: Concepts, Findings, Trends.* Oxford: Oxford University Press, 1989.
    Gordon, B. Memory systems and their disorders. In A. Asbury, G.M. McKhann, & W.I. McDonald (Eds.) *Diseases of the Nervous System (Vol I, 2nd ed.).* Philadelphia: W.B. Saunders, 1992.
    Neisser, U. (Ed.) *Memory Observed: Remembering in Natural Contexts.* San Francisco: W.H. Freeman, 1992.
    Yanagihara, T., & Petersen, R.C. (Eds.) *Memory Disorders: Research and Clinical Practice.* New York: Marcel Dekker, 1991.

A superb textbook on a wide range of topics in neuropsychology. Written at a technical but clear level:
    Kolb, B., & Whishaw, I.Q. *Fundamentals of Human Neuropsychology.* New York: Freeman, 1990.

Popular texts:
    Bolles, E.B. *Remembering and Forgetting: Inquiries Into the Nature of Memory.* New York: Walker and Company, 1988.

Memory training techniques:
For the general reader:
    Fogler, J., & Stern, L. *Improving Your Memory: How to Remember What You're Starting to Forget.* Baltimore: Johns Hopkins University Press, 1994.
    Lapp, D.C. *(Nearly) Total Recall: A guide to better memory at any age.* Stanford, CA: Stanford Alumni Association, 1992.

A professional's guide:
    Wilson, B.A., & Moffat, N. (Eds.). *Clinical Management of Memory Problems: 2nd ed.* San Diego: Singular Publishing Group, 1992.

ii. References, Credits, and Chapter Notes

Part I. MYTHS AND WORRIES

Chapter 1—Common Memory Myths—Debunked!
Preservation of nerve cells:
    Mann, D.M.A. Vulnerability of specific neurons to aging. In D.B. Calne, Neurodegenerative Diseases. Philadelphia: W.B. Saunders, 1994.
Loss of nerve connections:
    Huttenlocher, P.R., & de Courten, C. (1987). The development of synapses in striate cortex of man. *Human Neurobiology,* 6, 1-9.
Amnesia after violent crimes:
    Schacter, D. (1986). Amnesia and Crime: how much do we really know? *American Psychologist,* 41, 286-295.

Chapter 2—What Are You Worried About?
    Figure 1 data adapted from Bolla, K.I., Lindgren, K.N., Bonaccorsy, C., & Bleecker, M.L. (1991). Memory complaints in older adults: Fact or fiction? *Archives of Neurology,* 48, 61-64.

Part II. COMING TO KNOW YOUR OWN MEMORY

Chapter 5—Recognizing Old Memories
    Greta Garbo's 7AA shoe size: From Cecil Adams, *More of the Straight Dope,* New York: Ballantine, 1988, page 475.

Chapter 7—Familiarity, Déjà Vu, and the Other Déjàs.
    Definitions. Robert Gean Campbell. *Psychiatric Dictionary (6th Edition).* Oxford University Press, New York, 1989.
    Sno, H. & Linszen, D. The Déjà Vu Experience: Remembrance of Things Past? *The American Journal of Psychiatry,* 147: 1587-1595, 1990.

Chapter 13—How Your Memory Works—Everyday Examples
    Gordon, B. Memory systems and their disorders. In A. Asbury, G.M. McKhann, & W.I. McDonald (Eds.), *Diseases of the Nervous System (Vol I, 2nd ed.).* Philadelphia: W.B. Saunders, 1992.

Chapter 14—How Your Brain Remembers
Data and pictures courtesy Nathan Crone, M.D., who developed this technique together with John Hart, Jr., M.D., Ronald P. Lesser, M.D., and Barry Gordon, M.D., Ph.D.. Surendar Nathan, M.S., did the 3D MRI brain reconstruction and superimposition of the electrodes, and was also involved in the analysis of the brain electrical activity data.

Part III. IS YOUR MEMORY NORMAL?

Chapter 15— Spotting a Memory Problem—Checklists and Explanations
Arnold, S.E., & Kumar, A. (1993). Reversible dementias. *Medical Clinics of North America, 77,* 215-230.
Clarfield, A.M. (1988). The reversible dementias: do they reverse? *Annals of Internal Medicine, 9,* 476-486, 1988.

Chapter 16—How Forgetful Are You? Evaluating Your Own Memory
The questions used in this section, and the normative data, were adapted from those reported by the following:
Sunderland, A., Harris, J.E., & Gleave, J. Memory failures in everyday life following severe head injury. *Journal of Clinical Neuropsychology,* 6, 127-142, 1984.
Sunderland, A., Watts, K., Baddeley, A.D., & Harris, J.E. Subjective memory assessment test performance in elderly adults. *Journal of Gerontology,* 41, 376-384, 1986.

Other background sources:
Baddeley, A. *Your Memory: A User's Guide.* London: Prion, 1993.
Bennett-Levy, J. & Powell, G.E. (1980) The subjective memory questionnaire (SMQ). An investigation into the self-reporting of 'real life' memory skills. *British Journal of Social and Clinical Psychology,* 19, 177-188.
Broadbent, D.E., Cooper, P.F., FitzGerald, P. & Parkes, K.R. (1982) The cognitive failures questionnaire (CFQ) and its correlates. *British Journal of Clinical Psychology,* 21, 1-16.
Gilewski, M.J. & Zelinski, E.M. Questionnaire assessment of memory complaints. In Poon, L.W. (Ed.) *Clinical Memory Assessment.* Washington, DC: APA, 1986.
Gilewski, M.J., & Zelinski, E.M. (1988) Memory Functioning Questionnaire (MFQ). *Psychopharmacology,* 24, 665-670.

M.M. Gruneberg, P.E. Morris, R.E. Sykes (Eds.) *Practical Aspects of Memory.* New York: Academic Press, 1978.

Herrmann, D. (1982) Know thy memory: the use of questionnaires to assess and study memory. *Psychological Bulletin,* 92, 434-452.

Sunderland, A., Harris, J.E., & Baddeley, A.D. (1983) Do laboratory tests predict everyday memory? A neuropsychological study. *Journal of Verbal Learning and Verbal Behavior,* 22, 341-357.

Chapter 17—It's on the Tip of My Tongue!—Remembering and Forgetting Names and Faces
Face/name recognition survey questions, data, and quotations adapted with permission from:

Young, A.W., Hay, D.C., & Ellis, A.W. (1985) The faces that launched a thousand slips: Everyday difficulties and errors in recognizing people. *British Journal of Psycholgy,* 76, 495-523.

Forgetting rates:

Bahrick, H.P. Memory for people. In J.E. Harris, & P.E. Morris (Eds.) *Everyday Memory, Actions and Absent-Mindedness.* London: Academic Press, 1984.

Bahrick, H.P., Bahrick, P.O., & Wittlinger, R.P. (1975) Fifty years of memory for names and faces: A cross-sectional approach. *Journal of Experimental Psychology: General,* 104, 54-75.

General:

Bruce, V. *Recognizing Faces.* Hillsdale (NJ): Lawrence Erlbaum Associates, 1988.

Burke, D.M., MacKay, D.G., Worthley, J.S., & Wade, E.W. (1991). On the tip of the tongue: What causes word finding failures in young and older adults? *Journal of Memory and Language,* 30, 542-579.

Burton, A.M., & Bruce, V. (1992) I recognize your face but I can't remember your name: A simple explanation? *British Journal of Psychology,* 83, 45-60.

Cohen, G. (1990) Why is it difficult to put names to faces? *British Journal of Psychology,* 81, 287-297.

Harris, J.E., & Morris, P.E. (Eds.) *Everyday Memory, Action Slips and Absent-Mindedness.* Orlando: Academic Press, 1984.

James, W. The Principles of Psychology, Vol. 1. New York: Henry Holt, 1890.

Jones, G.V. Analyzing memory blocks. In Gruneberg, M.M., P.E. Morris, & R.N. Sykes (Eds.), *Practical Aspects of Memory: Current Research and*

Issues. Chichester: John Wiley & Sons, 1988.

Jones, S.J., & Rabbitt, P.M.A. (1994) Effects of age on the ability to remember common and rare proper names. *The Quarterly Journal of Experimental Psychology,* 47A, 1001-1014.

Reason, J. *Human Error.* Cambridge: Cambridge University Press, 1990.

Chapter 18—How Does Normal Memory Normally Behave?
sex differences:
McKelvie, S.J., Standing, L., St. Jean, D., & Law, J. (1993) Gender differences in recognition memory for faces and cars: Evidence for the interest hypothesis. *Bull. Psychonomic Society,* 31, 447-448.
waiting room study:
Silverman, I., & Eals, M. Sex differences in spatial abilities: Evolutionary theory and data. In J.H. Barkow, L. Cosmides, & J. Tooby (Eds.) *The Adapted Mind: Evolutionary Psychology and the Generation of Culture.* New York: Oxford University Press, 1992.
reunited women:
The Baltimore Sun (Associated Press), January 8, 1995
Challenger:
Neisser, U., & Harsch, N. Phantom flashbulbs: False recollections of hearing the news about *Challenger.* In E. Winograd & U. Neisser (Eds.) *Affect and Accuracy in Recall.* Cambridge (UK): Cambridge University Press, 1992.
Bricklayer under hypnosis:
Pfeiffer, J. *The Human Brain,* New York: Harper & Brothers, 1955, pg. 84.

General:
Cohen, G. *Memory in the Real World.* Hillsdale (NJ): Lawrence Erlbaum Associates, 1989.

Eaton, S.B., Shostak, M., & Konner, M. *The Paleolithic Prescription.* New York: Harper & Row, 1988.

Larsen, S.F. Potential flashbulbs: memories of ordinary news as the baseline. In E. Winograd & U. Neisser (Eds.) *Affect and Accuracy in Recall.* Cambridge (UK): Cambridge University Press, 1992.

Loftus, E.F., & Loftus, G.R. (1980) On the permanence of stored information in the human brain. *American Psychologist,* 35, 409-420.

Lumsden, C., & Wilson, E.O. *Genes, Mind, and Culture.* Cambridge: Harvard, 1981.

McFarland, D. *The Oxford Companion to Animal Behavior.* Oxford: Oxford, 1981.

Chapter 19—Truly Amazing Memories. What You Can Learn From Them. Why You Shouldn't Envy Them.

Barlow, F. *Mental Prodigies.* New York: Philosophical Library, 1952.

Brown, E., & Deffenbacher, K. Superior memory performance and mnemonic encoding. In L.K. Obler & D. Fein (Eds.) *The Exceptional Brain: Neuropsycholgy of Talent and Special Abilites.* New York: The Guilford Press, 1988.

Ericsson, K.A. (1985) Memory skill. *Canadian Journal of Psychology,* 39, 188-231.

Ericsson, K.A., & Chase, W.G. (1982) Exceptional memory. *American Scientist,* 70, 607-615.

Ericsson, K.A., Chase, W.G., & Faloon, S. (1980) Acquisition of a memory skill. *Science,* 208, 1181-1182.

Ericsson, K.A. & Faivre, I.A. What's exceptional about exceptional abilities? In L.K. Obler, & D. Fein (Eds.) *The Exceptional Brain: Neuropsycholgy of Talent and Special Abilities.* New York: The Guilford Press, 1988.

Ericsson, K.A., & Polson, P.G. A cognitive analysis of exceptional memory for restaurant orders. In M.T.H. Chi, R. Glaser, & M.J. Farr (Eds.) *The Nature of Expertise.* Hillsdale: Lawrence Erlbaum Associates, 1988.

Gordon, P., Valentine, E., & Wilding, J. (1984) One man's memory: A study of a mnemonist. *British Journal of Psychology,* 75, 1-14.

Hunt, E. & Love, T. How good can memory be? In A.W. Melton & E. Martin (Eds.) *Coding Processes in Human Memory.* Washington: Winston, 1972.

Luria, A.R. *The Mind of a Mnemonist.* Cambridge: Harvard University Press, 1968/1987.

Thompson, C.P., Cowan, T., Frieman, Jerome., Mahadevan, R.S., Vogl, R.J., & Frieman, J. (1991) Rajan: A study of a memorist. *Journal of Memory and Language,* 30, 702-724.

Wilding, J., & Valentine, E. (1985). One man's memory for prose, faces and names. *British Journal of Psychology,* 76, 215-219.

Wilding, J., & Valentine, E. Searching for superior memories. In Gruneberg, M.M., P.E. Morris, & R.N. Sykes (Eds.) *Practical Aspects of Memory: Current Research and Issues (Vol. 1).* Chichester: John Wiley & Sons, 1988.

Part IV. PEOPLE WITH PROBLEMS: WHAT CAN MAKE YOUR MEMORY WORSE.

Chapter 21—The Man with Too Many Mistresses, and one with Too Many Telephones—Too much to do.

This title and that of some other vignettes presented in this book owes an obvious debt to Oliver Sacks' groundbreaking book *The Man Who Mistook His Wife for a Hat.*

Letting your mind alone: James Thurber's essay on self-help books in *Let Your Mind Alone!* (Perennial Library, 1976) gave the same advice 50 years ago, in a more humorous way.

Chapter 23— You Never Know It's Enough, Until You've Had Too Much— Alcohol

Parker, E.S., Parker, D.A., Brody, J.A., & Schoenberg, R. (1982) Cognitive patterns resembling premature aging in male social drinkers. *Alcoholism: Clinical and Experimental Research*, 6, 46-51.

Victor, M. (1994). Alcoholic dementia. *Can. J. Neurol. Sci.*, 21, 88-99.

Chapter 24— Prescription Drugs

Bowen, J.D., & Larson, E.B. (1993). Drug-induced cognitive impairment: Defining the problem and finding solutions. *Drugs & Aging*, 3, 349-357.

Larson, E.B., Kukull, W.A., Buchner, D., & Reifler, B.V. (1987). Adverse drug reactions associated with global cognitive impairment in elderly persons. *Annals of Internal Medicine*, 107, 169-173.

Lowenthal, D.T., & Nadeau, S.E. (1991). Drug-induced dementia. *Southern Medical Journal*, 84, 1S-24-1S-31.

Chapter 25— "My Mind is Melting!"—Depression and Anxiety

Burt, D.B., Zembar, M.J., & Niederehe, G. (1995). Depression and memory impairment: A meta-analysis of the association, its pattern and specificity. *Psychological Bulletin*, 117, 285-305.

Kramer, S.I., & Reifler, B.V. (1992). Depression, dementia, and reversible dementia.

Chapter 26— "The Socialite Who Spilled Too Many Secrets"—Aging. When Your Memory Isn't As Good As It Was

Cerella, J. Aging and Information-Processing Rate. In J.E. Birren & K.W. Schaie (Eds.) *Handbook of The Psychology of Aging (3rd Ed.).* New York: Academic Press, 1990.

Grady, C.L., McIntosh, A.R., Horwitz, B., Maisog, J.M., Ungerleider, L.G., Mentis, M.J., Pietrini, P., Schapiro, M.B., & Haxby, J.V. (1995). Age-related reductions in human recognition memory due to impaired encoding. *Science*, 269, 218-221.

Hayflick, L. *How and Why We Age.* New York: Ballantine, 1994.

Hultsch, D.F., & Dixon, R.A. Learning and Memory in Aging. In J.E.

Birren & K.W. Schaie (Eds.) *Handbook of The Psychology of Aging (3rd Ed.)*. New York: Academic Press, 1990.

Kausler, D.H. *Learning and Memory in Normal Aging*. San Diego: Academic Press, 1994.

Koivisto, K., Reinikainen, K.J., Kanninen, T., Vanhanen, M., Helkala, E-L., Mykkanen, L., Laakso, M., Pyorala, K., & Riekkinen, P.J. Sr. (1995). Prevalence of age-associated memory impairment in a randomly selected population from eastern Finland. *Neurology*, 45, 741-746.

Larrabee, G.J., & McEntee, W.J. (1995). Age-associated memory impairment: Sorting out the controversies. *Neurology*, 45, 611-614.

Launer, L.J., Scheltens, Ph., Lindeboom, J., Barkhof, F., Weinstein, H.C., & Jonker, C. (1995). Medial temporal lobe atrophy in an open population of very old persons: Cognitive, brain atrophy, and socio-medical correlates. *Neurology*, 45, 747-752.

Mitrushina, M., Uchiyama, C., & Satz, P. (1995). Heterogenity of cognitive profiles in normal aging: Implications for early manifestations of Alzheimer's disease. *Journal of Clincial and Experimental Neuropsychology*, 17, 374-382.

Powell, D.H., & Whitla, D.K. (1994). Normal cognitive aging: Toward empirical perspectives. *Current Directions in Psychological Science*, 3, 27-31.

Salthouse, T. *Theoretical perspectives on cognitive aging*. Hillsdale (NJ): Erlbaum, 1991.

Schaie, K.W. Intellectual Development in Adulthood. In J.E. Birren & K.W. Schaie (Eds.) *Handbook of The Psychology of Aging (3rd Ed.)*. New York: Academic Press, 1990.

Schaie, K.W. (1994). The course of adult intellectual development. *American Psychologist*, 49, 304-313.

Schaie, K.W., & Willis, S.L. (1993). Age difference patterns of psychometric intelligence in adulthood: Generalizability within and across ability domains. *Psychology and Aging*, 8, 44-55.

Chapter 27— "Everybody Forgets Who Their Children Are"—Dementia and Alzheimer's Disease.

Petersen, R.C., Smith, G.E., Ivnik, R.J., et al. (1995). Apolipoprotein E status as a predictor of the development of Alzheimer's Disease in memory-impaired individuals. *JAMA*, 273, 1274-1278.

Cognex—Dr. Gordon has been a paid consultant to Parke-Davis, makers of Cognex, and a paid participant in Parke-Davis' Alzheimer's Disease National Speakers Bureau.

Chapter 28—The Unfinished Baseball Season—Pure Amnesia. Memory Loss From Other Brain Diseases

Gordon, B. Memory systems and their disorders. In A. Asbury, G.M. McKhann, & W.I. McDonald (Eds.) *Diseases of the Nervous System* (Vol I, 2nd ed.). Philadelphia: W.B. Saunders, 1992.

Note: The young man who had the "Unfinished Baseball Season", and his family, are eager to share their experiences with others, particularly about the process of recovery. They very much want to give support and encouragement to those who may have suffered a similar or related problem. You may contact them through the author.

Chapter 29—Temporary "Amnesias" and Everyday "Blackouts"

Gordon, B., & Marin, O.S.M. (1979). Transient global amnesia: An extensive case report. *Journal of Neurology, Neurosurgery, and Psychiatry,* 42, 572-575.

Chapter 31—"Girl Loses Identity, and Saves the Plot" — How the Media Portrays Amnesia

SOURCES USED FOR AMNESIA IN THE NEWSPAPERS:
Jim Cossan:
The New York Times, 12/14/80
New Orleans Times-Picayune, 12/13/80

John Hartman:
Houston Post, 7/21/81
Houston Post, 7/22/81
Los Angeles Times, 7/22/81
Houston Post, 7/19/82

Jim McDonnell:
Houston Post, 1/1/86
Houston Post, 12/28/85
Atlanta Journal-Constitution, 12/28/85
Houston Post, 12/29/85

Cheryl Tomiczek:
The New York Times, 3/22/81
The New York Times, 3/27/81
The New York Times, 4/29/81
New Orleans Times-Picayune, 9/14/81

Kihlstrom, J.F., & Evans, F.J. (Eds.) *Functional Disorders of Memory.* Hillsdale (NJ): Lawrence Erlbaum Associates, 1979.

Kopelman, M.D., Christensen, H., Puffett, A., & Stanhope, N. (1994). The great escape: a neuropsychological study of psychogenic amnesia. *Neuropsychologia,* 32, 675-691.

Schacter, D.L., & Kihlstrom, J.F. Functional amnesia. In F. Boller and J. Grafman (Eds.) *Handbook of Neuropsychology.* Amsterdam: Elsevier, 1989.

Chapter 32— Head Injury—Real and Imagined
Gordon, B. Postconcussional Syndrome. In R.T. Johnson (Ed.) *Current Therapy in Neurologic Disease.* New York: B.C. Decker, 1990.

Chapter 33— "Forever Fourteen" "An Affair to Forget"—Amnesia and Emotional Trauma
Treadway, M., McCloskey, M., Gordon, B., & Cohen, N.J. Landmark life events and the organization of memory: Evidence from functional retrograde amnesia. In S.-A. Christianson (Ed.) *Handbook of Emotion and Memory.* Hillsdale, NJ: Erlbaum, 1992.

Chapter 34— "A Shark Has Four Legs, Doesn't It?" A Bizarre—But Real— Form of Memory Loss, and the Brain's Odd Filing System
Hart, J., Jr., & Gordon, B. (1992). Neural subsystems of object knowledge. *Nature,* 359, 60-64.

Chapter 35— "I Raped My Children, But I Don't Remember It!"—The Unreliability of Recovered "Memories"
Bass, E., & Davis, L. *The Courage to Heal (3rd Edition).* New York: Harper Perennial, 1994.

Ceci, S.J., & Loftus, E.F. (1994). 'Memory work': A royal road to false memories? *Applied Cognitive Psychology,* 8, 351-364.

Gordon, B. (1995) Review of Loftus & Ketcham, The Myth of Repressed Memory. *New England Journal of Medicine,* 333, 133-134.

Herman, J.L. & Schatzow, E. (1987). Recovery and verification of memories of childhood sexual trauma. *Psychoanalytic Psychology,* 4, 1-14.

Lindsay, D.S., & Read, J.D. (1994). Psychotherapy and memories of childhood sexual abuse: A cognitive perspective. *Applied Cognitive Psychology,* 8, 281-338.

Loftus, E.F. (1993). Desperately seeking memories of the first few years of childhook: The reality of early memories. *Journal of Experiemntal Psychology: General,* 122, 274-277.

Loftus, E., & Ketchum, K. *The Myth of Repressed Memory.* New York: St. Martin's Press, 1994.

Loftus, E.F., & Kaufman, L. Why do traumatic experiences sometimes produce good memory (flashbulbs) and sometimes no memory (repression)? In E. Winograd & U. Neisser (Eds.) *Affect and Accuracy in Recall.* Cambridge (UK): Cambridge University Press, 1992.

Read, J.D., & Lindsay, D.S. (1994). Moving toward a middle ground on the 'false memory debate': Reply to commentaries on Lindsay and Read. *Applied Cognitive Psychology,* 8, 407-435.

Terr, L.C. (1983). Chowchilla revisited: The effects of psychic trauma four years after a school-bus kidnapping. *American Journal of Psychiatry,* 140, 1543-1550.

Usher, J.A., & Neisser, U. (1993). Childhood amnesia and the beginnings of memory for early life events. *Journal of Experimental Psychology: General,* 122, 155-165. (See Loftus, 1993, cited above)

Wagenaar, W.A., & Groeneweg, J. (1990). The memory of concentration camp survivors. *Applied Cognitive Psychology,* 4, 77-87.

Williams, L.M. (1994). Recall of childhood trauma: a prospective study of women's memories of child sexual abuse. *J. Consulting Clin. Psych.,* 62, 1167-1176.

Wright, L. *Remembering Satan.* New York: Knopf, 1994.

Part V. IMPROVING YOUR MEMORY

Chapters 36 and 37. What Really Works, or Why It Isn't Known to Work and What Really Works
Benedict, R.H.B., Brandt, J., & Bergey, G. (1993). An attempt at memory retraining in severe amnesia: An experimental single-case study. *Neuropsychological Rehabilitation,* 3, 37-51.

Brooks, J.O., Friedman, L., Gibson, J.M., & Yesavage, J.A. (1993). Spontaneous mnemonic strategies used by older and younger adults to remember proper names. *Memory,* 1, 393-407.

Buchner, D.M., Beresford, S.A.A., Larson, E.B., LaCroix, A.Z., & Wagner, E.H. (1992). Effects of physical activity on health status in older adults II: Intervention studies. *Annual Review of Public Health,* 13, 469-488.

Druckman, D., Bjork R.A. (Eds.) *In the Mind's Eye: Enhancing Human Performance.* Washington: National Academy Press, 1991.

Druckman, D., Bjork, R.A. (Eds.) *Learning, Remembering, Believing: Enhancing Human Performance.* Washington: National Academy Press, 1994.

Druckman, D., Swets, J.A. (Eds.) *Enhancing Human Performance Issues, Theories and Techniques*. Washington: National Academy Press, 1988.

Dustman, R.E., Ruhling, R.O., Russell, E.M., Shearer, D.E., Bonekat, W., Shigeoka, J.W., Wood, J.S., & Bradford, D.C. (1984). Aerobic exercise training and improved neuropsychological function of older individuals. *Neurobiology of Aging*, 5, 35-42.

Franzen, M.D., & Haut, M.W. (1991). The psychological treatment of memory impairment: A review of empirical studies. *Neuropsychology Review*, 2, 29-63.

Higbee, K.L. Practical aspects of mnemonics. In Gruneberg, M.M., P.E. Morris, & R.N. Sykes (Eds.) *Practical Aspects of Memory: Current Research and Issues*. Chichester: John Wiley & Sons, 1988.

Lachman, M.E., Weaver, S.L., Bandura, M., Elliot, E., & Lewkowicz, C.J. (1992). Improving memory and control beliefs through cognitive restructuring and self-generated strategies. *Journal of Gerontology: Psychological Sciences*, 47, 293-299.

Neely, A.S. & Backman, L. (1995). Effects of multifactorial memory training in old age: Generalizability across tasks and individuals. *Journal of Gerontology: Psycholoigcal Sciences*, 50B, 134-140.

Robinson-Riegler, B., & McDaniel, M.A. (1994). Further constraints on the bizarreness effect: Elaboration at encoding. *Memory & Cognition*, 22, 702-712.

Schaffer, G., & Poon, L.W. (1982). Individual variability in memory training with the elderly. *Educational Gerontology*, 8, 217-229.

Sheikh, J.I., Hill, R.D., & Yesavage, J.A. (1986). Long-term efficacy of cognitive training for age-associated memory impairment: A six-month follow-up study. *Developmental Neuropsychology*, 2, 413-421.

Wagner, E.H., & LaCroix, A.Z., Buchner, D.M., & Larson, E.B. (1992). Effects of physical activity on health status in older adults I: Observational studies. *Annual Review of Public Health*, 13, 451-468.

Yates, F.A. *The Art Of Memory*. Chicago: University of Chicago Press, 1966. (A historical review)

A sampler of books written for a general audience:

Brown, A.S. *How to Increase Your Memory Power*. Glenview (Ill.): Scott, Foresman, 1989.

Crook, T., & Allison, C. *How to Remember Names*. New York: Harper Perennial, 1992.

Fogler, J., & Stern, L. *Improving Your Memory: How to Remember What You're Starting to Forget*. Baltimore: Johns Hopkins University Press, 1994.

Herold, M. *You'll Never Forget a Name Again!* Chicago: Contemporary Books, 1992.

Higbee, K.L. *Your Memory: How It Works and How To Improve It (Second Edition)*. New York: Prentice Hall, 1988.

Lapp, D.C. *(Nearly) Total Recall: A guide to better memory at any age*. Stanford, CA: Stanford Alumni Association, 1992.

Lorayne, H., & Lucas, J. *The Memory Book*. New York: Stein & Day, 1974.

About the Authors

Barry Gordon, M.D., Ph.D., is a behavioral neurologist, cognitive neuro-scientist and experimental psychologist who specializes in memory and language disorders. He heads the division of Cognitive Neurology at the Johns Hopkins University School of Medicine in Baltimore, where he is also the director of the Cognitive Neurology, Neuropsychology and Memory Disorders Clinic. He has authored or co-authored over 50 papers and 26 book chapters. Dr. Gordon diagnoses and treats a variety of brain conditions. He and his colleagues also help devise strategies for coping with memory problems.

Dr. Gordon's work has received international media attention. His work in Alzheimer's disease was featured on the PBS series *The Brain.* Dr. Gordon has also served as an expert on a number of legal matters dealing with higher mental functions, including serving as a consultant to the prosecution's medical team in the trial of John Hinckley, Jr.

Rachel Wilder, formerly the senior science writer for the Johns Hopkins University School of Medicine, has been an editor at *U.S. News and World Report, Self,* and *Science Digest,* where she wrote a monthly column on animal and human behavior. She has also published articles in *USA Today* and *Cosmopolitan,* contributed to four travel books, and appeared on *The Merv Griffin Show.*

Martha P. Trachtenberg is a graduate of Syracuse University. She splits her time between music—song writing and jingle singing—and editorial work. Her research credits include the recent biographies of Calvin Klein, John F. Kennedy, Jr., and Trisha Yearwood. She lives in New York City with her husband and son.

Dr. Barry Gordon is available for speaking engagements. Please contact MasterMedia's Speaker's Bureau for availability and fee arrangement. **Call Tony Colao at (800) 453-2887.**

OTHER MASTERMEDIA BOOKS

To order additional copies of any MasterMedia book, send a check for the price of the book plus $2.00 postage and handling for the first book, $1.00 for each additional book to:

MasterMedia Limited
17 East 89th Street
New York, NY 10128
(212) 260-5600
(800) 334-8232 please use MasterCard or VISA on phone orders
(212) 546-7638 (fax)

AGING PARENTS AND YOU: A Complete Handbook to Help You Help Your Elders Maintain a Healthy, Productive and Independent Life, by Eugenia Anderson-Ellis, is a complete guide to providing care to aging relatives. It gives practical advice and resources to adults who are helping their elders lead productive and independent lives. Revised and updated. ($9.95 paper)

BALANCING ACTS! Juggling Love, Work, Family, and Recreation, by Susan Schiffer Stautberg and Marcia L. Worthing, provides strategies to achieve a balanced life by reordering priorities and setting realistic goals. ($12.95 paper)

BREATHING SPACE: Living and Working at a Comfortable Pace in a Sped-Up Society, by Jeff Davidson, helps readers to handle information and activity overload and gain greater control over their lives. ($10.95 paper)

THE CONFIDENCE FACTOR: How Self-Esteem Can Change Your Life, by Dr. Judith Briles, is based on a nationwide survey of six thousand men and women. Briles explores why women so often feel a lack of self-confidence and have a poor opinion of themselves. She offers step-by-step advice on becoming the person you want to be. ($9.95 paper, $18.95 cloth)

HOT HEALTH-CARE CAREERS, by Margaret McNally and Phyllis Schneider, offers readers what they need to know about training for and getting jobs in a rewarding field where professionals are always in demand. ($10.95 paper)

LIFETIME EMPLOYABILITY: How to Become Indispensable, by Carole Hyatt is both a guide through the mysteries of the business universe brought down to earth and a handbook to help you evaluate your attitudes, your skills, and your goals. Through expert advice and interviews of nearly 200 men and women whose lives have changed because their jobs or goals shifted, *Lifetime Employability* is designed to increase your staying power in today's down-sized economy. ($12.95 paper)

LIFE'S THIRD ACT: Taking Control of Your Mature Years, by Patricia Burnham, Ph.D., is a perceptive handbook for everyone who recognizes that planning is the key to enjoying your mature years. ($10.95 paper, $18.95 cloth)

THE LIVING HEART BRAND NAME SHOPPER'S GUIDE, by Michael F. DeBakey, M.D., Antonio M. Gotto, Jr., M.D., D.Phil., Lynne W. Scott, M.A., R.D./L.D., and John P. Foreyt, Ph.D., lists brand-name supermarket products that are low in fat, saturated fatty acids, and cholesterol. ($12.50 paper)

THE LOYALTY FACTOR: Building Trust in Today's Workplace, by Carol Kinsey Goman, Ph.D., offers techniques for restoring commitment and loyalty in the workplace. ($9.95 paper)

MANAGING YOUR CHILD'S DIABETES, by Robert Wood Johnson IV, Sale Johnson, Casey Johnson, and Susan Kleinman, brings help to families trying to understand diabetes and control its effects. ($10.95 paper)

MANAGING YOUR PSORIASIS, by Nicholas J. Lowe, M.D., is an innovative manual that couples scientific research and encouraging support, with an emphasis on how patients can take charge of their health. ($10.95 paper, $17.95 cloth)

OFFICE BIOLOGY: Why Tuesday Is the Most Productive Day and Other Relevant Facts for Survival in the Workplace, by Edith Weiner and Arnold Brown, teaches how in the '90s and beyond we will be expected to work smarter, take better control of our health, adapt to advancing technology, and improve our lives in ways that are not too costly or resource-intensive. ($12.95 paper, $21.95 cloth)

PAIN RELIEF: How to Say No to Acute, Chronic, and Cancer Pain!, by Dr. Jane Cowles, offers a step-by-step plan for assessing pain and communicating it to your doctor, and explains the importance of having a pain plan before undergoing any medical or surgical treatment; includes "The Pain Patient's Bill of Rights," and a reusable pain assessment chart. ($14.95 paper, 22.95 cloth)

REAL LIFE 101: The Graduate's Guide to Survival, by Susan Kleinman, supplies welcome advice to those facing "real life" for the first time, focusing on work, money, health, and how to deal with freedom and responsibility. ($9.95 paper)

SIDE-BY-SIDE STRATEGIES: How Two-Career Couples Can Thrive in the Nineties, by Jane Hershey Cuozzo and S. Diane Graham, describes how two-career couples can learn the difference between competing with a spouse and becoming a supportive power partner. Published in hardcover as *Power Partners.* ($10.95 paper, $19.95 cloth)

STEP FORWARD: Sexual Harassment in the Workplace, What You Need to Know, by Susan L. Webb, presents the facts for identifying the tell-tale signs of sexual harassment on the job, and how to deal with it. ($9.95 paper)

STRAIGHT TALK ON WOMEN'S HEALTH: How to Get the Health Care You Deserve, by Janice Teal, Ph.D., and Phyllis Schneider, is destined to become a health-care "bible." Devoid of confusing medical jargon, it offers a wealth of resources, including contact lists of healthlines and women's medical centers. ($14.95 paper)

TAKING CONTROL OF YOUR LIFE: The Secrets of Successful Enterprising Women, by Gail Blanke and Kathleen Walas, is based on the authors' professional experience with Avon Products' Women of Enterprise Awards, given each year to outstanding women entrepreneurs. The authors offer a specific plan to help women gain control over their lives, and include business tips and quizzes as well as beauty and lifestyle information. ($17.95 cloth)

TWENTYSOMETHING: Managing and Motivating Today's New Work Force, by Lawrence J. Bradford, Ph.D., and Claire Raines, M.A., examines the work orientation of the younger generation, offering managers in businesses of all kinds a practical guide to better understand and supervise their young employees. ($22.95 cloth)

YOUR HEALTHY BODY, YOUR HEALTHY LIFE: How to Take Control of Your Medical Destiny, by Donald B. Louria, M.D., provides precise advice and strategies that will help you to live a long and healthy life. Learn also about nutrition, exercise, vitamins, and medication, as well as how to control risk factors for major diseases. Revised and updated. ($12.95 paper)

YOUR VISION: All About Modern Eye Care, by Warren D. Cross Jr., M.D., and Lawrence Lynn, Ph.D., reveals astounding research discoveries in an entertaining and informative handbook written with the patient in mind. ($13.95 paper)